ACRES of FLINT

Sarah Orne Jewett and Her Contemporaries

REVISED EDITION

Perry D. Westbrook

The Scarecrow Press, Inc.
Metuchen, N.J., & London
1981

Acres of Flint was originally published
by The Scarecrow Press in 1951.

Library of Congress Cataloging in Publication Data

Westbrook, Perry D.
    Acres of flint.

    Bibliography: p.
    Includes index.
    1. American literature—New England—History and criticism. 2. American
literature—19th century—History and criticism. 3. American literature—Women
authors—History and criticism. 4. Jewett, Sarah Orne, 1849–1909—Criticism and
interpretation. 5. New England in literature.
    I. Title.
PS243.W4   1980   810'.9'974   80-20501
ISBN 0-8108-1357-2

Manufactured in the United States of America

For Myrtle

CONTENTS

PREFACE TO THE REVISED EDITION

Almost thirty-five years ago as a student at Columbia University I suggested to Professor Lionel Trilling that I write my Ph.D. dissertation on the village and rural authors of New England. Five years later a book deriving from the dissertation, under the title *Acres of Flint: Writers of Rural New England, 1870–1900*, appeared in print as one of the first volumes to be published by Dr. Ralph Shaw's newly founded Scarecrow Press. I was fortunate from the start. Professor Trilling had been agreeable to my general idea for a dissertation on New England so-called "local colorists," and for the sake of compactness we narrowed the time span of the subject to roughly the post–Civil War generation. The reason for choosing that particular period was that in those years, we thought, the writing about the New England countryside and seacoast by authors native to the region had reached a high point both in quantity and quality. Authors like Sarah Orne Jewett and Mary E. Wilkins Freeman were producing short stories and sketches that, as studies of character and evocations of a traditional though vanishing way of life, transcended the limits of mere "local color." These prose writers, moreover, had found a ready market and thus enjoyed a significant readership in a number of the distinguished periodicals of the time—among them the *Atlantic Monthly, Harper's Monthly*, and the *Century Illustrated Monthly*.

The village-bred poets did not fare so well, though two of them—E. A. Robinson and Emily Dickinson—are among the four or five greatest poets the nation has produced. Emily Dickinson saw only seven of her poems in print during her lifetime; not until the 1890s did collections of her verse appear and win the acclaim that their extraordinary genius deserved. Robinson, beginning to publish in the '90s, achieved no reputation until after 1900. Professor Trilling and the two other members of my dissertation committee—Professors Emery Neff and Henry Steele Commager—agreed with me that I should not get too deeply involved with these two major poets, both of whom had received much scholarly and critical attention already. If I had attempted to deal at all thoroughly with them, I should have had little space left for the ten or twelve other authors whom I intended to discuss. Thus I gave Robinson and Dickinson only brief notices, which are, of course, in no way commensurate with their importance in American letters.

On its publication in 1951 *Acres of Flint* received generally favorable reviews. It has been out of print for many years; but recently interest in it has revived sufficiently to warrant its being brought out in a second and somewhat revised edition. Most of the revisions are routine—corrections of any errors in fact or typography, occasional changes in diction and phrasing, the conforming of the footnotes and bibliography to present-day practice. In content, changes have been few and for the most part minor. I cannot say that in all cases I still agree wholeheartedly with some of my conclusions and attitudes as expressed in the book. For example, in my estimate of some aspects of rural New England character I may have been overly enthusiastic, as I may have been, also, in regard to the quality of life in the back-country villages. Today I should at least be more restrained in making value judgments.

Most of the writing of *Acres of Flint* I did on Swan's Island, situated in Blue Hill Bay, on the coast of Maine. Swan's Island, though surely no Utopia, is a compact New England township retaining many of the centuries-old characteristics of such communities. Moreover, its location within view of the Mt. Desert Hills is one of the loveliest on the Atlantic seaboard. In such surroundings one could not but write with enthusiasm. At any rate, my decision has been to leave the affirmative tone of the book unmodified.

The renewal of reader interest in *Acres of Flint* is attributable in large degree, I think, to an aspect of its subject matter that in the late 1940s struck me as purely incidental and not especially significant sociologically or aesthetically. I refer to the fact that most of the authors I was writing about were women. As an explanation of this phenomenon I accepted William Dean Howells's statement that in America in the last century cultural pursuits like reading and writing were more or less the province of women, while men devoted their energies and talents to the professions and to business and industry—careers and activities from which the mores of the times rather strictly excluded women. The arbitrariness and injustice of this rigid assignment of roles according to sex was, and is, obvious. Yet in the first edition of *Acres of Flint* I did not dwell on what today would be called the sexist aspects of my subject. I noted the simple truth that women were predominantly the interpreters of rural New England culture, the recorders of its mores, and the guardians of its values. In this revised edition, however, I feel that I should emphasize, and attempt more fully to account for, the feminine domination of the body of literature that I am discussing. This I have tried to do in an added section at the end of Chapter I.

In general I have adhered to the plan of documentation followed in my first edition. For each author discussed at length I provide in a footnote a list of important sources of biographical information and critical comment. Since 1950 much new material has appeared on the writers I have dealt with. I call attention to some, but not all, such writings in appropriate footnotes, whether or not I have actually drawn from them myself in the new edition. My bibliography contains full entries for all items mentioned either in my text or in my footnotes.

Much of the Chapter IX, "Controversy with Nature: Celia Thaxter," appeared in the *New England Quarterly*, December, 1947, and is reprinted with permission of the editor.

With the exception of the photograph of Sarah Orne Jewett's house, the illustrations in this revised edition have been reproduced from books and periodicals contemporary with the period covered in *Acres of Flint*. I am indebted for the reproductions to Arlen R. Westbrook, my wife.

PERRY D. WESTBROOK

Department of English
State University of New York at Albany

PREFACE TO THE FIRST EDITION

This book is an attempt to describe the literary expression of rural New England during that region's period of greatest social and economic upheaval, the generation following the Civil War. Considerations of space and unity have suggested that I confine myself strictly to writers of rural background in one or another of the six New England States; hence the omission of any detailed treatment of the early Howells and James, both of whom had much of interest and significance to say within the scope of my subject but who wrote from a more urban and generally broader context. They are not the indigenous voices of the region I wish to study.

My reasons for treating relatively briefly Emily Dickinson and the E. A. Robinson of the '90's are perhaps less tenable. Still, able and lengthy studies of these two, by such scholars as George Whicher and Emery Neff, are available and familiar to all students of American literature. Not one of the least failings of literary scholarship is the piling up of repetitious material. Thus in the case of such major figures as Dickinson, Robinson, and Frost I have confined myself to rather few pages of comments strictly apropos to my subject.

And do not the lesser writers deserve their day in court? All of the eight or ten authors whom I discuss at length had something to say to the Americans of their times. Occasionally what they said was inadequate, but more often, I think, it is still well worth our attention. Furthermore, the majority of these voices were endowed with real literary grace and effectiveness. I am not recording a series of disinterments. Rather I am attempting to introduce the reader to personalities who still live in their writings but have merely got pushed into a corner at the literary cocktail party of our generation. Let's force our way through the throng of Gibson-drinkers and see what this neglected, but by no means abashed, group from Down East have to say.

A literary-historical pundit who has successfully adapted the Taylor system to the mass production of anthologies and quasi-philosophical treatments of American life in all its phases once staggered me by asking me what the thesis of my book was. I didn't know then and I don't know now. All I know is that the rural sections of a certain rather small region of the United States produced (not so long ago) an interesting group of writers, of whom, I found, no one had yet given an adequate account. As

I progressed I thought I discovered a certain unity of mood and purpose within the group. This concept, or feeling, is expressed in the title, *Acres of Flint*, and in the Emily Dickinson poem that suggested the title. But above all, these men and women are individuals: individualism is part of their heritage. Why outrage their identities by forcing them into the confines of a succinctly worded thesis?

When one finishes a volume, even a thin one, and stops to take cognizance of the activity, one is at once surprised at how little credit—or discredit—one personally can assume. Were I to acknowledge all the influences that went into the making of this book, I should have to begin with the circumstances and friends of my New England boyhood. But once so started I would have another book. To turn to those persons who directly aided me I should like to name gratefully the following, who gave the manuscript a careful and critical reading: Professors James Gutmann, Frederick W. Dupee, Herbert Wallace Schneider, Henry Steele Commager, Ralph Leslie Rusk, Elliot Van Kirk, Dobbie, and Dorothy Brewster, all of Columbia University. For several careful readings and much encouragement and helpful suggestions I wish particularly to thank Professor Emery Neff. For meticulous chapter by chapter and page by page guidance I am deeply indebted to Professor Lionel Trilling, who generously shared his time and critical insight.

Expressions of sincere gratitude are due also to Vivian Hopkins, the Emerson scholar, who read my manuscript word for word with critical but kindly eye; to Shields McIlwaine, the Southern regionalist, who shared with me the fruits of his long experience in the regional approach to literature; to Joseph Wheeler, former Librarian of the Enoch Pratt Free Library, and Arthur Wallace Peach, director of the Vermont Historical Society, for their advice regarding matters of publication; to Herbert Brown, editor of the *New England Quarterly*, who helped me much in matters of style; and to my father, Francis A. Westbrook, and to Mr. and Mrs. Graham Carey, all three of Benson, Vermont, for examining the manuscript and providing for me their discerning comments as New England intellectuals of the present day.

For help in gathering the volumes needed in this enterprise I wish to thank the Librarians of the University of Maine, of Columbia University, of the New York State College for Teachers at Albany, and of the New York State Library. Above all I wish to call attention to my debt to Harmon Lockrow of Albany, outstanding among booksellers specializing in Americana, for his indefatigable efforts in providing me with volume after volume of primary source material otherwise almost unobtainable.

My ultimate debt is acknowledged in the Dedication.

I. "THE TIDE RISES, THE TIDE FALLS"

> Some stonger nature once ruled these neglected trees and this fallow
> ground. They will wait the return of their master as long as roots can
> creep through mould, and the mould make way for them. The stories of
> strange lives have been whispered to the earth, their thoughts have
> burned themselves into the cold rocks . . . .
>
> SARAH ORNE JEWETT, The Gray Man[1]

1. Migration to the North

In 1824 Seth Hubbell, an obscure New England farmer, published a little
pamphlet recounting, under solemn oath of truthfulness, his "sufferings"
as a first settler in what is now the mountain township of Wolcott,
Vermont. But the solemn oath was unnecessary. Seth Hubbell's experiences, however unbelievably harrowing, were so typically American
and so typically New England that no one would question them.

Like so many early Vermonters, including Ethan Allen, Hubbell was a
native of Connecticut. He does not give us his reasons for leaving his farm
in the long-established community of Norwalk, but we can reasonably
conjecture what they were. The New England seaboard, at the time of the
settlement of the uplands of Vermont, New Hampshire, and Maine, had
been inhabited for a hundred and fifty years by a thrifty and highly prolific
people. Cellar holes, miles of stone walls, milldams, all still to be found
throughout the now wooded sections of Connecticut and Massachusetts,
tell how thickly the land was settled. Present-day fishermen along Seth
Hubbell's own Silvermine River and its tributaries in Norwalk and New
Canaan, Connecticut, find a millsite every mile or two—the mossy
abutments of the dams, the half-filled foundations, and, until the suburban
depredations of the last fifty years, the Cyclopean, time-eaten millstones
themselves hidden deep in the grass and underbrush. Seth undoubtedly
had his wheat ground at one of these mills and caught trout in the pool
below the dam, where today one still has the best chances of a strike.

By the end of the Revolution the population of this area was too dense
for successful farming —almost as dense in the rural parts as it has now
become under the influx of suburbanites, who have trucked away

1

Hubbell's miles of stonewalls to convert them into durable fieldstone villas. What occurred in those days immediately following the Revolution has been compared to the swarming of bees. The first hive of New England was filled; a new hive must be established. Seth Hubbell was one of the tens of thousands who in a few years swarmed over the new lands to the north, now free of the French, the Indians, and the Proclamation Line, and within three decades gave many of the up-country counties the most numerous population they have ever had.[2]

Thus in the summer of 1788 Seth Hubbell, according to his own account, traveled by ox team the three hundred miles of hilly, winding road from Norwalk to Wolcott. On this first trip he was alone, his purpose being to clear some land on which later to settle his household. After a summer of preparation he returned to Norwalk, leaving his oxen with a nearby settler. In late February of the following winter he set out again for Vermont, this time with his wife and five daughters, and another yoke of oxen, a horse, and some cows. Within a hundred miles of Wolcott one of the oxen failed, so that Hubbell himself had to spell it at the yoke. Eventually the sick ox had to be abandoned, while the family pushed on through four feet of snow to Hyde Park, the last inhabited place on their journey. Here they "laid over," while for ten days Seth carried hay back several miles to the ailing ox in an attempt to save it, so serious would its loss be to his plans. But at last the animal died; and with his wife and two eldest children, the younger ones staying at Hyde Park, Seth snowshoed the last eight miles of the blazed trail to Wolcott. Here he found that, for reasons he fails to specify, he had lost ownership of the land that he had cleared the previous summer and that one of the oxen left behind for the winter had died.

Miraculously the family got through the spring and summer. Without food or money, Seth was fortunate enough to kill a sable, which he carried fifty miles to trade for a half bushel of wheat. Later he got a moose from an Indian. To buy land he had to sell all his livestock except one indispensable cow. Lacking his horse, he had to carry his younger children on his shoulders from Hyde Park, and until the first harvest had to "back" all his provisions from New Hampshire, sixty miles away. That first summer, having only an axe and an old hoe to work with, he cleared and planted two acres of land. It was five years before he could afford a team. Among the calamities to follow was the loss of his wife and two daughters in a great epidemic. Writing about his life in 1824, Seth makes this comment:

> When I reflect on those past events, the fatigue and toil I had to encounter, the dark scenes I had to pass through, I am struck with wonder and astonishment at the fortitude and presence of mind that I then had to bear up under them.[3]

Seth Hubbell is not the only one to be "struck with wonder and astonishment" at the vitality of the American pioneer. When we do begin to understand it, especially as its inherited potentialities operate in the frontierless America of today, we may better understand why contemporary Americans behave as they do. Vast stores of energy, when denied a legitimate outlet, sometimes burst forth in unhappy manifestations despite all restraint. When the marketplace rather than the forest becomes the outlet for American vigor the story is frequently one for amazement but not always for approbation.

But Seth Hubbell and the other thousands of participants in this swarming of the New England hive did not lack outlets for their energies, no matter how intense. These men and women, who had left well-ordered communities along the coast and in the big river valleys, were not content with mere log huts in a clearing, as apparently were the settlers of the Southern mountains. A subsistence was merely the beginning; the next most necessary step was to establish the two great bulwarks of New England civilization—religion and education. In 1821 and 1822, President Timothy Dwight of Yale reports in his famous *Travels in New England and New York*[4] that he had seen school houses in New England all the way to the Canadian border, even in communities that had not yet outgrown the log-cabin stage. Moreover, education was thriving beyond the elementary level. Dwight found the northern states well supplied with academies where advanced Latin, French, Greek, English, and mathematics were taught. Colleges too were already established—institutions like Middlebury and the University of Vermont and the medical school, now extinct, at Castleton, Vermont. But all this was only a replica of the older down-country life. Middlebury with its college had its counterpart in Litchfield, say, with its law school and its girls' academy.

Thus within the thirty years following the Revolution, families like that of Seth Hubbell had spread New England village civilization over at least twice its former area. Built around the school and the church, this civilization nurtured at its best a population of literate and intelligent small landholders. Dwight, again, speaks of the many social libraries he found on his travels and the great amount of reading done by men and women in every sphere of New England society.[5] Thomas Low Nichols in his *Forty Years of American Life* describes his native town of Orford, New Hampshire, far up the Connecticut Valley, as being almost a perfect democracy. Every man was a property owner, landlords were unknown, hired men were accepted on terms of complete equality in the family, and men of large fortune were only less rare than those who could not make both ends meet.[6]

Most enthusiastic of all, Harriet Beecher Stowe found among New Englanders a Hebrew piety combined with a Greek simplicity.

The state of society in some of the districts of Maine, in these days, much resembled in its spirit that which Moses labored to produce in ruder ages. It was entirely democratic, simple, grave, hearty, and sincere, —solemn and religious in its daily tone, and yet, as to all material good, full of wholesome thrift and prosperity. Perhaps, taking the average mass of the people, a more healthful and desirable state of society never existed. Its better specimens had a simple Doric grandeur unsurpassed in any age.[7]

In villages like this, several generations of the finest American type were produced. There are many descriptions, for example, of the girls who worked in the textile mills at Lowell, whither they had been recruited from the farthest sections of New England. Writers on the subject—Lucy Larcom, Charles Dickens, and Thomas Low Nichols[8]—found these mill girls from the backcountry to be educated, talented, and comely. Most of them did much reading; many were musical; their contributions to the mill paper, the *Lowell Offering*, won the praise of Dickens himself; they had the initiative to call and win impromptu strikes when they felt they had been treated unfairly.

2. Exodus

Like the Hebrews, to whom they were fond of comparing themselves, the Yankees were given to seeking promised lands; a study of the map of New England will reveal a generous sprinkling of Canaans from Long Island Sound to Canada. The backcountry and the remoter coastal districts flourished through the first quarter of the nineteenth century, but after that the decline began. In the farming villages the fertility of the New England family, so greatly in contrast with the sterility of the New England soil, had again created a desperate population problem. Tramp through the hills of Vermont and New Hampshire, and you will find stonewalls and cellar holes—literally whole villages of them with the inevitable lilac bushes and apple trees—on hilltops and forty-five–degree slopes, where only the most intense population pressure could have driven families to attempt farming. Competition on the wheat market by more fertile regions and increasing importation of foreign wool were even worse handicaps than the subarctic climate and glacier-gutted terrain. No wonder that the reports of deep, stoneless soil on the Ohio and beyond set in motion a second exodus, one that was not to stop till the major portion of New England had been restored to the forest.

As an example of what this exodus meant let us trace the history of the typical northern New England town of Benson, in hilly and broken, but by no means exceptionally sterile, country near the head of the Champlain Valley in Vermont. The first inhabitants began to creep into this township immediately after the Revolution, about the time Seth Hubbell settled in Wolcott. The oldest headstones in the graveyard date back to the 1780's; the oldest existing houses, to the 1790's. The town grew from 658 in 1791 to 1,159 in 1800 and had its greatest population, over 1,500, in 1810. From then on every census showed a decline, at first slight, but steadily increasing in acceleration. By 1890 the town numbered about 1,000 and by 1940 only 600 persons, or fewer than at the time of the first census in 1791. During the nineteenth century there were in the town two churches, eight schools, several doctors, a hotel; now there are one half-filled church, four schools, no doctors, no hotel. And farms are still being abandoned. On a casual walk in the township one passes as many deserted as inhabited houses. As it takes only thirty or forty years for an abandoned house, if uncared for, to disappear almost entirely, it is evident that since about 1850, when the emigration got well started, the countryside in this town has continuously presented the disheartening aspect of desertion and steady decay.

But the period of greatest depression, when the Greek and Hebrew democracy of the nineteenth century seemed to be undergoing utter disintegration, was from the end of the Civil War till the end of the century. Added to the other causes of depopulation, many of the soldiers who were not killed did not return to their home towns, having been struck with postwar restlessness and the lure of easy money in the West and in the cities. The already-stagnant backwaters of New England were on the verge of being drained dry. A contemporary account of a New England village during this period accomplishes more than pages of statistics.

> Midway between Williamstown and Brattleboro, I saw on the summit of a hill against the evening sky what seemed a large cathedral. Driving thither, I found a huge, old-time, two-story church, a large academy (which blended in the distance with the church), a village with a broad street, perhaps 150 feet wide. I drove on and found that the church was abandoned, the academy dismantled, the village deserted. The farmer who owned the farm on the north of the village lived on one side of the broad street and he who owned the farm on the south lived on the other, and they were the only inhabitants. All the others had gone —to the manufacturing villages, to the great cities, to the West. Here had been industry, education, religion, comfort, and contentment, but there remained only a drear solitude of forsaken homes. . . .The deserted village was the old-fashioned "Centre" of the town, on a high hill, remote from railways and mill-streams, unknown to summer boarders —an agricultural village, dependent upon the agriculture around it and from which it sprang.[9]

The picture is even more bewildering when we realize that barely a hundred years before the date of this account the first settlers had inched their way up the inland valleys with their ox teams to establish this town in a wilderness. Was ever a commonwealth built with such difficulty and so quickly thrown away?

3. Ebb-Tide

Conditions along the coast, with the exception of the great ports, were analogous to those in the remoter inland sections. In his true account of John Gilley, one of the gems of local-color realism of the last century, President Charles W. Eliot of Harvard has told a story of hardship and humble heroism equal to anything in the life of Seth Hubbell. As early settlers on the rocky islands off Mt. Desert, John Gilley and his father William before him, made fruitful an environment even more unfavorable than that of northern Vermont. John got his start in life by carrying paving stones to Boston in a leaky schooner that he owned with two other seamen. Anchoring their vessel on the seaward side of one of the outer islands, the men would land their dories on the surf-pounded beaches. On the Maine coast a beach is usually a heap of cobblestones slanting upwards from the water at a twenty- or thiry-degree angle. The stones, ranging in size from that of an egg to that of a basketball, have been worn smooth and round by the breakers, which incessantly churn and grind them with a roar that can be heard miles away. From one of these shambles the men would select a doryful of cobbles of the size proper for the streets of Boston. Launching the dory through the icy surf was a dangerous, back-breaking job. When the schooner was reached each stone would have to be handed over the side and carefully stowed. Then there would be another trip to the beach, and many more, till the ship's cargo of one hundred tons had been put aboard. There followed the two-hundred–mile trip up to Boston in hazardous, badly charted waters, and finally the unloading at the Stone Wharf in Charlestown.

This was considered one of the easier ways of hewing a living from the granite coast of eastern New England.[10] The more colorful story of the New England coastal village in the early days of the Republic, each one with its thriving shipyard and fleet of whaling, merchant, or fishing vessels is familiar in fiction and history. Lucy Larcom's description in *A New England Girlhood* of her home town of Beverly, Massachusetts, or Sarah Orne Jewett's essays and stories in such books as *Country By-Ways* or *Deephaven* give piquant and nostalgic pictures of these times. Around the harbors all along the coast one would find that a farmer ploughing behind his oxen in his meadow was, likely as not, a traveled mariner as well, a familiar of Calcutta, Hongkong, and Valparaiso. In many homesteads would be Canton shawls, Smyrna silks, Turkish satins, green parrots, Java sparrows, and Russian kopecks, and in the richer homes would be Mongolian and African servants. On the wharves at almost every New England rivermouth would be rolling cocoa-nuts, exotic spices, and tamarinds.[11] Added to the Hebrew piety and Greek democracy of the inland towns, here on the seacoast one also found a Phoenician cosmopolitanism. Observing a little Down-East community, Stowe justly commented:

> A ship-building, a ship-sailing community has an unconscious poetry ever underlying its existence. Exotic ideas from foreign lands relieve the trite monotony of life; the ship-owner lives in communion with the whole world, and is less likely to fall into the petty commonplaces that infest the routine of inland life.[12]

But the decline was as rapid and disastrous as that which overtook the farming communities. First, the British blockade of 1812–15 dealt New England shipping a blow from which it never fully recovered, driving many shipowners to smuggling for a livelihood. Later, in rapid succession, came the loss of the whale fishery, owing to the substitution of coal oil for whale oil; the depletion of the forests on which the shipbuilding had depended; the railroad, which made it cheaper to distribute goods from several large ports rather than from many little ports; and finally the obsolescence of the sailing vessel for transoceanic commerce. By 1870 a hundred once-thriving little seaports from Eastport to Greenwich had been reduced to decadent fishing villages with a population as provincial as that of the remotest hamlet among the hills. Where formerly half a dozen ships in world trade lay in the harbor, now only an occasional moth-eaten square-rigger or an unpainted coaster would be tied to a crumbling wharf.[13]

The effects of such change on community life were of course disastrous, and are today everywhere apparent on the New England coast. The spot where this book is being written, the island township of Swan's Island, Maine, is typical. Since the Civil War the population of this island has dropped from over a thousand to about three hundred. Wharves where oceangoing vessels once tied up are now only piles of rocks and half-rotted, barnacled timbers. Public buildings, once scenes of gay and wholesome recreation, are sagging in disrepair. The population, formerly owners and masters of vessels, now hire out as common seamen on other men's ships, spend their time tinkering with worn-out Ford motors on leaky lobster craft, or serve as lackeys for the summer visitors. Even those who continue to fish independently are at the mercy of shaky, speculative markets to a much greater extent then the proprietor of an independent cargo ship of a hundred years ago.

4. Predominance of Women Writers

The writers discussed in this book are for the most part women. The reasons for this "feminization of literature," as Van Wyck Brooks calls it,[14] are many—among them the preoccupation of men with money-making rather than with the arts; the simple numerical inferiority of men as a result of the slaughter of the Civil War; the emigration of men to the West; and, lastly, the confinement of women to traditional roles that excluded them from many activities open to men and thus forced them into cultural pursuits, such as writing, which could be followed in the home during intervals between household chores. These causes and others were doubtless at work, and perhaps, more decisively, in New England villages than in the nation as a whole. War casualties were high among village men, and many of those who had survived, no longer attracted to their former life on their rocky, unproductive farms, sought more rewarding occupations elsewhere, whether on the land or in the cities. Thus many women, unable to find husbands, were left more or less stranded in their native villages. Of course, few of these women became writers, but many of them became readers who would naturally be drawn to writing that dealt with their own way of life. Obviously the village environment was one that women authors who were acquainted with rural New England would be best qualified to interpret.

Given their background, their sympathies, and their subject matter, the woman writers of rural New England perforce wrote primarily about women and their problems and satisfactions and compensations. Writings so oriented attracted attention far beyond the areas they dealt with; for these areas, despite their social and economic decline, still represented attitudes and values that had been influential, and continued to be so, in shaping American civilization. The fact is that women had been left as custodians of a village culture that traced its descent from the early seventeenth century. The men who remained on the countryside willingly left this custodial function to their women; and, if we can believe writers like Sarah Orne Jewett and Mary Wilkins Freeman, it is well that this was the case, since by these authors the men are usually depicted as weak in character or warped in will. Yet the men retained political power, for women could legally neither hold office—except perhaps on school committees—nor vote in town meetings. Furthermore, though in the congregations of the churches women had for generations outnumbered men by at least two to one,[15] they had no vote in church elections and were, of course, excluded from religious ministry.

Despite these obvious injustices and handicaps, women had long dominated New England rural culture. This was especially the case in that body of literature that originated in or dealt with the countryside. The authors centering around Boston, Cambridge, and Concord were mainly men; and until well beyond the middle of the nineteenth century they received most of the acclaim. But shortly after the Civil War this admittedly brilliant group of writers—Oliver Wendell Holmes, James Russell Lowell, Henry Wadsworth Longfellow, Ralph Waldo Emerson— were past their artistic prime; and a decade or so later we are told that the literary center of the nation had shifted from Boston to New York. New England was believed to be in a cultural decline along with its very real economic one.

And one of the symptoms of decline was thought by many to be the fact that most of the remaining writers were women—a judgment that even such perceptive cultural historians as Van Wyck Brooks[16] and Vernon Parrington[17] supported. This implied slur upon women writers did not necessarily stem from a conviction of any innate intellectual or creative inferiority in women. Rather it was based on the belief that by education and experience women, especially in rural New England, were ill-equipped for the role of literary representatives of their region. It is true that the educational opportunities in the academies and the colleges were not as available to women as to men, though throughout the century progress was being made in eliminating this disparity. It is also true that a broad spectrum of experience—politics, large-scale business enterprise, agriculture, all the professions except teaching on elementary levels—was virtually closed to women. Yet the results, so far as literature goes, were not as disastrous as Brooks and Parrington seemed to think. In the restricted environments of the New England countryside or on the remote stretches of the coast such writers as Sarah Orne Jewett, Mary Wilkins Freeman, Rose Terry Cooke, and Celia Thaxter found the materials for dramatic stories of human strengths and frailties and poignantly evocative descriptive sketches of their region. Few writers of prose in America in their century surpassed these authors in literary skill; and as for poetry, Emily Dickinson, who lived all but a few months of her fifty-six years in the country town of Amherst, took her place—albeit after her death— among the greatest poets in the English language.

A capacity for compensating for misfortune or deprivation is a remarkable human attribute, and it seems particularly strong among persons endowed with creative talents. Emerson, indeed, found compensation to be one of the laws of life, operating almost independently of an individual's effort. The major thesis of the present study—expressed in the poem by Emily Dickinson from which the title is taken—is that, with an apparent paucity of material and experience to draw from, a group of New England rural writers, most of them village-bred women, produced a uniquely distinguished body of literature. James Fenimore Cooper, Nathaniel Hawthorne, and Henry James complained of the lack of material and inspiration afforded the novelist by the American scene. Henry James's extensive list of these lacks is famous: "no state, in the

European sense of the word, ... no sovereign, no court, no personal loyalty, no aristocracy, no church, no clergy, no army, no diplomatic service, no country gentlemen, no palaces, no castles, nor manors, nor old country-houses, nor parsonages, nor thatched cottages. ..."[18] The list goes on and on—as remarkable for its length as for its inaccuracies. Yet James, before he permanently fled from the Great American Cultural Desert, had known the comparative sophistications of New York, Newport, and Cambridge. It is difficult to imagine what his list might have included had he been living in a small New England town.

The village authors themselves, however, found subjects to write about and did so with such success that even James found words of praise for Sarah Orne Jewett and Mary Wilkins Freeman.[19] But the New England these two were writing about was in fact culturally deprived, and they had to make the best of what was at hand. It must also be emphasized that the writers with whom I am dealing were themselves women living under the restrictions that their society and its customs imposed on their sex. That they and many of the women they wrote about felt and to some extent resented these restrictions is evident in many stories, e.g., Freeman's "A Village Singer," Cooke's "Mrs. Flint's Married Experience," and Jewett's "The Town Poor." But resentment and a sense of injustice has sparked much of the world's literature and art.

In the late nineteenth century women were not, of course, newcomers to the New England literary scene. Indeed, in the mid–seventeenth century Anne Bradstreet had achieved a reputation not yet extinguished. In the late eighteenth century Mercy Warren of Boston had written a number of plays and in 1805 had published her three-volume *History of the Rise, Progress, and Termination of the American Revolution.* In the 1820's Catharine Maria Sedgwick of the Berkshire village of Stockbridge had inaugurated New England rural writing with *A New England Tale* (1822) and *Redwood* (1824). A contemporary of Cooper, she produced in her historically based *Hope Leslie, or Early Times in the Massachusetts* (1827) a novel superior in style and plot to any of Cooper's historical novels, and in her generation she achieved a popularity comparable to his. During the 1830's Harriet Beecher Stowe, born and brought up a parson's daughter in Litchfield, Connecticut, began her career as a writer of fiction dealing with New England rural and village themes. And Margaret Fuller, though frowned upon by the convention-bound, had proved to be the most discerning literary critic the country had produced up to her time. Large numbers of other women—whom Hawthorne sourly referred to as a "damned mob of scribbling women"[20]—were wielding their pens on various levels of literary accomplishment. The women writers of and about rural New England to be discussed in the following chapters were carrying on a feminine literary tradition of long standing and were of a numerous company.

10

II. "ART FOR TRUTH'S SAKE":

The Atlantic Monthly, T. W. Higginson,
Elizabeth Stuart Phelps, Whittier, and
Harriet Beecher Stowe

> And here let us say that the mere dilettante and the amateur ruralist
> may as well keep their hands off. The prize is not for them. He who
> would successfully strive for it must be himself what he sings,—a part
> and parcel of the rural life of New England,—one who has grown strong
> amidst its healthful influences, familiar with all its details, and capable of
> detecting whatever of beauty, humor, or pathos pertain to it,—one who
> has added to his book-lore the large experience of an active participation
> in the rugged soil, the hearty amusements, the trials and the pleasures he
> describes.
>
> JOHN GREENLEAF WHITTIER, *Robert Dinsmore*[1]

1. Moral Earnestness

The ordeal of New England, grim as it has been pictured by various
historians, has seldom been realized in all its catastrophic effects. But the
few mitigating features that usually accompany any calamity have been
even more seriously neglected. In the gloomy citation of statistics and
examples we have overlooked that most important aspect of any disaster,
the manner in which the people involved met their misfortunes and
continued to live through them. Trite as it sounds, the final value is always
the human value; and this is always the most difficult to estimate, because
it can be judged only from actual contact with the people themselves. For
example, Eugene O'Neill, born in Times Square, attempted to depict New
Englanders during this time in terms of the philosophy of Sigmund Freud
of Vienna. While *Desire Under the Elms* and *Mourning Becomes Electra* are
worthwhile expositions of the Freudian outlook, they cannot be taken as
serious documents in the sociology of New England.[2] What we should
look for in writers of the period of decline is the same intimate contact
with their subject matter as Frost has with a later period. E. A. Robinson,
as we shall see, had this close relationship. But his response was so violent
and he so early fled his native environment that his accuracy cannot be
implicitly relied on.

There are, however, many fully qualified "recorders of the New England decline," as Fred Pattee has called them. Some of them, such as Mary Wilkins Freeman and Sarah Orne Jewett, are important figures in American letters. Others, such as Rowland Robinson and Celia Thaxter, are mainly of local interest. But taken together they give a detailed and accurate contemporary picture of New England during the times of stress. Between the Civil War and the beginning of the twentieth century these writers were busily describing the life unfolding around them and, perhaps more important, were recording their own feelings as actors in the drama. The composite story that they tell is a complete one; and it is an interesting one because it is of an exciting period. Its accuracy is ensured by the literary creed by which these men and women wrote, the creed of local-color realism.

The keynote for local-color writing was struck by William Dean Howells in the *Atlantic Monthly* during 1870. In a review of the translations of several of Björnson's novels—favorites among the New England local colorists and in a way prototypes for the worldwide movement in peasant literature that includes such works as Tolstoy's *Master and Man*, Knut Hamsun's *Growth of the Soil*, and V. S. Reymont's *The Peasants*—Howells suggests that the time has come for Americans to cease copying the situations and catastrophes of English authors. He particularly abominates Luise Mühlbach's "blond romances." How much better it would be, he goes on to say, to drink inspiration from these "fresh, wonderful tales of Norwegian life," with their "simplicity, reticence and self-control." In these stories the artificiality of the drawing room, the "pathetic fallacy," the melodrama of the back alley, and tedious, oversubtilized analysis of emotion—the staples of American fiction of the time—give way to a portrayal of humble everyday folk, an objective description of nature, and simple narration. New England writers, the reviewer believes, could derive a peculiar benefit from Björnson's stories, since the conscientious, thrifty fishermen and farmers of Norway and the rugged climate and barren soil they contend with are so reminiscent of New England.[3]

In a highly influential essay, "Americanism in Literature," published in the *Atlantic* in the same year, Thomas Wentworth Higginson again sounded the Emersonian plea for a native literature. Quoting from David Wasson, the preacher, he finds that "the Englishman is undoubtedly a wholesome figure in the mental eye; but will not 20,000,000 copies of him do for the present?" He suggests that we investigate the work of other cultures—of Norway, perhaps—but above all he demands American energy, heartiness, and action to be embedded in our literature. Moreover, while he does not wish us always to remain Puritans, he feels that the Puritan earnestness of purpose would aid in building a strong national literature. The lack of such purpose is best exemplified, Higginson thinks, in the timidity of the upper and urban classes, who refused, for example, to hear lectures by Wendell Phillips and Theodore Parker, two of New England's greatest orators, though these men were repeatedly invited to lecture before less elite rural audiences. One had to go to the country to find people who were still not afraid of a new idea or one that did not come from England.[4]

There was nothing essentially new in these strictures voiced by the *Atlantic;* Emerson in his "American Scholar" and Whittier in an essay on Robert Dinsmore, to mention but two, had been saying the same things to New Englanders for the past forty years. The idea of an objective, indigenous, realistic literature, expressive of the lives of the people rather than of the upper classes, had at last taken hold, not only in New England but in the nation as a whole. The suggestions laid down in the review on Björnson were followed perhaps too sedulously. But in New England the particular suggestion of Higginson, that there be earnestness of purpose, fell on naturally fertile ground. Because generally the New England local colorists felt it their duty to present their localities and neighbors as truthfully as they possibly could, we have from these authors a most useful and effective type of writing. A few New England local colorists, of course, did not live up to Higginson's ideal. One of these was the Bostonized, genteel Thomas Bailey Aldrich, whose most famous story is the artificial "Marjorie Daw." Aldrich, of course, had another talent—that of *The Story of a Bad Boy,* based on his Portsmouth childhood. Yet much of his effort was directed to the writing of rather vapid *vers de société* and "pretty" short stories. One would not find Mary Wilkins Freeman squandering her talent on such literary dawdling; or Sarah Orne Jewett, who agreed with Wordsworth's dictum that "existence is the most frivolous thing in the world if one does not conceive it as a great and continual duty,"[5] and had said to Willa Cather, "To work in silence and with all one's heart, that is the writer's lot."[6] When devoted to realistic writing the New England sense of duty was bound to produce results.

2. Ethicism

Elizabeth Stuart Phelps—later Mrs. Ward—the writer of many mediocre stories of uplift, but a better critic than she was an artist, has written a typical New England condemnation of the vacuous prettiness of such writers as Aldrich. In her autobiography—in a chapter entitled "Art for Truth's Sake"—she attempts to defend the writers of New England, both past and present, for what Howells called their "ethicism," that is, their preoccupation with morals and conduct. Quoting Matthew Arnold's statement that conduct is "three fourths of life," she goes on to show that the realists, among whom she incorrectly numbers herself, must give a proportionate ethical content to their works.

> In a word, the province of the artist is to portray life as it is; and life *is* moral responsibility. Life is several things, we do not deny. It is beauty, it is joy, it is tragedy, it is comedy, it is psychical and physical pleasure . . .; but it is steadily and sturdily and always moral responsibility.[7]

The moral, of course, even in Phelps's view, should never be made obvious. It will be inherent in every realistic transcription of life.

> "Helplessly to point the moral" is the last thing needful or artistic. The moral takes care of itself. Life is moral struggle. Portray the struggle, and you need write no tract. In so far as you feel obliged to write the tract, your work is not well done. One of the greatest works of fiction ever given to the world in any tongue was *Les Miserables* . . . . Did Victor Hugo write a tract? He told an immortal story. Hold beside it the sketches and pastels, the etchings, the studies in dialect, the adoration of the incident, the dissection of the cadaver, which form the fashion in the ateliers of schools to-day![8]

The opinions of Phelps are valuable not because she herself is a distinguished writer but because by background and upbringing she is so much in the New England tradition. Though born in Boston, she escaped that city's intellectual climate by being moved at the age of three to Andover, where her father was a professor of sacred rhetoric. On both sides she was descended from Calvinistic ministers, and the Theological School of Andover was the last stonghold of the old religion against the Unitarianism and Transcendentalism of Boston and Concord. Though only twenty miles from Boston, Andover represented in its religious outlook as well as in its aspect of a college and academy town the best that the small New England community had to offer. Since it represented the kind of culture that migrating Yankees had carried from the Mohawk Valley to the Kansas plains, Andover was also more typically New England than the metropolis, which had outgrown its rural roots.

The consequence was that Phelps found herself willy-nilly in perfect rapport with the great masses of reading Americans. To write of life from the Andover point of view was to write of life from the dominant American point of view. Thus her *The Gates Ajar* with its evangelical assurance of salvation and immortality and the actual glimpses it gave of Heaven was, for all its mawkishness, one of the most popular books ever published in America. Appearing after the Civil War and growing out of its author's own grief for her brother killed in battle, the book appealed to every bereaved man or woman who had the same religious background as she.

The Gates Ajar and similar religious effusions that followed it can scarcely be classed as attempts to record New England life and thus concern us little here. But Phelps could not refrain from having a fling at local color, taking Gloucester, where she had spent over twenty summers, as her special province. Unlike most "summer people," Phelps had mingled intimately with the "natives." Having witnessed the misery caused by the murder of a father of twelve children in a barroom brawl in Gloucester, she suddenly was awakened to the evils of the liquour traffic. The Sunday following the murder she held a religious service in the bar where the brawl had occurred. The fishermen were favorably impressed both by the service and by Phelps, a fact that the modern intellectual will be surprised to hear but that any one acquainted at first hand with Americans en masse will find quite natural. For many years thereafter Phelps worked among the men of Gloucester in their Reform Clubs, speaking to them herself and bringing to them such outstanding lecturers as Phillips Brooks.

Out of this experience came a number of stories of Gloucester life that combined local color with all the "moral earnestness" and "ethicism" that this intense modern Puritan could command. Of these pieces The Madonna of the Tubs is typical; and in it, we presume, is an example of the moral that inheres but should not obtrude, to paraphrase its author's own critical beliefs. Unfortunately the moral in The Madonna of the Tubs is not so latent as it might be. As the title rather blatantly implies, the thesis is that among the lowliest persons one may find saints and madonnas, there being one of each in this particular tale of the New England fisherman. The basic goodness of common folk is of course as valid as it is a common theme for local-color stories. But in real life, which local-color writing is supposed to follow, canonization usually occurs only many years after the candidate's death, not during childhood, as is the case with the little crippled boy in Phelps's tale. Furthermore, the author allows her prohibitionist sentiments to loom too prominently in the remorse of the drunken father, who quarrels alcoholically with his family the night of his departure on a voyage that almost costs him his life.

One need not give a detailed summary of The Madonna of the Tubs to indicate that it is inferior as art and as realism. Phelps is important in what she tried to do rather than in what she succeeded in doing. She was the most articulate theorist of her group and the worst practitioner. A dozen other local colorists of her time in New England surpassed her in artistry and in truth to life, if not in national popularity. Yet all of them contain the ethical counterpoint that Phelps and Higginson advocated but that Phelps, at least, allowed too often to become the melody itself. The result is a hysteria that forfeits her her reader's confidence—a shrillness that pervades whole works and renders them obnoxious to a sensitive ear, as in this passage from *The Madonna of the Tubs.*

> Their eyes clashed, retreated, advanced, united, and held gloriously. They defied each other, they adored each other, taunted and blessed, challenged and yielded, blamed and forgave, wounded and worshipped, as only a few men and women may in all the world, and love the better for it. The story of years was told without a word; the secret of anguish was said in silence; the torrent of joy poured past dumb lips, and there by the winter sea, on a Christmas Eve, in the dismal hotel entry, by the light of the smoky kerosene, two souls without speech or language met, perhaps for the first time in all their lives.[9]

Yet "ethicism" in a writer like Howells, who indeed originated the term, could be most effective, as in the following passage from *Their Wedding Journey.* Basil March has been gazing over the Plains of Abraham at Quebec.

> The red stain in Basil's thought yielded to the rain sweeping across the pasture-land from which it had long since faded, and the words on the monument, "Here died Wolfe victorious", did not proclaim his bloody triumph over the French, but his self-conquest, his victory over fear and pain and love of life. Alas! when shall the poor, blind, stupid world honor those who renounce self in the joy of their kind, equally with those who devote themselves through the anguish and loss of thousands? So old a world, and groping still![10]

3. Country vs. City

Henry Ward Beecher has written that

> the remote neighborhoods and hill-towns yet retain the manners, morals, institutions, customs and religion of the fathers. The interior villages of New England are her brood-combs.[11]

In any consideration of New England civilization the rural areas should receive due attention. Too many persons have the notion that Boston is the region's only cultural repository. Nothing could be further from the truth. A majority of the great men and women of New England—Edwards, Longfellow, Hawthorne, Thoreau, Alcott, Horace Greeley, Bryant, T. B. Aldrich, Emily Dickinson, Noah Webster, E. A. Robinson, Daniel Webster, Whittier, the Beechers, the Stowes, Edward Bellamy—were products of country villages or smaller seaports. Boston and Cambridge became merely convenient places for them to congregate. But it is not sufficient to judge localities by prominent people alone. The New England countryside's greatest contribution to American life is the Yankees themselves —the most dominant type, because of their far-flung emigrations, in the whole nation and the type by which America is known to the world. From them have come in large measure the energy, the humor, the earnestness, the love of education that are a considerable part of our national character. The occasional condescensions of Bostonians like Holmes or Lowell are simply not justifiable. For example, the jargon spoken by Hosea Biglow in Lowell's *Biglow Papers* is little more than a stage dialect, reflecting the author's sense of superiority rather than his accuracy of observation—a fact noted by E. A. Robinson and Robert Frost in the '90's. Many a New England farmer spoke, and sometimes still speaks, as pure and sonorous English as has been heard on this side of the Atlantic. Similarly, Holmes's harping on the fact that in the country people say "store" when a Bostonian would say "shop" is far from creditable to him.

The place of the rural Yankee as the central figure in New England life has, moreover, always been recognized by most New England writers, whether rural or Bostonian. The interest of Emerson, Thoreau, and the rest of the Concord group in country life and character need only be mentioned. Even the Brahmins tacitly admitted the greater vitality of country people by using them over and over again in their poems and stories. The wisdom of Lowell's Hosea Biglow, for all the violence done his speech, is rural wisdom. Holmes felt his novels had a better chance of coming to life if they were infused with rural blood. John Macy, in an essay entitled "The Passing of the Yankee," has summed up the case effectively:

> Almost all New England fiction that has a flicker of vitality deals with the non-urban Yankee, the farmer, the villager, the fisherman, the country doctor, the minister, and their womenfolk . . . . New England has thriven, in every way that it ever did thrive, by virtue of its rural and semi-rural population.[12]

The fact that most of the native writers of any merit in New England during the post–Civil War generation were born and bred in the country not only bears out Macy's statement but lends weight to the opinion that a study of New England culture, particularly during these later days, must perforce be focused on the countryside and villages rather than on the parlors of Boston and Cambridge. As St. Petersburg was once Russia's window to the West, so was Boston New England's window to the East. In studying the culture of Russia one would make a mistake to emphasize solely the brilliance of the old Baltic capital. If one did not wish to get merely a dim reflection of Paris, one would have to venture back into thousands of miles of hinterland, where Tolstoy, Dostoevsky, and Chekhov were living among the peasants and the small-town provincials and recording their lives. Similarly, to catch the full flavor of New England,

and not a diluted aroma of contemporary German, English, and French culture, one must push backward from Boston—northward, southward, and westward—among the upland valleys and along the ragged, granite coast, where the sombre native hues of the old way of life had not faded out completely under the refulgence streaming through the eastern window.

4. Whittier

Interest in the New England countryside and its life was not a development of the post–Civil War years. At the beginning of the century, Catharine Sedgwick had successfully incorporated into her tales an authentic New England atmosphere. Timothy Dwight, as already mentioned, wrote enthusiastically and voluminously of his travels through his native region. Later, the Unitarian novelist Sylvester Judd crammed his transcendental novels with realistic etchings of rural life and customs, as would be expected from the subtitle of his most famous work, *Margaret: A Story of the Real and the Ideal.* But the direct literary inspiration to such later writers as Sarah Orne Jewett, Rowland Robinson, and Celia Thaxter came from two famous predecessors, John Greenleaf Whittier and Harriet Beecher Stowe.

In the pastoral country along the Merrimack in northeastern Massachusetts a Quaker farmer's son had become awakened to the beauty of the life into which he was born. When not writing on religion and slavery, Whittier recreated the past and present of New England, its people and its scenery. Like Longfellow and Hawthorne, he often wandered far into colonial and Indian times, as in "Mogg Megone" and "The Bridal of Pennacook." But in such poems, as Whittier himself says, "the story . . . has been considered by the author only as a framework for sketches of the scenery of New England, and of its early inhabitants."[13] The interest is in local color, rather than in narrative. Other poems, like "Telling the Bees" and "Snowbound," go back to the author's own childhood and youth, but again the interest is in scenes, people, and customs. Finally there are innumerable poems on the New England of his adulthood, poems like the deeply felt "The Meeting" on New England Quakerism, the "Songs of Labor," and "Among the Hills." The "Prelude" to "Among the Hills" in a sense sets the key for later New England local-color writing because in it is struck a typical balance between the sordid and the happy sides of rural life. The poem begins with a conventional picture of the somnolent beauty of the countryside on a summer day—a "pervading symphony of peace." It next eulogizes a farmer's son who is

Proud of field-lore and harvest craft, and feeling
All their fine possibilities, how rich
And restful even poverty and toil
Become when beauty, harmony, and love
Sit at their humble hearth as angels sat
At evening in the patriarch's tent, when man
Makes labor noble, and his farmer's frock
The symbol of a Christian chivalry
Tender and just and generous to her
Who clothes with grace all duty . . . .[14]

But like Emerson, Whittier realized "the lofty land breeds little men";
he knew, and with customary honesty admitted that he knew

Too well the picture has another side,—
How wearily the grind of toil goes on
Where love is wanting, how the eye and ear
And heart are starved amidst the plenitude
Of nature, and how hard and colorless
Is life without an atmosphere. I look
Across the lapse of half a century,
And call to mind old homesteads, where no flower
Told that the spring had come, but evil weeds,
Nightshade and rough-leaved burdock in the place
Of the sweet doorway greeting of the rose
And honeysuckle, where the house walls seemed
Blistering in sun, without a tree or vine
To cast the tremulous shadow of its leaves
Across the curtainless windows from whose panes
Fluttered the signal rags of shiftlessness;
Within, the cluttered kitchen-floor, unwashed
(Broom-clean I think they called it); the best room
Stifling with cellar damp, shut from the air
In hot midsummer, bookless, pictureless . . . .
And, in sad keeping with all things about them,
Shrill, querulous women, sour and sullen men,
Untidy, loveless, old before their time,
With scarce a human interest save their own
Monotonous round of small economies,
Or the poor scandal of the neighborhood;
Blind to the beauty everywhere revealed,
Treading the May-flowers with regardless feet . . . .
Church-goers, fearful of the unseen Powers,
But grumbling over pulpit-tax and pew-rent,
Saving, as shrewd economists, their souls
And winter pork with the least possible outlay
Of salt and sanctity . . . .[15]

It is little wonder that the Connecticut local colorist Rose Terry Cooke should have dedicated to Whittier, "my friend . . . master and maker of New England poetry," *Somebody's Neighbors,* a volume of sketches chilled with the bleaker side of the New England character. Many others also—Sarah Orne Jewett, Celia Thaxter, Elizabeth Stuart Phelps—were friends and followers of Whittier, who was always lavish in his praise of young, and especially female, writers who paid court to him.

In Whittier's own artistic life there were influences that tie him in with the British romantic movement. As a young farmer he had read the poems of Robert Burns and had been immediately struck both with their freshness and with the recognition of human dignity, even in the lowliest persons, that pervades them. The idea that great poetry could be created out of such humdrum occupations as ploughing and haying was fascinating to the Amesbury farm boy and immediately started him writing verse himself and sending it to the local newspapers, one of them William Lloyd Garrison's in Newburyport close by. Soon, under the inspiration of Burns, he had arrived at a theory of realism that was to last a lifetime. In an essay on his friend, the elderly and little-known Robert Dinsmore, a Scottish dialect poet long settled in New Hampshire, Whittier wrote a passage that might have been pinned over the desk of every realist since his day:

> He [Robert Dinsmore] calls things by their right names; no euphemism, or transcendentalism,—the plainer and commoner the better . . . . Never having seen a nightingale, he makes no attempt to describe the fowl; but he has seen the night-hawk, at sunset, cutting the air above him, and he tells of it. Side by side with his waving corn-fields and orchard-blooms, we have the barn-yard and pigsty.[16]

Robert Dinsmore, in his poems of farm life and village customs in New Hampshire, was one of the very first New England local colonists, though he has now passed into complete oblivion.

All his life Whittier had before him the same ends as did Burns: to describe with loving accuracy the countryside in which he lived and worked; to celebrate the people and customs of his homeland and to glorify its history; to assert, whenever possible, human worth, especially that of the farmer; to broaden through his abolitionist poetry, as did Burns through his espousal of the French Revolution, the sway of human freedom. The difference between "Snowbound" and "The Cotter's Saturday Night" and between "The Moral Warfare" and "A Man's a Man for A' That" is one of genius rather than of purpose or of spirit. The famous stanza from the "Epistle to John Lapraik" applies to Whittier as well as to Burns:

> Gie me ae spark o' nature's fire,
> That's a' the learning I desire'

Then tho' I drudge thro' dub an' mire
  At pleugh or cart,
My muse, tho' hamely in attire,
  May touch the heart.

As a matter of fact, the purposes and manner of Burns, from the desire to ennoble the common people down to the use of dialect, have from the time of Whittier crept into all our local-color writing. Burns has influenced American writing on nature and rural life more even than Wordsworth, and his manner is to be found in such recent poets as Robert Frost. Nor is it surprising that those who attempt to describe country life should be inspired by this most democratic of poets. Interest in local color is a natural outgrowth of a faith in the democratic way of life, even when we find, as did Whittier, that the rules of realism compel us to paint such life as less ideal than we should like it to be.

5. Harriet Beecher Stowe

Whittier's partner in firmly establishing New England regional literature was Harriet Beecher Stowe. Concerned, like Whittier, with the problem of slavery and writing her most important works on that burning topic, she also turned out at least four memorable and lengthy books on New England life. Again like Whittier, she tended to go back into the past, the pre-railroad past, for her settings, though her aim was to create authentic New England scenes and characters. Born in Litchfield in the hills of western Connecticut, she had known New England village life at its ripest. Litchfield, when Parson Beecher lived and reared his famous family there, had already seen several generations of American life. It had been swept over by the great migration into the northern hill country, and one of its most famous sons, Ethan Allen, had been a leader against the British and the Yorkers in the struggle to expand the borders of New England. But despite the emigrations Litchfield remained serenely on its hilltop, with its churches, its law school, its girls' academy—an embodiment of the best and most durable in New England life.

The daughter of a respected and scholarly minister in such a town could easily find this world a good place, even if the oldtime Calvinism had not to some extent relaxed, as it had particularly in the Beecher household. We are told of the pleasant freedom of the life of the students of both sexes in this village—young people conspicuously free of the restrictions of Puritanism. Harriet Beecher Stowe has told the story of her Litchfield girlhood in *Poganuc People*, one of her finest works, in which members of the Beecher family appear as characters, she being the heroine, Dolly.

Before writing *Poganuc People* Stowe had published *Oldtown Folks,* a re-creation of her husband's hometown of Natick, Massachusetts, about twenty miles west of Boston. Calvin Stowe, a natural storyteller, had spun so many tales about the human oddities of this old Indian town where the Reverend John Eliot had once preached the gospel, that his wife decided to make a book of the material. Professor Stowe himself appears as Horace Holyoke, the narrator. Added to her husband's stories were many observations that she herself had made during frequent visits to the village,[17] and a rather mawkish love story doesn't quite spoil the book. Typically, she wrote *Oldtown Folks* with a purpose.

> It was more to me than a story; it is my résumé of the whole spirit and body of New England, a country that is now exerting such an influence on the civilized world that to know it truly becomes an object.[18]

Oldtown Folks was such a success that is was followed by *Sam Lawson's Oldtown Fireside Stories,* in which the most lovable character in the former work, the whittling, lying, loafing, untidy Sam Lawson—village laureate of yarn-spinning—tells four or five hundred pages of stories, tall and otherwise. Sam Lawson with his shambling gait and mighty drawl has been called the truest Yankee in fiction; he is certainly Stowe's masterpiece in characterization

Two other New England novels of Harriet Beecher Stowe are *The Minister's Wooing,* laid in Newport at the beginning of the nineteenth century, and *The Pearl of Orr's Island,* laid on the Maine coast as she knew it during her husband's professorship at Bowdoin College. This latter work, which was the inspiration of Sarah Orne Jewett's Maine writing, was highly influential among the next generation of New England authors. Unfortunately, like most of Stowe's work, it is marred by sentimentality, this time in the form of an improbable and ridiculous plot involving a shipwrecked castaway, who after being reared into a solid citizen by a Maine fisherman's family, discovers that he is heir to a vast fortune left him by his West Indian father, from whom his mother was fleeing at the time of the shipwreck that cast him upon the rocks of Maine . . . added to which is a love story involving an orphaned fisher-girl named Mara, who distressingly dies before she can marry the exotic hero.

Despite this excrescence of trashiness and the endless arguments on such theological subjects as free will and grace, which had become obsessions with Stowe and mar all her works, *The Pearl of Orr's Island* is built on a solid basis of skillfully presented local realism. Written about a Maine seacoast community at a time when the shipyards were humming and almost every male had sailed in foreign parts, the book is well ventilated with salt breezes and the breath of spruce forests. The fisherfolk, too, have tar on them, with the notable exceptions of the dandified hero and phthisic heroine. Although there is no Sam Lawson, there are the two women, Roxy and Ruey Toothacre, who board out around the neighborhood as nurses, sempstresses, watchers, layers out of corpses, and midwives. Miss Roxy is the typical Yankee realist, exuding common sense, practicality, independence and pithy speeches:

> "I was always homely as an owl," said Miss Roxy. . . . "I always had sense to know it, and knew my sphere. Homely folks would like to say pretty things, and to have pretty things said to them, but they never do. I made up my mind pretty early that my part in the vineyard was to have hard work and no posies."[19]

No writer except Sarah Orne Jewett has so successfully caught the rhythms of Down-East speech; and in reproducing the continuous scriptural allusion that flowed through such speech in the days when people still went to meeting twice every Sabbath day, Sarah Orne Jewett has not approached her predecessor. Much of the picturesqueness of Yankee speech of former generations lay in this liberal sprinkling of biblical metaphor. As a minister's daughter deeply concerned with religion, Stowe was perhaps at an advantage, but at any rate she has mastered one of the secrets of the dialect spoken by her characters. Another example, again from Miss Roxy, though it is typical of all Stowe's characters, is worth giving. For those who wish to know, the allusion is to Jonah 4: 6–9, though it came naturally to Miss Roxy, without any thought of verse and chapter. The Moses referred to is the hero of the novel—not the Hebrew prophet.

> "Well, Master Moses'll jest have to give up his particular notions . . . and come down in the dust, like all the rest on us, when the Lord sends an east wind and withers our gourds."[20]

This is a far cry from the stagy squawkings and misspellings of Hosea Biglow. For this is true Yankee, in rhythm, grammar, and imagery. Yet, oddly enough, Lowell was able to give Stowe the best advice she ever ignored. If she had followed it she would have ranked high among American novelists. In a letter to her he wrote:

> My advice is to follow your own instincts—to stick to nature, and avoid what people commonly call the "Ideal"; for that, and beauty, and pathos, and success, all lie in the simply natural. . . . There are ten thousand people who can write "ideal" things for one who can see, and feel, and reproduce nature and character.[21]

One will find, as John Erskine has, that these books of Stowe are still worth reading, contain much of "the simply natural."[22]

An important influence in the works of Stowe must be mentioned. Like Whittier, she found in Scotland the writer who spoke most convincingly to her. When she was a child in Litchfield her father had relaxed the Calvinistic ban against novels to the extent of allowing his children to read Sir Walter Scott, who was so historical in content and earnest in spirit that he could hardly be classed as a worldly writer. Like the rest of their generation, the Beecher children gulped Scott by the volume. *Ivanhoe*, for example, they read seven times in one summer.[23] Just before the writing of *Uncle Tom's Cabin* in Brunswick, Stowe reread Scott in his entirety, this time aloud to her children in stints of two hours a day.[24]

The influence of Scott on Stowe is obvious, not only in *Uncle Tom's Cabin*, where it is most frequently pointed out, but to an even greater extent on her New England writings. In a novel like *The Heart of Midlothian*, for example, Scott had set out to tell a story from recent Scottish history embellished with a plot from his own imagination. But more important than the plot or historical content were the reproductions of Scottish dialect, scenery, life, and, above all, character. Analogous material was abundantly available in New England. There was a picturesque recent past; there was superb scenery; there was a distinctive dialect; and there was a yeomanry fully as interesting as Scottish peasants and quite similar to them in their religion, honesty, and sturdiness. Stowe is not, of course, to be compared with Scott artistically. Farthest from him in the mawkishness of her plots, she comes nearest to him in her burning pride of locality, which is voiced by one of her characters.

> You have the greatest reason to bless the kind Providence which has cast your lot in such a family, in such a community. I have had some means in my youth of comparing other parts of the country with our New England, and it is my opinion that a young man could not ask a better introduction into life than the wholesome nurture of a Christian family in our favored land.[25]

Substitute Scotland for New England and this could be Scott's Mr. Deans speaking to his daughter Effie.

The impact of Scott, like that of Burns, on New England literature has perhaps never been fully appreciated. His influence on writers like Simms and Cooper has of course often been pointed out; and Mark Twain in *Life on the Mississippi* has blamed Scott for the ridiculous pseudo-feudalism— false notions of honor, a sense of *noblesse oblige*, a tendency toward Gothic architecture—that assuaged the conscience of the South for the great wrong of slavery. But Scott has had a most salutary effect also, particularly on the local-color movement in the North. Writing fiction in the guise of history, he became the first respected novelist in the Calvinistic atmosphere of the region, and thus set a cogent example of truth to life for the writers nurtured on his works.[26] The influence flowed not only from the medieval novels, but from books like *The Heart of Midlothian*, a story not far different in spirit from the peasant writing of such continental writers as Tolstoy and Björnson, who were being recommended as models of realism by organs like the *Atlantic* and such influential critics as Howells. Usually in thinking of Scott one calls to mind *Ivanhoe, The Talisman, Kenilworth;* but Scott also wrote on more closely contemporary themes and in these books appear his finest characterization and most authentic atmosphere. Even in the medieval novels, the humble people—such as the Saxon peasants in *Ivanhoe*—live longer in the memory than the lords and ladies. It is not surprising that earnest authors like Stowe, Whittier, and Rowland Robinson, who wrote of the country people of New England, virtually adulated Scott, as did indeed most English-speaking readers of the nineteenth century.

III. NOSTALGIA:

Rowland E. Robinson and the Hill Country

> With these changes in business and methods, and this constant intercourse with all inhabitants of the republic, the quaint individuality of the earlier people is fast dissolving into commonplace likeness, so that now the typical Green Mountain Boy of the olden time endures only like an ancient pine that, spared by some chance, rears its rugged crest above the second growth, still awaiting the tempest or the axe that shall lay it low; yet as the pine, changing its habit of growth with changed conditions, is still a pine, so the Vermonter of today, when brought to the test, proves to be of the same tough fibre as were his ancestors.
>
> ROWLAND ROBINSON, *Vermont: A Study of Independence*[1]

1. Life

One of the keenest—and least known—interpreters of New England rural life was the Vermonter Rowland Robinson. Born in the Champlain Valley in 1833, he lived on the New England countryside from the days of its youthful vigor through the bloodletting of the Civil War and the drainage of its best manhood into the Ohio and beyond. The circumstances, as well as the chronology, of Robinson's life strangely parallel the catastrophe and the gradual readjustment that New England underwent in the nineteenth century. A student of the region during its critical days could make no more rewarding study than that of the life and works of this neglected author.

Robinson was born into a Quaker family—Hicksite, in his day—that had come to Vermont from Newport, Rhode Island, in 1791, about the time of the migration of Seth Hubbell from Connecticut. Settling first in Vergennes, the family later moved a few miles northward to Ferrisburgh, establishing there the old Robinson homestead, Rokeby, which is still standing, a distinctive landmark in the Champlain Valley. It is a house of Quaker dignity and simplicity, set well back from the road among its shade trees. Here Robinson lived out his years, dying in the room of his birth. His formal schooling was acquired in a little shingled school house standing on the Robinson farm, and later in the Ferrisburgh Academy, a now-extinct monument to the early New Englander's respect for education. But he was more of a reader than a student. In his home he found and devoured the works of Scott and other historical novelists, a genre of which he was always passionately fond and to which he was to make his own contribution.

His most vital education came from his environment rather than from books and paid teachers. From his parents he learned an admiration for the stolid idealism of the old-fashioned Quaker. In an *Atlantic* article of 1901, "Recollections of a Quaker Boy," he describes in as poignant language as he ever wrote the Quakerism of his region before the Hicksite Separation, when the old garb was worn, the old language spoken, and the old high-thinking observed.[2] One is reminded of Whittier's poem:

> The Quaker of the olden time!—
>   How calm and firm and true,
> Unspotted by its wrong and crime,
>   He walked the dark earth through.
> The lust of power, the love of gain,
>   The thousand lures of sin
> Around him, had no power to stain
>   The purity within.[3]

Also from his parents he learned a lesson concerning human freedom. Rokeby was a busy station on the Underground Railway; the elder Robinson, like most Quakers, was an ardent abolitionist, even having had William Lloyd Garrison as a guest in his house. Often as a child Rowland was conscious of mysterious doings in the secret "slave chamber" behind the chimney upstairs; and this chamber figures prominently in some of his historical stories. He always felt pride in the fact that his family realized the great truth about liberty: that we must see that all men enjoy it before we can rest secure in it ourselves.

Older events of the French Wars and the Revolution, in which Vermont and the Champlain Valley had played such prominent parts, also made their impression on the young farm boy. Samuel Goodrich, the author of the Peter Parley books so popular in the last century, tells in his *Recollections of a Lifetime* how an aura of romance was spread about his boyhood by the story of the Revolutionary battle that had taken place in his hometown of Ridgefield, Connecticut, and that had left its mark in the scars of cannon balls on houses still standing.[4] Robinson had a like feeling of contact with the past when he heard the stories of Ticonderoga and Plattsburgh, the latter at least still fresh in the memory of living men. The carpenters shingling the roof of his own Rokeby had heard the thunder of MacDonough's cannon on Lake Champlain. In the country stores an occasional superannuated Green Mountain Boy was still spinning yarns of Bennington and Ticonderoga. For this past of his native state Robinson had a love like Scott's for the history of Scotland. One of the characters in his stories, a young schoolmaster boarding with a veteran of Ethan Allen's campaigns, might be Robinson himself:

> The young man had pleasanter intercourse with his aged host when, settled for the long evening in his armchair with his pipe alight, he told of the bitter feud of the Green Mountain Boys and the New York land speculators, of scouts and battles in which he had borne a part, or repeated, as he heard them told by actors and eyewitnesses, the bloody tragedies of the old French war, whereof the schoolmaster made careful and copious notes with a view to future use in his projected "Early History of Vermont". His finger slipped from its place in the shut volume of the Iliad, and he forgot the battles of Greeks and Trojans as he listened, with pride swelling his heart, to the unsung heroic deeds of his own humble ancestors.[5]

At the age of eighteen Rowland had already written "Some of Grandfather's Stories," after the grandfather's death in 1851.

Robinson had some talent in art, which he attempted to develop during a residence in New York as a young man, the only years he ever spent away from his beloved Ferrisburgh. Although he sold illustrations to standard magazines of the day, *Harper's Monthly*, among them, he was never notably successful. However, his ability at drawing enabled him to illustrate some of his own articles and, more important, trained his eye for the close observation that makes him an outstanding nature essayist. He was soon back in Vermont and in 1870 had married Anna Stevens of East Montpelier. Under her encouragement he first broke into print with the article "Fox Hunting in New England," which appeared in *Scribner's Magazine*. Other articles on New England life—bearing such titles as "Merino Sheep," "New England Fences," and "A Vermont Marble Quarry"—appeared in *Lippincott's*, the *Atlantic Monthly*, and the *Century*.

Robinson at this time was a farmer and outdoorsman rather than author. An orchardist, gardener, and sheep-raiser, he prided himself most on his skill in butter making and decorated the tubs he sent to Boston with comic drawings, much to the delight of the freight handlers along the route. But his passion was for tramping, fishing, hunting. Sam Lovel, the woodsman of Robinson's stories, states his author's case rather well:

> "... It comes nat'ral for me tu run in the woods. 'F I du git more game tu show fer it 'n' some does, I git suthin' besides 't I can't show. The air o' the woods tastes good tu me, for 't hain't ben breathed by nothin' but wild creeturs, 's 'n ole feller said 'at useter git up airly daown in Rho 'dislan', where my folks come from."[6]

On his camping and hunting trips Robinson came to know Ferrisburgh and its surrounding townships as well as Thoreau knew Concord. The settings of his stories, for the most part laid in this territory, have the accuracy of a government topographic map.

The last years of Rowland Robinson's life were spent in total blindness. As Early as 1887, when he was fifty-four, his vision was badly impaired; and despite operations in New York he was in darkness by 1893. During the previous half-century of his life he had come to know Vermont as well as any one could. He had seen it in the flush time of its prosperity, the days of the famous Merino sheep and Morgan horses, and he had witnessed the decay of its prosperity, the emigration to the West, the coming of the railroad with its disruption of the old village life, the steady decline in quality as well as quantity of the population. During the thirteen years of his blindness he did the bulk of his writing, on the gentle insistence of his wife, who knew the spiritual necessity for such occupation, and with the aid of a grooved writing board devised by the Perkins Institute for the Blind. This writing was a means of livelihood in the truest sense, for it made his blindness a triumph rather than a tragedy. From the strictly personal side, it constituted a many-volumed reappraisal of his life and the forces that had played upon it. The result is a peculiarly perspicacious, tolerant, and convincing estimate of the New England village: of what it once had to offer and of what it still has in by no means exhausted abundance. In the apparent wreckage of his own life Robinson searched the wreckage of New England and in each he found much worth salvaging and perpetuating. But the pervasive tone was one of nostalgia for an order that had passed its prime and which could be completely lost only at great detriment, he thought, to the state and the nation.

2. Place and People

Take a map of Vermont and locate Addison County, about midway down Lake Champlain. On the northern boundary of the county is Ferrisburgh, the home of Rowland Robinson. To the east and southeast are Starksboro and Lincoln, which are the models for the hill village of Danvis in Robinson's works. To the south is Vergennes at the head of navigation on the Otter Creek. Roughly these towns embrace the northern third of the county, yet they contain a thoroughly typical slice of inland New England. Starksboro and Lincoln are in the hill country, the granite, steep-sloped lands of the Green Mountains. Ferrisburgh and Vergennes are in the heart of the Champlain Valley, land rivaled for fertility in New England only along the bigger rivers. In Starksboro and Lincoln one would find the earliest and most severe symptoms of the decline of the New England countryside. These are the towns that helped swell the population of Vermont's insane asylums during the nineteenth century till proportionately they were the fullest in the nation. Ferrisburgh and Vergennes, however, with their orchards and their dairy farms, have in comparison always prospered, the shock of the calamities that overtook the hillier regions being cushioned by the richness and flatness of the soil. This is rich country historically, too. Here, at the mouth of Otter Creek, that main thoroughfare for immigration into Vermont from Southern New England, some of the most decisive contact with the encroaching Yorkers was made. At Vergennes, also, MacDonough's fleet was built and defended Fort Cassin from British attack. This northern strip of Addison County is New England in microcosm.

Robinson's writings comprise essentially a single seven-volume work. They are a geographical, historical, sociological, zoological study of northern Addison County from the French and Indian Wars till the late nineteenth century. With the wealth of local detail of Thoreau, Robinson has compiled a three- or four-generation human saga comparable in scope, if not in quality, with that of Trollope's Barsetshire novels. In an age when the eighteenth-century White of Selborne's voluminous account of the human and natural life of the English village where he lived was the model for so many New England localists, Robinson confined himself more rigorously to his region than any other writer except Thoreau. Not even Sarah Orne Jewett has adhered so tenaciously to her Maine coast, or Celia Thaxter to her beloved Isles of Shoals, as has Robinson to his tiny corner of Vermont.

The capital of Robinson's demesne is the mythical hill village of Danvis, suggested by his visits to Lincoln and Starksboro. The chief resources of Danvis are a view of Camel's Hump, blueberries, hunting that once was better than it is, a flinty soil on which some corn can be grown with great difficulty, some fairly good trout streams, and a very neighborly atmosphere. The main public building of this town is Uncle Lisha Pegg's cobbling shop, where the leading citizens meet nightly to discuss neighbors, crops, and hunting, spin yarns, and crack jokes. The more important of these Danvis folk who ramble in and out of most of Robinson's works are worth an introduction.

First is Uncle Lisha himself, moderator of the group, who has given his name to two of Robinson's books, *Uncle Lisha's Shop* and *Uncle Lisha's Outing.* He is a dry-skinned and dry-humored, bespectacled old cobbler, who himself is lured into the immigration to "Westconstant" (Wisconsin), only to return in a few years with a sharp reprimand for Vermonters who run down Vermont in comparison with the West:

> "It's a dirty bird 'at faouls his own nest. . . . I druther hev the leetle chunk o' V'mont sile 'at's going tu kiver my ol' bones 'n tu hev the hull splatteration o' yer West."[7]

Solon Briggs is the malaprop of the group, "a man of big if not weighty words."[8]

Joseph Hill is a henpecked nonentity. He is the son of Joziah Hill, a nonagenarian commonly known as Gran'ther Hill, a veteran of Ticonderoga, Hubbardton, and Bennington, who according to himself had been on intimate terms with that Holy Trinity of the Green Mountain Boys—Remember Baker, Seth Warner, and Ethan Allen. As a believer in historical realism, he profanely corrects Ethan Allen's account of his words to the British commander at Fort Ticonderoga. According to Gran'ther Hill, who was second only after Ethan to enter the fort, the true words were, "Come aout o' yer hole, you damned ol' skunk, or by the Gre't Jehover I'll let daylight through ye!" rather than the formal demand in "the name of the great Jehovah and the Continental Congress"[9] so dear to Fourth of July speakers. He is a blasphemous, hearty old sinner. When heckled by female relatives who would have him mend his ways at his time of life with one foot in the grave, he roars fiercely: "I hain't a man o' my time o' life, an' I hain't nary foot in nothin."[10] Though he has no high regard for the civilization he has helped to establish, he has served it for sixty years as a farmer and even as wielder of the birch in the district school, where we may feel sure that the history he taught was confined entirely to his own exploits and those lesser ones of Ethan Allen. Finally, he is a self-appointed physician who recommends "callymill" and bleeding for his sick daughter-in-law. When the doctor says "Callymill is pizon, an' tew much bleedin' is what kills hawgs," Gran'ther Hill answers, "Pizon is good when it's took proper . . . an' folks hain't hawgs, not all of 'em hain't. . . ."[11]

Peletiah Gove is the juvenile of the saga, a youth who, in the Civil War, finds an early resting place under Virginia soil.

Samuel Lovel is a great woodsman, who will not forego his hunting even on Thanksgiving Day.

Joel Bartlett, the "clark of the deestrick," is a Quaker "whose mouth was made up for a whistle that the strictness of his religious views had never permitted him to utter"[12] and who dressed like George Fox. He is an efficient conductor on the Underground Railroad.

Antoine Bissette, commonly designated as Ann Twine, is a Canadian—"not a voter but interested as a furnisher of scholars"[13] to the district school, whose student body he augments by one a year. He is a teller of toweringly tall stories involving "man Canada"—meaning "a man from Canada"—who would surpass even Gran'ther Hill in his mighty exploits. His outlandish French Canadian dialect is the despair of his acquaintance and of Robinson's readers.

Jerusy Peggs (née Chase) is Uncle Lisha's wife, whom he was able to marry only because his rival suitor had stepped on a skunk the eve of a critical sugaring party. She is a faithful and sensible woman, but does not figure largely in Robinson's stories, which mainly concern the doings of men.

Last is Mrs. Purington, a gossip and busybody, the bane of Gran'ther Hill, whom she attempts to reform from his heathenish ways.

The language of Danvis is as distinctive as its citizenry, and one that readers who have an aversion to dialect stories will find an almost insurmountable barrier to the enjoyment of Robinson. Mark Twain has praised Harris, the author of Uncle Remus, as being the greatest master of the black dialect in which he writes. In backwoods Yankee speech Robinson has been fully as successful. The mere look of this speech on the page, as Robinson transcribes it, is alarming, so grotesque is the spelling and so drastic are the elisions. However, it may be a comfort to know there is a reason for these monstrosities, as is often not the case in such writing. For example, Lowell, despite his learned researches into New England dialect, would occasionally lapse into such needless misspellings as *fees'ble* and *sez* where *feas'ble* and *says* would be equally phonetic. If the misspellings add to the humor, as with Josh Billings's writings, all well and good; but in these instances cited from Lowell it is difficult to see how they do. However, when Robinson writes *caow* for *cow,* he is reproducing the "five-syllabled" pronunciation that Calvin Coolidge, from the heart of Vermont's hills, is said to have given that word. Robinson's Yankee speech, in fact, is consistently more accurate, if more difficult to read, than that of Lowell. Lowell tends to limit himself to a few stock peculiarities—like *wuz* for *was, ez* for *as, ketch* for *catch*—which are justifiable so far as they go but do not denote a much keener ear than that of the average character actor doing a conventional Yankee part. Robinson attempted to catch the idiosyncrasies in every vowel and consonant, particularly as regards elision: *Rho 'dislan'* for *Rhode Island* and *I druther* for *I'd rather*—difficult reading perhaps but phonetically exact. Furthermore, like Sarah Orne Jewett and Harriet Beecher Stowe, Robinson has caught the rhythm of his people's talk. Though many phrases and pronunciations that Robinson uses have now passed out of existence, any one who has heard a Vermont farmer speak will recognize the rhythms of the following utterance of Uncle Lisha made in a controversy on the naming of Sam Lovel's boy.

> "Good airth an' seas! what be you a-makin' sech a rumpus 'baout a young un's name for? If he's a good boy his name'll be good, and if he's a bad boy George Washin't'n wouldn't saound good wi' him a-bearing' on't. We hain't much more'n worms anyways, an' it hain't but precious leetle 'caount what names we hev while we're squirmin' 'raound here. The' hain't one name in ten thaousand but 'll be forgot a hundered years f'm naow, an' folks 'at sees 'em scratched on gre't stuns 'll wonder why anyb'dy bothered tu du it, more 'n they will who we was or what we done .... So don't fret your gizzard 'baout the boy's name, Eunice Pur'n't'n."[14]

Robinson's most remarkable feat in dialect has been in rendering Ann

Twine's French Canadian mutilation of English. In this difficult and seldom-tried field, Robinson is the undisputed master; but only an acquaintance with the French Canadian immigrant will indicate how successful Robinson has been. Just what the task was he has indicated in one of his prefaces:

> The Canadian who learns English of the Yankee often outdoes his teacher in that twisting of the vowels which, no doubt brought over in the Mayflower, became so marked a characteristic of New England speech.[15]

Like Mark Twain, Lowell, and others of his century, Robinson was fascinated by dialects. In the preface quoted above he gives a brief glossary of odd and already almost extinct phrases used in his writings: *julluk* for *just like; luftu* and *lufted tu* for *love to; hayth* for *height (hayth o' land); toro* and *cruttur* for *bull; to shool* for *to wander aimlessly; a heater piece* for *a triangular piece of land,* like a flatiron; *to flurrup* for *to move in a lively, erratic manner; a linter* for *a lean-to.* The passing of this speech Robinson mourned as he did all the disappearing individualisms of New England's past.

> . . . And though the dialect is yet spoken by some in almost its original quaintness, abounding in odd similes and figures of speech, it is passing away; so that one may look forward to the time when a Yankee may not be known by his speech, unless perhaps he shall speak a little better English than his neighbors.[16]

Before leaving the subject of dialect, it would be worth hearing a typical bit of conversation in Uncle Lisha's shop:

> [Uncle Lisha says] "Fish! Yes; fish 'n' inyuns 'n' terbacker's baout all a Canuck keers for. Ann Twine, you're the furderest Canuck f 'om where ye c'n ketch bull-paouts an' eels 't I ever see. Give 'em them an' inyuns an' terbacker, an' an ole hoss, 'n' a wuthless dog, 'n' they're happy."
> [Antoine answers] "You call it ma dog don't good for some 'ting, Onc' Lasha? You tole him dat he bit you, den he show he good. He fus' rate dog, sah. He lay in haouse all a time honly w'en he barkin' at folks go 'long on road, 'n' he jes' fat as burrer."
> "Good qualities, all on 'em", said Lisha, "p'tic'ly in a Canuck dog, being' as fat's butter".
> "Those 'ere French", Solon Griggs remarked to Pelatiah, who sat beside him, "is a joe-vial an' fry-volous race."
> "Yus," said Pelatiah, sadly regarding the palms of his mittens, much soiled with handling cord-wood since sledding had come, "I s'pose they be pooty smart to run."
> Solon, disgusted with his unappreciative listener, raised his voice and

addressed the Frenchman. "Antwine, didn't your antsisters come from France?"

"No, M'sieu Brigg, ma aunt seesters and brudder, too, all bawn in Canada. Ma mudder one of it, seester to ma aunt, prob'ly."

"You misconstrowed my inquirement, Antwine," said Solon. "I meant to ast you, wa'n't their prosperity 'at was borned before 'em natyves of France—reg'lar polly voo Franceys, so tu speak?"

"Ah do' know—yas, Ah guess so, Ah guess yes," Antoine replied at random, having no idea of Solon's meaning.

"Shah! fur's any conjoogle satisfactualness is consarned, if a man hain't a lingoist he might's well talk to a sawmill as one o' these furrin Canucks," said Solon, and added, "I b'lieve I'll take my department an' go hum."

"Ah do' know 'f Ah got it raght, zhontemans," said Antoine, as the wooden latch clattered behind the departing wise man, "but Ah tink wat you call Solum in Anglish was dam hole foolish, an't it?" There was no dissenting voice, but Lisha said apologetically, "Oh, wal, Solon means well!"

"I'll be darned if I know what he does mean." Sam Lovel said.

"Wal," said Lisha, "I s'pose he's a well-read man, an'—"

"Dum the *well* red men!" Sam broke in, "I wish 't they was all sick 'n' dead, consarn 'em! See haow they're cuttin' up aout West 'n' in Floridy!"

"Oh, wall," Lisha continued, "We're well red o' him an' them, so le's don' bother!"

"I don' keer what you say 'baout red men, ef I was a Ninjun as I be a white man," cried Peletiah, rising and smacking his mittens together, "while 't there was a pale face on the face of the U-nited States of Ameriky, I wouldn't never lay daown my bow-arrers, my tommyhock, an' my wampum: never, no never!"[17]

3. Works

The history of Danvis and the surrounding countryside is unfolded through the lives of the inhabitants. Gran'ther Hill, of course, is the embodiment of the far past. The story of his life is told in *A Danvis Pioneer.* In a tavern in Connecticut before the Revolution Joziah Hill is approached by a sharper who is offering for sale a tract in the New Hampshire grants along Lake Champlain. Engaging himself on the spot to marry the landlord's daughter, Joziah closes the deal and the next day sets out for Vermont with a veteran scout and woodsman. Arriving at the mouth of the Otter Creek near Vergennes, the two discover that the sharper in Connecticut had not owned the land he had sold; but arrangements are made whereby Hill can remain and establish himself on a clearable piece. Many vicissitudes follow. The Yorkers with rival claims attempt to chase off the settlers, but Ethan Allen and others frustrate their efforts. Later Hill learns that his sweetheart has deserted him down in Connecticut and he gives up his land to become a woodsman and trapper. When the Revolution comes he joins the Green Mountain Boys in their fights at Ticonderoga, Hubbardton, and Bennington. At Hubbardton he saves a girl from the Indians and soon marries her. Later he returns to the Champlain Valley, where he becomes the first settler of Danvis at the foot of the Green Mountains. Here as Gran'ther Hill he thrives throughout the other Danvis stories.

In *A Danvis Pioneer* Robinson has used the essence of his knowledge of the early history of his region, and the result is a deeply felt historical novel, which for some reason is relatively unheard of today. In the boy's book *A Hero of Ticonderoga* and the brief *In the Greenwood*, books not directly involving Gran'ther Hill, he has again made use of Revolutionary material, but not nearly so successfully—probably because his chief character doesn't come to life so vividly.

Another group of historical novels is based on the activities of the Underground Railroad conducted by Champlain Valley Quakers. Here Robinson was drawing on his own experiences as a boy, when runaway slaves were sheltered in his home. In all these stories Joel Bartlett, the Quaker of the Danvis group, figures more or less importantly. In the best of them, however, *Out of Bondage*, he is not the important person, but is simply mentioned as keeping the next station on the route to Canada. The plot is as melodramatic as the original occurrences must often have been. One winter evening the Quaker Zebulon Barclay takes in a runaway slave ill with pneumonia, bedding him in a secret chamber like that in the Robinson house. Most non-Quaker Vermonters, Robinson is proud to say, were sympathetic toward the underground movement. Though they might not actively help in its functioning, they would seldom hand over a fleeing slave. But in this case one mean spirit, Hiel James, who suspects where the slave is, agrees to help the closely pursuing Southern owner. Meanwhile in the Barclay household a French Canadian hired man, Jerome, hears the coughing of the fugitive and decides to earn a reward by turning informer. Because of the sudden illness of Zebulon the family is unable to get the slave to the next station. Realizing the danger, Bob Ransom, a sweetheart of Zebulon's daughter, whose wooing has been handicapped because he is not a Quaker, undertakes to remove the sick Negro to his father's sugar house nearby, there to keep him warm and care for him himself. The housekeeper cooperates by giving the Canadian Jerome a potion to render him too sick to inform the owner. The next day, however, Jerome notices smoke in the nearby sugar house, investigates, and informs Hiel. That night the posse arrives at the hiding place, but before they can batter down the door, which young Ransom refuses to open, the Negro, weakened by illness and exposure, dies of fright, thus finding his way "out of bondage." The story is fast moving as well as authentic in atmosphere and detail; it entitles Robinson to recognition as a writer on slavery.[18]

Another abolitionist story is "The Mole's Path," in which a typically independent New England woman—of the type that Mary Wilkins Freeman writes about so often—carries on the work of the underground that her late father had been devoted to. Having taken in a slave woman and her daughter, she has to get word to the next station, that of Joel Bartlett. She persuades the crippled mail-carrier, Joseph Bagley, to take the message. Bagley, though in need of the reward money to buy a new horse, is too good a Vermonter to trade in human lives. Meeting the sheriff and the owner of the fugitives, he misdirects them and removes a linchpin from their carriage, causing a breakdown and a helpful delay in their seach. The black woman and child are successfully carried to the next stop, and Joseph is given a mare by the old woman for his faithfulness.

In addition to other shorter stories on the Negroes and their efforts to escape from bondage, the book-length *Uncle Lisha's Outing*, though primarily devoted to descriptions of hunting along Lake Champlain, contains an interesting episode involving a runaway slave. One is sure that in this story Robinson had the definite purpose of showing his Danvis folks in nobler stature than they could appear in their village get-togethers and on their hunting and fishing trips. For here Ann Twine, Joseph Hill, Uncle Lisha, and Sam Lovel show that when human decency is involved they know their stand. While rummaging around the Champlain swamps they come upon a Negro hiding in a hut arranged for him by Joel Bartlett, who comes into his own in this story. A little later they meet the posse. By various ruses, possible only to capable woodsmen, they get the Negro aboard a Canadian apple boat, to be carried, according to arrangements made by Ann Twine, the rest of the way to Canada. The passage money is one dollar. The theme here is the same as in the other stories of the underground: the life that the Vermonter leads, whether abolitionist or not, makes for an intuitive sense of justice, exactly as it makes for neighborliness and good humor.

It is as the historian of everyday matters, however, that Rowland Robinson has made his mark. In such books as *Uncle Lisha's Shop, Danvis Folks, Sam Lovel's Camps,* and *Sam Lovel's Boy,* he has reproduced in painstaking detail life—particularly the life of men and boys—as it was lived in the New England hills just before the coming of the railroad, the period that, like Harriet Beecher Stowe, he found to be the golden age of rural New England. This must not be taken as a senescent yearning for the good old times. The blind Robinson, living over his days with the aid of his writing board, had reasons other than a constitutional fear of change for his choice of the era of his boyhood as the one richest in human values. Unlike most Americans, but like many New Englanders, he was not completely convinced that progress and the passing of time are synonymous terms. It seemed to him that time occasionally brought retrogression as well as progress. He writes in the preface to his best-known work, *Uncle Lisha's Shop:*

> ... People are losing the neighborly kindness of the old times when none were rich and none were poor, and all were in greater measure dependent on each other. In fact, the Danvis folk are not better now than their lowland neighbors, who therefore no longer despise them.[19]

Thus for the setting of these books that form the backbone of his work Robinson quite naturally chose the hills, where change came slowest and the old ways lingered longest.

His technique is a most simple one, based on that prehistoric genre, the campfire yarn. Robinson will get three or four of his characters together— say Ann Twine, Gran'ther Hill, Uncle Lisha, Sam Lovel—on a camping trip, at a sugaring-off party, at a woodcutting or moving bee, at a turkey shooting, or, most often, in Uncle Lisha's cobbling shop. After assembling the characters and describing carefully the activity that is going on—there is here room for much local color and description of old customs—some action, usually humorous, takes place, as when the appearance of several raccoons on the road outside the school house breaks up the bitter debate at the No. 4 district school meeting. Or, especially if the setting is Uncle Lisha's shop or an evening campfire, one of the characters will spin a yarn, which is usually topped by a taller one by Ann Twine, who revels in his reputation as the greatest liar in Danvis. Thus the books are unencumbered with plot; they are simply a series of sketches involving the same characters and describing various aspects of old-time rural life. Readers interested in ancient American customs and atmosphere should not, and cannot, miss these volumes. They will find that Robinson has overlooked no custom or oddity of Vermont lore. Everything from an old-time wolf-hunt to a quilting bee is painstakingly depicted.

It must not be thought that Robinson was overawed by the quaintness of the old days. The hill-country, then as later, had its meanness and its tragedy. The short story "Fourth of July at Highfield Poorhouse"[20] does not gloss over the starkness of the paupers' lives in that most sordid of New England institutions, the town poor farm. With all his fondness for Vermonters, Robinson paints the woman keeper of the establishment at Highfield as a stingy, heartless bigot far beyond the possibilities of reform. As a description of the lot of those who have been forced "to go on the town," this piece should be compared with Mary Wilkins Freeman's grim story on a similar subject, "Sister Liddy."[21] In another story, "The Purification of Cornbury,"[22] Robinson portrays the cruel bigotry of a female member of the Moral Reform Society. This unpleasant lady, the wife of the head selectman, forces her husband to drive out-of-doors in midwinter a woman who has been living in sin with a widowed farmer of the neighborhood. Later the reformer is herself reformed of her inhumanity. She forces the sinners to marry and then compels her own husband to hire the couple to work on his farm. The spinelessness of the selectmen, who permit themselves to commit an act of cruelty, is one of the most damning factors in the situation. Finally, in the story of "The Shag Back Panther"[23] is the portrait of a French Canadian as mean as Ann Twine is big-hearted. A habitual bullier of little children, this character attempts by tales of a fierce catamount to keep neighboring boys and girls off a blueberry patch on Shag Back Mountain, till he himself, through a hoax arranged by his indignant neighbors, has reason to believe the "painter" actually exists and is thus afraid to pick in the patch himself.

To round out his pictures of Danvis and its environs Robinson has written many essays describing the plants, fish, animals, and geography of the area. The bulk of these, originally published in *Field and Stream Magazine*, are collected in the volume *In New England Fields and Woods*. A longer piece, "Along Three Rivers,"[24] gives almost a stone-by-stone and tree-by-tree catalogue of the area where the Otter, the Little Otter, and the Lewis Creeks flow into Lake Champlain. As in Thoreau's descriptive writings, every cellar hole, every old boundary, every channel in the marshes is carefully located and described.

As a descriptive artist, Robinson is not only accurate and detailed, but highly picturesque. From a little essay called "A New England Woodpile" we have a typical example:

> As conveniently near the shed as possible, the pile of sled-length wood is stretching itself slowly, a huge vertebrate, every day or two gaining in length; a joint of various woods, with great trunks at the bottom, then smaller ones, gradually growing less to the topping out of saplings and branches. Here is a sugar-maple, three feet through at the butt, with the scars of many tappings showing on its rough bark. The oldest of them may have been made by the Indians. Who knows what was their method of tapping?[25]

As might be expected of an old and blind man writing of his youth, Robinson is highly successful in evoking the mood of nostalgic reminiscence. The titles of many of his shorter pieces suggest their tone: "The Land of Memory," "The Shut-In Sportsman," "Making the Most of It." His descriptions of the winter landscape are usually his most poignant.

> Gradually the change comes, the glory of autumn passes away, the brown leaves drift and waver to the earth, the summer birds fly southward to lands of perennial leaf and blossom, and leave to us but the memory of song in a desolate silent land, when the brooks must sing

only to themselves under crystal roofs, and you only know they are singing by the beads of elastic pearl that round and lengthen and break into many beads as they slip along the braided current.

There are only the moaning of the wind among the hills and the rustle of the withered leaves along the dun earth. A week ago it was full of life —now there is only desolation and death, yet so imperceptibly have these come that we know not when the other ceased, and we are not appalled. Then comes the miracle of snow, the gray sky blossoms into a white shower of celestial petals that bloom again on withered stem and bough and shrub until the gray and tawny world is transformed into universal purity. Where there was no life are now abundant signs of it, the silent record of many things. Mouse, weasel and squirrel, hare, skunk and fox have written the plain story of their nightly wanderings, red-poll, bunting, crow, and grouse have embroidered the history of their alighting and their terrestrial journeyings on the same white page. The jay of many voices proclaims his presence, the chickadee lisps his brief song, the nuthatch blows his reedy clarionet, a white flock of snow buntings drift by with a creaking twitter like the sound of floating ice, a crow sounds his raucous trumpet . . . .[26]

In this somewhat lengthy description, it will be noticed, Robinson employs a rather old-fashioned conventional diction ("the glory of autumn passes away"), which is saved from the compost pile of all such writing by an accuracy of observation unsurpassed in American nature writing ("beads of elastic pearl that round and lengthen and break into many beads as they slip along the braided current"). And combined with this facility of visual imagination—so often the compensation of the blind—is an equally accurate aural observation ("the nuthatch blows his reedy clarionet").

Often, however, Robinson gains his effect with a single stroke. At the end of *Uncle Lisha's Shop*, after Uncle Lisha and his wife Jerushy have boarded the lake and canal boat that is to carry them to Wisconsin, Sam Lovel returns to the deserted shop. The scene is one too often repeated in the New England of those times.

> When Sam looked into the empty shop, where nothing was left to tell of its former use but a faint waft of the old familiar odor, the sconce and its mouse-nibbled candle-end, a broken last and a rubbishy heap of leather scraps, a partridge sprang from the floor and, hurtling through the open window, went sailing away to the woods.[27]

The wilderness, symbolized by the partridge, had already taken over where once had been the fellowship and friendliness of goodly human society. Despite his passion for the woods and fields, Robinson valued humanity more highly. The way in which he most differs from his fellow nature lover, Thoreau, is in his farmer's realization that nature is often unfriendly.

There is nothing of the Transcendentalist in Robinson. Like Celia Thaxter, he had lived in too close dependence on nature to deify it, however much he might love it.

4. Philosophy of Life

The present-day Vermont poet and essayist Arthur Wallace Peach has perhaps best interpreted the philosophy of life implied in Robinson's writings.[28] As has been said, this philosophy is more than an impotent lament for the good old days. It is a reaffirmation, as Professor Peach points out, of a life built on fundamental values, whether such life finds existence in past, present, or future. The pervasive nostalgia of Robinson's pages results from the feeling that the present marked a falling-off from the past. Yet he was never the black pessimist. Human beings could get from life what they sought. There were always the common things—the outdoors, companionship, work, and play.

It is hard not to be trite about fundamental things. Realizing this, Robinson tried to explain his way of life in the pithy language of the sportsman.

> Let us school our desires to moderation, and learn to be satisfied with whatever these limited hunting grounds may give us, and they will surprise us with their bounty. We may study the book of nature the closer when the pages are few and always at hand.
>
> Gilbert White found an ample field of observation in his own parish, and Thoreau discovered more in the fenced acres of Concord woodland and its tamed river than in the vast forests and wild streams of Maine . . . .
>
> If we may not have salmon nor [sic] trout nor grayling, nor so much of as bass, there are pickerel and perch and bream in the streams we know. The fewer there are, the warier and the greater the skill that is needed to take them, and . . . the more time for contemplation, which is part of the true angler's pastime, and let us be content if it is the larger part, and so in all our recreations make the most and best of what is vouchsafed us.[29]

Thus Robinson could not understand the latter-day scramble for wealth, symbolized in his books by the merchant Bascom, to whose wiles Sam Lovel falls victim, only to be saved by the pitching in of all his neighbors. Nor does he comprehend the burning desire of Vermonters to go West. Perhaps they will find more valuable lands, but they will leave behind something priceless. Again Robinson resorts to figurative language. In a story called "The Goodwin Spring" Jerry and Asenath Goodwin are getting too old to cultivate their rockpile of a hill farm.

40

"I don't see haow we're a goin' tu sell the place if we want tu"
[Asenath says]. "The' hain't nobody wants tu buy it, erless it's some o'
them French, an' I can't stand the idee o' them a-gabbin' an' a-swearing'
an' a-dancin' in the haouse, like's not in the square room where aour
little Jerry was sick so long, an' makin' it all smell o' onions the hul
endurin' time.[30]

Moreover, there is on the place a spring of a purity unequaled in the
region. Jerry fetches a bucket of cool, sparkling water and they drink
deeply of it. The water becomes for the old couple a symbol of the deep
draughts of life they have drunk on their sterile old farm, and they decide
not to sell, but to end their days there.

And this was the attitude of the majority of those who remained behind
in the Western migrations; Robinson and the other rural writers of his day
were only the spokesmen of many. The determination to stay with what
was left of the old times has been called all sorts of unflattering names—
degeneracy, stubbornness, shiftlessness. But this disparaging attitutde is
beginning to change. Those who elected to remain the guardians of the old
way of life, however vitiated it may be, have become modern heroes. For
example, Bernard DeVoto, in the article "New England, There She
Stands,"[31] goes to considerable pains to explain why he has chosen New
England as his home. Writing in the depths of the Great Depression,
DeVoto tells of a Vermont farmer who has managed to keep his life
independent of the forces that make depressions. This self-sufficient farmer
of a few rocky acres such as Gran'ther Hill first settled on has actually done
a very simple thing. He has merely kept his life free of nonessentials, while
carefully guarding the essentials. He eats well; extends his hospitality to his
friends; keeps his sense of humor; respects his neighbors; enjoys the
hunting and fishing offered him free by nature; governs himself in town
meeting, and as often as not, in the State assembly; and rears and educates
his children either to farm the land after him or to go to the cities as a life
giving transfusion into the anemic urban blood. Among such people
DeVoto says he would prefer to live. He and Robinson would see eye to
eye.

IV. NOSTALGIA:
Sarah Orne Jewett and the Maine Coast

... It was easy to be much disturbed by the sad discovery that certain phases of provincial life were fast waning in New England. Small and old-fashioned towns ... were no longer self-subsistent, as in earlier times; and while it was impossible to estimate the value of that wider life that was flowing in from the great springs, many a mournful villager felt the anxiety that came with these years of change. Tradition and time-honored custom were to be swept away together by the irresistible current. Character and architecture seemed to lose individuality and distinction. ... The well-filled purses that were scattered in our country's first great triumphal impulse of prosperity often came into the hands of people who hastened to spoil instead of to mend the best things that their village held.

SARAH ORNE JEWETT, Deephaven[1]

1. 148 Charles Street, Boston

In 1908 Willa Cather, then managing editor of *McClure's Magazine*, visited her contributor Sarah Orne Jewett in the home of Annie Fields at 148 Charles Street, Boston. Willa Cather had already written several of her outstanding short stories—"Paul's Case," "The Wagner Matinee," "The Sculptor's Funeral." Yet she was not entirely satisfied with her achievement. She had been attempting to put into her stories the Bohemians and Swedes who had been her neighbors in Nebraska, but thus far the attempt had been unsuccessful.

Some instinct drew her to Sarah Orne Jewett—a right instinct, as later events proved. It is true that her first novel, *Alexander's Bridge*, which appeared in 1912, was a poor imitation of Henry James's international manner. But in the following year *O Pioneers* was published—the first in a series that was to place Willa Cather among the major novelists of her times. This story of Alexandra Bergson, an immigrant Swedish girl who through sheer strength of character keeps her family together after the death of the father, resembles in theme many of Jewett's tales of New England farm women who wring success out of apparent failure. We are told, moreover, that Willa Cather discussed the characters of the book with her older friend. It was with good reason that *O Pioneers* was dedicated to Jewett, who was fast becoming an influence in a large segment of American fiction, the segment represented by such women writers as Ruth Suckow, Ellen Glasgow, Dorothy Canfield, who conducted during the 1920's a painstaking and effective search for values in American life.[2]

Willa Cather herself considered her visit to 148 Charles Street significant enough to write an essay on it.[3] It was like a spiritual homecoming, so congenial to her was the atmosphere of this famous old house where the Boston publisher James Fields had entertained America's and Europe's great during half a century. Here, occupying rooms where Dickens, Emerson, and Hawthorne had been familiar guests, were two old ladies, Jewett and Annie Fields, inseparable friends for forty years and embodiments of a disappearing way of life.[4] Here an American from the "raw" West could first become aware of her colonial heritage. In every nook and corner of that house the past not only was protected but was actually alive. The crassness, the rush, the dissonance of the modern world were carefully shut out. The transitory and the cheap were excluded, and only the lasting values received due attention. Here, as in few other houses in America, Milton, Donne, Shakespeare, and Arnold were read aloud, and the teachings of Aristotle were taken off the shelves and used as maxims for daily living. Such, in paraphrase, is Willa Cather's description of a backwater of American life that she had not hitherto discovered. In Henry James's words, in another connection, what she had seen was "the last link in a tradition . . . the age of plain living and high thinking, of pure ideals and earnest effort, of moral passion and noble experiment."[5] Willa Cather remarks that on the death of Annie Fields 148 Charles Street became the site of a garage.

Jewett died only sixteen months after this momentous meeting, but in that time Willa Cather had found the theme on which her most effective work is built. Essentially her novels are a lament for the past. As a motto for *My Antonia* she has chosen from Vergil's *Georgics* the quotation *Optima dies prima fugit*. But it is not only in *My Antonia* that the passing of the old West with its simple virtues of honesty, piety, and hard work is lamented. This is also the theme of *A Lost Lady, O Pioneers, One of Ours,* "Neighbor Rosicky," *The Professor's House,* and other stories decrying the effect of a selfish commercialism on Western life.

This nostalgia for the past is not the result of a blind conservatism or an impotent rage against the shopkeepers and speculators of the new order. It is a deliberate weighing of two sets of values—the old and the new. Because the balance tips toward the old we should not cry "Tory." The Menckens, also, have found the new to be contemptible, though they find the past to be little better, if not worse.

In Jewett and Cather we find full and closely reasoned case for the American past. For example, to their interest in tradition is directly attributable the preoccupation of both with rural life and characters. A Roman poet has said that in the country the Golden Age lingered longest before its disappearance from the world. In her preface to *Deephaven* Jewett quotes a similar thought from George Sand's Preface to *Légendes Rustiques:*

> Le paysan est donc, si l'on peut ainsi dire, le seul historien qui nous reste des temps antehistorique. Honneur et profit intellectuel á qui se consacrerait á la recherche de ses traditions merveilleuses de chaque hameau qui rassemblées ou groupées, comparées entre elles et minutieusement disséquées jetteraient peut-être de grandes lueurs sur la nuit profonde des âges primitifs.[6]

This passage might well serve as a motto for all local colorist. But Jewett fortifies the quotation with a remark of her own:

> There will also exist that other class of country people who preserve the best traditions of culture and of manners, from some divine inborn instinct towards what is simplest and best and purest, who know the best because they themselves are of kin to it.[7]

In this extension of the Wordsworthian faith in the basic goodness of the rustic we find the reason why both Cather and Jewett wrote about people of "obscure destinies" in remote corners of the nation, people in whom the ancient human goodnesses remained relatively untouched by the modern blight of greed and self-seeking. For Jewett such people were to be found in abundance among the islands and in the coves of her own Maine coast. But the Yankees, by the time they reached Nebraska, had been badly infected by the virus of commercialism. Thus Cather turned to the immigrants fresh from Europe—the Bohemians of *My Antonia*, the Swedes of *O Pioneers*—for many of her examples of unspoiled humanity. Perhaps even here the hint came from Jewett, who in stories like "The Luck of the Bogans" and "The Little Captive Maid" had written sympathetically of the big-heartedness, the industry, the engaging simplicity and humor, the ardent religious faith of the Irish immigrants in New England.

At any rate the immigrant farmers of Nebraska became the favored children of Willa Cather. Flinging back in his face Theodore Roosevelt's exhortations to all newcomers to America to give up their old ways, Cather regretted the Americanization of her Bohemians, Russians, and Swedes, for too often this Americanization meant a substitution of cynical money grabbing, the love of luxury, the loss of faith, for the old peasant values of honest labor, plain-living, and sincere religion. So far did Cather carry this idea that in her historical novels, *Death Comes for the Archbishop* and *Shadows on the Rock*, she finds the Spanish and French settlers on this continent, with their faithful adherence to the traditions and values embodied in their Catholic religion, to be the moral superiors of the English colonists and their later descendants, the Western pioneers, who settled the wilderness too often with the sole purpose of fattening their bankrolls rather than spreading the best of Christian civilization.

The veneration of the past plays a part even in the use of dialect. Cather found the language of Jewett's characters to be the most effective idiom any writer can employ. But she quarrels with the use of the word *dialect*, considering it a term of condescension on the part of city-dwellers for what they cannot understand. They cannot understand the country people's talk because they can't understand their temper, their scale of values. Speech, to Cather, reflects by its tempo, its inflections, its rhythms, and its accents the character of the speaker. The new-style, urban Americans, to whom the rural Yankees with their taciturn honesty are almost foreigners, would naturally consider the soft cadences of the old-time New Englanders to be "hickish," just as they would find the contentment with the mere subsistence afforded by an ancestral farm to be "lack of ambition" or "plain mulishness."[8]

From Jewett, Cather may have received inspiration for many of her other distinctive qualities: her simple, idiomatic style; the use of material close to her heart and experience; the high level of idealism and integrity on which, as consistently as any American of this generation, she kept her art. Yet it is only fair to say that she far outstripped her teacher. Though Cather sincerely names *The Country of the Pointed Firs* with *Huckleberry Finn* and *The Scarlet Letter* as the three American works of fiction most likely to endure, we of today would place *My Antonia* or *A Lost Lady* in the trio sooner than Jewett's book.

Perhaps it would be juster to say that Sarah Orne Jewett was a stimulus rather than an influence on her young friend. The affinity between the two is quite understandable, for there was a curious similarity in their backgrounds, however great the geographical difference between Maine and Nebraska. Both were children of professional men devoted to ends other than the filling of their pocketbooks. As the daughter of a country doctor, Jewett would be educated to standards of conduct and duty not radically different from those that Cather learned as the daughter of a Presbyterian minister. Both were born of patrician stock, one of New England, the other of Virginia origin. Both had grown up in rapidly changing rural environments, where the change had usually been for the worse. In the Nebraska of Cather the pioneer's industry and devotion to duty had given way to a crass materialism combined with a crabbed Calvinistic orthodoxy. In the New England of Jewett the aristocratic families with their wealth of property and culture and the steady ancient yeomanry were being driven out by factories, immigrants, and summer visitors. Both had watched the heroic eras of their localities pass into history, giving place to an order of things that they at least considered vastly inferior. It was such conditions and influences that fostered their similar outlooks and formed their similar styles of writing. In Emerson's phrase, each valued qualities more and magnitudes less.

2. South Berwick, Maine

Sarah Orne Jewett had not acquired her views of life at 148 Charles Street. Born in 1849 in the old shipbuilding town of South Berwick, Maine, at the head-of-tide of the Piscataqua River a few miles above Portsmouth, she could trace her family roots far into the pre-Revolutionary past of New England. The house she had been born in and in which she spent her days—the house described in her first book, *Deephaven*—had been built in 1740, a model of Georgian capaciousness and purity of line. On the paternal side, her family had been Cavalier rather than Puritan, and "mistaken but honest" Tories during the Revolution. Her ancestors had long been prosperous and influential squires of South Berwick and nearby Portsmouth and Exeter man of culture and masters in the art of living; men who like her ship-captain grandfather were citizens "of the whole geography" and not merely of Maine.[9] In Jewett's lifetime only the remnants survived of this past that seemed to her so much more livable than the present. Only a few rotting wharves remained as evidence that South Berwick shipping was once familiar in Archangel and Marseilles. Only the old elm-shaded mansions like the Jewetts' were left from the former Tory splendor. On the countryside the abandoned houses, the ubiquitous cellar holes, the miles of tumbled-down stone walls that laced the woods told the story of the great western migration and the scores of young men lost by the town in the Civil War. Of the old yeomanry, as ancient in its lineage as the shipbuilding patricians, the casual observer would find only the human wreckage—rheumatic solitaries, superannuated single women, poverty-stricken families with hordes of dirty-faced, undernourished children on stony farms. One of Jewett's first tasks as a writer was to reveal whatever worth still lingered in these derelicts.

The two chief influences on Jewett's girlhood were her environment and her father; and the two ran counter to each other, for the environment kept her attention on the glamour of the past while her father kept her conscious of the possiblilities of the present. The tidewater region of New England in which she lived was mellow with age. Speaking of prewar days, she says in one of her letters,

> I look upon that generation as the one to which I really belong,—I who was brought up with grand-fathers and grand-uncles and aunts for my playmates.[10]

In another letter, touching on her visits to relatives in Exeter, her mother's girlhood home, she writes:

> . . . I always find my childhood going on as if I had never grown up at all, with my grand-aunts and their old houses and their elm-trees and their unbroken china plates and big jars by the fireplaces . . . . There are electric cars in Exeter now, but they can't make the least difference to me![11]

This flavor of the past was most pungent in South Berwick—in the beloved family homestead, in the great square aristocratic houses above on the river, in the legends of John Paul Jones, who had outfitted the *Ranger* in their neighborhood. Like Rowland Robinson and Samuel Goodrich, Jewett exulted from her earliest days in a sense of belonging to a great and venerable tradition. " . . . I am always delighting," she wrote, "in reading the old Berwick, picturesque as it was, under the cover of the new life which seems . . . so dull and unrewarding in most ways."[12]

This reading of the past can lead in its exaggerated forms to a crabbed antiquarianism or a silly preoccupation with genealogy, as it often did in New England. Fortunately there was in Jewett's girlhood a powerful antidote to the genealogical addiction. This was the common sense and the robust humanity of her father, the chief doctor of Berwick township. Dr. Jewett was one of those skillful, dignified, yet lovable horse-and-buggy doctors that appear often in books and occasionally in real life. Added to a grasp of theory that had qualified him to teach obstetrics at Bowdoin College was all the unbookish knowledge that comes with years of general practice—wisdom like that described by Holmes in his novel *The Guardian Angel* as belonging to the nonagenarian practitioner Dr. Hurlbut, who could diagnose the ailments of his village patients by reference to hereditary influences that he had observed in their families during four generations. Because she was delicate, Sarah was not sent to school, a fortunate circumstance for one of her potentialities. Instead of learning life from books, she learned it during years of accompanying her father on his country calls.

Jewett tells of her companionship with her father in the auto-biographical novel *A Country Doctor*. Like the heroine of her book, she entered the homes of the doctor's patients, made lifelong friendships with them, observed their sicknesses, learned of their pasts, followed the year-by-year vicissitudes of their lives. She became herself a student of her father's medical books. If there is any truth in the theory, entertained by Thomas Mann and Dostoevsky, that character reveals itself most vividly in illness, then this Maine village girl was receiving the best education possible for a future writer. A systematic study of Shakespeare and Milton and the mastering of Latin and Greek could well take second place to these

47

bedside visits in lonely farmhouses and the discerning comments of the wise old doctor during the rides home in golden summer evenings or crimson winter twilights. Nor could a girl thus educated ever find fulfillment solely in the intellectual tangents of genealogy or local antiquarianism—those pastimes of so many small-town fogies, both male and female. Superimposed on the picturesque past would be the human present, blending into the past perhaps but never obliterated by it.

Nor could an intelligent girl thus educated become a snob. One of the most unfair charges ever brought against Jewett—and it is made by most of her commentators—is that she was condescending toward the country people of South Berwick. Though she was a Brahmin of Brahmins (for as Dr. Holmes points out in *Elsie Venner* the original habitat of the Brahmin was the small New England seacoast town[13]), she was also a thoroughgoing democrat in the social sense of that word. Till her death she was proud to have a countrywoman say to her on the street, "You're one of the doctor's girls, ain't ye?" Her first book, *Deephaven* (1877) was written as a protest against those condescending summer visitors, who, already swarming along the coast and inland as far as the White Mountains, "mistook a selectman for a tramp, because he happened to be crossing a field in his shirt sleeves."[14] Her understanding studies of the Irish immigrants, written after long residence in Irish-hating Boston, are a final proof that she liked all people too well to condescend toward any of them.

In *A Country Doctor* Jewett dramatically traces the two forces that molded her life. Her heroine, the orphaned child of an unhappy marriage between a farmer's daughter and a boy of aristocratic background, spends her early childhood on a farm under the care of her kindly and capable grandmother. The local doctor, who promised the mother at the deathbed that he would always look out for her baby, takes her to his own bachelor home when the grandmother dies. As she accompanies him on his rounds, her admiration for the country people among whom she started life is transformed into a desire to help them, and she herself plans to study medicine and become a country doctor. When she reaches womanhood she receives a friendly letter from her father's sister. She begins to wonder about the paternal half of her heritage, concerning which the bitterness engendered by her parents' marriage had caused her grandmother to keep her in ignorance. She decides, with the doctor's permission, to pay this conciliatory aunt a visit in the nearby seaport where she lives. Arriving in her father's city, she finds her unmarried aunt inhabiting with aristocratic regimen the ancestral mansion. The two immediately take to one another, the aunt lavishing upon her niece all her thwarted maternal affections. The girl is quickly introduced to her birthright. She attends the Episcopal church where her family have worshipped since Colonial times. She is shown the decaying grandeurs of the old city where her people had been leading burghers. She is made acquainted with broken-down mariners who had sailed on her grandfather's vessels long ago. She is introduced to the society of the town and becomes one of its most popular members. She learns that her new position entails not only an honored name but also a substantial fortune, which had previously been withheld from her.

The girl is at first overwhelmed. But later bewilderment gives way to pride. She has a feeling of belonging to something more important and finer than she had ever known; she feels herself merging with a great tradition. For a time she forgets the country town where she grew up and the doctor who had been her foster father. It is so easy to fall into this secure and ready-made niche and to luxuriate there in the pride of an ancestry that flows like old madeira through the veins. Then comes a proposal of marriage from a rising young lawyer of good family and the trance is broken by the sudden realization of all this new life will involve. If she accepts this man she foresees a lifetime of guardianship of something that is fine but is no longer so vital as it was—a lifetime of subtle but deep frustration. Former ties and plans reassert themselves. Strengthened by her knowledge of belonging to a heroic and respected tradition, the girl chooses to return to the country village of her girlhood and to the old doctor whose work and life have always been of the present. Happier, more self-assured for her experience, she studies medicine and realizes her dream of being a country doctor herself. The urgings of life are stronger in her than the claims of ancestry and the lure of the past.

3. The Outside World

Sarah Orne Jewett was always a woman of culture as well as breeding; a lady "in the old high sense," Willa Cather describes her. In the 1870's, after she became famous as a writer, she began to visit extensively in Boston and elsewhere and became acquainted with the other New England writers of her day—William Dean Howells, Thomas Bailey Aldrich, Celia Thaxter, John Greenleaf Whittier. The deepest friendship of her life was with Annie Fields, born an Adams and widow of the Boston publisher James Fields. One-forty-eight Charles Street and the Fieldses' summer house at Manchester-on-the-Sea became second homes for Jewett. The two women traveled frequently and widely in Europe, where Fields introduced her friend to many of the great in art and intellect— Arnold, Tennyson, Christina Rossetti.

Jewett's interests in reading were always broad. Proud of a trace of French blood in her own veins, she mastered French and read widely in Balzac, George Sand, Flaubert, and Daudet. Anything in these writers that seemed applicable to her own art she quickly assimilated. Over her secretary in South Berwick she kept pinned "two wonderful bits of Flaubert—'Écrire la vie ordinaire comme on écrit l'histoire' and the other,

'Ce n'est pas de faire rire—mais d'agir à la façon de la nature, c'est à dire de faire rêver'."[15]

She shared Howells's enthusiasm for the great Russians. At first preferring *Pendennis* to *Anna Karenina*, she was later kept awake till morning by a story of Tolstoi. "I have felt something of what Tolstoi has been doing all the way along," she wrote to Fields. "I never felt the soul of Tolstoi's work till last night, something of it in Katia, but now I know what he means."[16] It is not surprising that the great chronicler of Russian peasant life should have something to say to this friend of Maine farmers and fishermen. With Turgenev too she felt a kinship. In a preface to *Rudin* Stepniak had characterized Turgenev as being a lover of "light, sunshine, and living human poetry," who "on the fringe of his pictures, or in their background, just for the sake of contrast . . . will show us the vices, the cruelties, even the mire of life."[17] These words, she thought, aptly described her own aims in writing.

Thus, like her voyaging ancestors, Sarah Orne Jewett, for all her village upbringing, was in no sense a provincial. She represented, in her own life, the best of these old-time New England qualities whose passing she so deplored. Unlike Thoreau, who felt he could best know Concord by refusing to go elsewhere, she once said to Willa Cather that one must know the world before one could know the village. But she never forgot the village; virtually all her literary efforts were devoted to its depiction. The South Berwick mansion was always her home and there she did most of her writing. Till she died in 1910, of injuries sustained in a fall from a carriage, she was never long away from that lingering atmosphere of the past that she describes so poignantly in her sketches and stories.

4. "Deephaven"

Her interest in tradition led Jewett into several attempts at historical writing; in *The Story of the Normans* she wrote history. More important efforts were in fiction, particularly the historical novel *The Tory Lover*, suggested by the old Hamilton house on the Piscataqua River, and the connections of John Paul Jones with the Portsmouth region. Like Rowland Robinson, however, she wrote more successfully on the old order as it still lingered in the village life of her own girlhood. In a book of sketches called *Country By-Ways* she has told how she came face to face with the past in her drives and rides—she was an accomplished horsewoman—in the country around South Berwick. "There are still a good many examples of the old manner of out-of-door life and customs, as well as a good deal of the old-fashioned provincial society, left in the eastern parts of the New England States,"[18] she writes. In her first book, *Deephaven*, she records with youthful conservatism these vestiges of an older and disappearing culture.

Deephaven, as we have seen, was conceived with the purpose of explaining the country people to the summer boarders. "There is a noble saying of Plato," she wrote, "that the best thing that can be done for the people of a state is to make them acquainted with one another."[19] Direct inspiration came from the first chapters of Harriet Beecher Stowe's *Pearl of Orr's Island.* Writing in 1860, Stowe had found that the older Hebrew-like society of New England was still existent on the Maine coast; there was a simple pious dignity in the life here not to be found among other Americans. In Sarah Orne Jewett's own words,

> *The Pearl of Orr's Island* gave the young author . . . to see with new eyes, and to follow eagerly the old shore paths from one gray, weatherbeaten house to another where Genius pointed her the way.[20]

Before writing *Deephaven* Jewett had published several pieces under the pen name of Alice Eliot. Her first efforts were stories of plot, a form in which she herself realized she was inept. But soon came the *Atlantic* story "The Shore House," an account of a New England colonial mansion in the town of Deephaven, which Jewett stoutly declared was a composite of all lesser New England seaports, but which is unquestionably inspired by South Berwick and perhaps nearby York. "The Shore House" won the unstinted praise of William Dean Howells. In describing the spacious, elm-shaded, cupolaed mansion, so typical of coastal towns from New Haven to Wiscasset, she accomplished something as memorable as had Mark Twain in his descriptions of the plantation homes along the lower Mississippi. For several years additional Deephaven sketches—one cannot call them stories —appeared in the *Atlantic,* each stamped with the truth born of a deep knowledge and love of subject. In 1877, on the urging of Howells, the sketches were gathered and published as a book. The sales were good, and criticism throughout the nation was favorable. Jewett had become an established writer.

The plan of the book is very simple and very typical of its author. Helen Denis, a young girl who is actually Jewett, is companion to her friend Kate Lancaster during a summer spent in the colonial mansion of Kate's deceased aunt, Miss Brandon, at Deephaven on the Maine coast. Through the eyes of these two impressionable Boston girls we learn everything worth knowing about Deephaven. We are shown the mansion itself, the ancestral home of Kate's kinsmen: the garret with its mysterious old chests and boxes, one of which contains Kate's grandmother's love letters; the great paneled lower hall with its archway and its door at either end opening onto vistas of lilacs and plum trees; "the best chamber" with its immense canopied bed, its ponderous chairs, its ceiling-high mirror, and its pink and maroon wallpaper captured from a French vessel a hundred years ago; the west parlor with its blue and white Dutch-tiled fireplace depicting the treatment of good and bad souls, and its knickknack cabinet full of Chinese carvings, Swiss woodwork, and other gewgaws picked up by Brandons during four generations of seafaring; the sentimental contents of the late Miss Brandon's escritoire—a blue-ribboned packet of letters, a miniature on ivory, a lock of brown hair, and the crucifix, massbook, and rosaries of a favorite brother who had staggered the family by turning Catholic while studying in Europe.

In the town we are introduced to the deaf and arthritic captains who, long since beached by the decline of New England shipping, may "be found every pleasant morning sunning themselves like turtles on one of the wharves,"[21] and who talk as casually of a particular bargain they had made in buying a piece of cloth in Bombay as a housewife would of her achievements in the local grocery store. There is the landlocked Captain Lant, who has been farming for twenty years and who spins the girls a remarkable yarn involving mental telepathy. There is old Captain Sands, one of the prominent citizens, who sits out his days in an old warehouse surrounded by as great a variety of curios—old figureheads, unbelievable shells from the South Seas, a swordfish's sword imbedded in the planking of a ship—as one could find in Miss Brandon's knickknack cabinet.

Among the women, also, are interesting characters. Mrs. Kew, the hard-working, methodical, self-sufficient wife of a lighthouse keeper, is a great reader and, despite her isolated life, an engaging talker. There is also widow Mrs. Patton, known locally as the Widow Jim, the faithful servant and confidante of the late Miss Brandon. Self-appointed village genealogist and historian, she is also one of those indispensable female rural factotums who can do everything from fancy needlework to laying out a corpse. Despite years of brutal abuse from the drunken husband to whose memory she is nevertheless loyal, she remains a cheerful and entertaining companion to the girls who continually seek her company. There is finally the recluse, Miss Bonny, who inhabits a shanty on the side of a nearby mountain. An impoverished gatherer of herbs who smokes a pipe for her "nerves," she is self-reliant and appreciative of the beautiful views from her doorstep:

> "Real sightly, aint it? . . . But you ought to be here and look acrost the woods some morning just at sun-up. Why, the sky is all yaller and red, and them lowlands topped with fog!"[22]

There are pathetic characters, too. In the nearby East Parish, a smaller edition of Deephaven, the crazed Miss Chauncey lives alone in the wreckage of the once stately home of her forefathers. The sole remnant of a great shipbuilding family, she is under the delusion that the ancient grandeur is still surrounding her. All the family misfortunes, including the suicide of a brother, are forgotten, and she is still the lady of the manor, graciously receiving her visitors and refusing to leave her draughty and leaky halls. Miss Chauncey, it is interesting to note, was a real person, and Sarah Orne Jewett made her first visit to her exactly as described in *Deephaven*.[23]

Less melodramatic is the account, also based on fact, of an impoverished family living on one of those bleak, granite-shored coves that make the Maine coast resemble a huge saw blade. In this sketch, called "In Shadow," Jewett writes with an unsentimentalized compassion that reminds one of the Russian writers she so much admired.

> We succeeded in making friends with the children, and gave them some candy and the rest of our lunch . . . . They looked thin and pitiful; but even in that lonely place, where they so seldom saw a stranger or even a neighbor, they showed there was an evident effort to make them look like other children, and they were neatly dressed, though there could be no mistake about their being very poor. One forlorn little soul, with honest gray eyes and a sweet, shy smile, showed us a string of beads which she wore round her neck; there were perhaps two dozen of them, blue and white, on a bit of twine, and they were the dearest things in all her world.[24]

When they give the father a dollar for caring for their horse he says, "I hope ye may never know what it is to earn every dollar as hard as I have. I never earned any money as easy as this before." Late that fall the two girls return again to this desolate cove, only to find a funeral in progress. The man and his wife have died and the children have been farmed out around the neighborhood. There follows a description of the "walking funeral"—the indoors ceremony dominated by the dismal tones of "China," the lining up of the procession outside, and the slow walk behind the corpse to the little burying plot fenced off from the rocky, autumnal fields. The squat, gray house is now left deserted on the shore.

> It is not likely that any one else will ever go to live there. The man to whom the farm was mortgaged will add the few forlorn acres to his pasture-land, and the thistles which the man who is dead had fought so many years will march in next summer and take unmolested possession.
> I think today of that fireless, empty, forsaken house, where the winter sun shines in and creeps slowly along the floor; the bitter cold is in and around the house, and the snow has sifted in at every crack; outside it is untrodden by any living creature's footstep. The wind blows and rushes and shakes the loose window-sashes in their frames, while the padlock knocks—knocks against the door.[25]

The secret of Jewett's description is in making her reader feel what she describes as she herself has felt it—the ache in the presence of killing poverty, as symbolized in the puny girl with her cheap necklace, or the shapeless dread that makes one walk on tiptoe about an abandoned farm.

5. An English Village in New England

Harriet Beecher Stowe was much impressed by the Hebraic qualities of New England, qualities that resulted from centuries of living as closely as possible by the stern letter of the Old Testament.[26] But Jewett, who was of Cavalier descent, was not interested in these vestiges of the old Puritan theocracy. To her it was that other heritage of colonial times, the lingering English tradition, that distinguished New England and rural life. She was, in fact, one of the most ardent anglophiles in a region and period of anglophilism; and in her *Story of the Normans,* her sole attempt at actual history, she gives vent to her admiration for the English and her sense of kinship with them. Proud of her own trace of French blood, she believed that in England after the Conquest a nearly perfect racial composition developed:

> It is the Norman graft upon the sturdy old Saxon tree that has borne best fruit among the nations—that has made the England of history, the England of great scholars and soldiers and sailors, the England of great men and women, of books and ships and gardens and pictures and songs! . . . To-day the Northman, the Norman, and the Englishman, and a young nation on this Western shore of the Atlantic are all kindred who, possessing a rich inheritance, should own the closest of kindred ties.[27]

In America the English tradition existed in its purest form and lingered the longest, Jewett feels, in the region in which she grew up. "For many years," she writes, "New England was simply a bit of Old England transplanted."[28] In her own day many of the older people, still mindful of their ancestry, thought and lived like Englishmen. But in the nation as a whole, where the distinctive American characteristics were no longer those of New England but of the West, this vestigial colonialism had become outdated. The gentry of the old school had been relegated to the status of museum pieces except in a few Eastern backwaters.

> If one of our own [New England's] elderly ladies were suddenly dropped into the midst of provincial English society, she would be quite at home; but west of her own Hudson River she is lucky if she does not find herself behind the times, and almost a stranger and a foreigner.[29]

Jewett, of course, regretted this dominance of Middle Western Americanism. The atmosphere of South Berwick was much more congenial to her. She was delighted to find the characters in Jane Austen's novels to be like the people in her own town before the Civil War. She deceived herself into thinking that the Boer War strengthened the ties between Old and New England. She was touched by a memorial service in the South

Berwick church on the death of Queen Victoria, when in the same town, in which there had once been bitter anti-British feeling, the congregation wept for the dead British sovereign, whose portrait they framed in evergreen. [30] The Queen, indeed, seemed the focal point in New England anglophilism. Jewett symbolized the feeling toward her in the story "The Queen's Twin." A childless old widow, living alone on a remote farm on the Maine coast, Abby Martin experiences the only pleasure of her solitary life by imagining herself the twin sister of Victoria. The Queen and Mrs. Abby Martin had been born at the same hour of the same day, both had married men named Albert, and once while on a voyage with her seafaring husband to England Mrs. Martin had caught a glimpse of her "twin." From these coincidences the Widow Martin creates a dream-life that she shares with her unknowing reginal sister. She familiarizes herself with the affairs of the royal family, and she fills her house with pictures of Her Majesty. Every Sunday, for a special treat, she reads the Queen's book on the Highlands. She celebrates the Jubilee and other royal anniversaries as if they were her own.[31]

The feelings of Jewett, who sympathized with Abby Martin, were typical. Perhaps no divergence better symbolized the differing outlooks of the American of the West from the New Englander than their opposite attitudes toward the English. Compare the rather cocksure Americanism of the early Mark Twain with the deep attachment of Jewett to the mother country, and the difference will be clear. An amusing anecdote is told by Oscar Laighton, who was the brother of Celia Thaxter, a friend and fellow writer of Jewett's. On a voyage with his sister to England on a British ship Oscar Laighton gave a dinner address in which he described English shipping and English girls as the finest in the world. All the diners applauded enthusiastically, except a man from Chicago, who sat in glum silence. During the rest of the evening the unappreciative Chicagoan was ostracized. To the irate Laighton, the incident was typical of Western boorishness.

It is not surprising, then, to find Jewett glorying in the fact that "Deephaven seemed more like the lazy little English seaside towns than any other. It was not in the least American."[32] There were lacking the bustle and excitement of American life. Most of the buildings, from the manor house itself to the tiniest fisherman's cottage, which were so English in their lines, had been built before the memory of the living inhabitants, as would be the case in a seaport of Devon or Cornwall. In the little fenced-in gardens the roses and apple trees had, as like as not, grown from stock brought from the mother country. The population itself, with the exception of several stranded sailors, was purely of English descent and nurtured on English traditions. Lucy Larcom, in *A New England Girlhood*, points out that in her native Beverly and other eastern New England towns "it was the voice of a mother country more ancient than their own, that little children heard crooning across the sea in their cradle hymns and nursery songs."[33] Indeed, the relationship with England was so close that the children were sometimes confused as to their nationality. Larcom describes rather whimsically her puzzlement over a verse in her spelling book, which like many of their texts was printed in England.

> I thank the goodness and the grace
>   That on my birth has smiled,
> And made me, in these latter days,
>   A happy *English* child.[34]

The social stratification of Deephaven reminded Jewett delightfully of Cranford, and the comparison is most apt. At the top were a handful of elderly representatives of the first families, the occupants of the elm-shaded, manor-like houses that lined the main street. Most of them were celibate, for the human race found it hard to multiply in such an exalted sphere. Among them the female dominated morally as well as numerically, though the chief feminine activities seemed to be playing whist and the hoarding of old brocades and lace. The males, of whom the minister, of course, was the most prominent, kept themselves locked in their libraries most of the time, where they sipped sherry and devoted themselves to continuous but apparently unproductive "studies." On the fringe of this upper circle but never securely in it clung various nondescripts who because of bad grammar or unfirmly rooted family trees could not establish their repectability conclusively enough for full acceptance. In dress and appearance the nobility and gentry, as Jewett calls them, were as old-fashioned as in their living. One deaf old gentleman, Mr. Joshua Dorsey, even wore his hair in a queue. The chief conversational topics, when it was necessary to talk, were theology and the former grandeur of Deephaven—the days of Governor and Lady Chantrey, when there were five families in town who rode in their own coaches.

In *Deephaven* Jewett's nostalgia for the past becomes almost a disease. Her own genteel blood flows for the moment in harmony with the sluggish circulations of the broken-down aristocrats whom she describes.

> Deephaven is utterly out of fashion. It never recovered from the effects of the embargo of 1807, and a sand-bar has been steadily filling in the mouth of the harbor . . . . But nobody in Deephaven cares for excitement; and if some one once in a while has the low taste to prefer a more active life, he is obliged to go elsewhere in search of it, and is spoken of afterward with kind pity . . . . There lingered a fierce pride in their family and town records, and a hardly concealed contempt and pity for people who were obliged to live in other parts of the world. . . . The people had nothing to do with the present, or the hurry of modern life.[35]

At times one is distressed for Jewett, as when she records approvingly the stuffy Miss Honora Carew's gratification that there is "no disagreeable foreign population"[36] in Deephaven, or perhaps when she finds

> it a great privilege to have an elderly person in one's neighborhood, in town or country, who is proud, and conservative, and who lives in stately fashion; who is intolerant of sham and of useless novelties, and clings to the old ways of living and behaving as if they were a part of her religion.[37]

Yet such stuffiness was prevalent in New England at the time—and has not totally disappeared in the twentieth century. We cannot be too hard on Jewett for reflecting the attitudes of her place and period. Furthermore, as we shall see in a later chapter, Jewett soon outgrew her scorn of foreigners —certainly the most reprehensible side of Deephaven narrowness.

If *Deephaven* were devoted solely to a description of decaying aristocracy, it would be a much inferior book. By far the greater and more vital part is devoted to the lives of the fishermen and farmers of the community; and in leaving the class with which she identifies herself, Jewett also leaves whatever smugness she may be accused of. The memories of her childhood visits with her father to country sickbeds return and vitalize her writing; one feels as if he had emerged from a museum into real life, for Jewett's common folk are always brilliantly alive. But if she drops her smugness, she does not drop her admiration for the English. As a matter of fact, she quite correctly believes the commoners of Deephaven to be even more English than the run-out quality folks. A comparison between the characters of *Deephaven* and those of George Eliot's great novel of English rural life, *Adam Bede*, will make Jewett's belief clearer. In *Deephaven*, the genteel persons—for example, Miss Honora Carew with her constant preoccupation with teacups and ancestors, and the broken-down merchant, Mr. Dick Carew, with his mysterious and time-consuming studies—make sorry counterparts to the proud, headstrong, if perhaps not wholly admirable, Donnithornes in George Eliot's tale. Nor would the whist-playing Parson Lorimer stand up against the philosophical, liberal, humane Mr. Erwine. But now compare the common people of both books. George Eliot's marvelous yeomen, the carpenters Seth and Adam Bede, and the farming Poyser family, are true first cousins to the sturdy, literate freemen of Jewett's New England. On this democratic level is the real bond between old and New England.

In her preface to *Deephaven* Jewett says that provincial and rustic influences the world over produce the same effects on character. Perhaps that is the explanation of the close likeness she finds between the country people of Maine and those of England. At any rate, in the New England of *Deephaven* the likeness amounts to an exact reproduction. Thus among the fishermen and farmers of the community we find the English villager's respect for social station. The moth-eaten gentry may have been, "like the conies of Scripture, a feeble folk,"[38] but when they tottered into Deephaven church on Sundays, they received all the respectful attention that the British Squire could demand on like occasions. But more significant, in these people of Deephaven there lived what Jewett called "the strength of the hills and the voice of the waves,"[39] that calm vigor of character that attains its full growth only in a race that has lived for generations in close intimacy with the land or sea. When that growth flowers, as it did briefly in New England and during centuries in Old England, it produces human beings like George Eliot's Seth and Adam Bede, Mrs. Poyser, and Dinah Morris, or like Sarah Orne Jewett's Miss Kew, Mrs. Patton, and Captain Sands, all of whom are marked by the same great human qualities of kindliness, self-control, deep religious feeling, independence, self-reliance, and an immense folk-wisdom, some-times misnamed common sense. It is also one of the qualities of such people, so long as their basic rights are not infringed upon, to venerate tradition. Thus it is that in Deephaven, as in England, the aristocracy was respected as being representative of an honored past. The ultimate standard, however, was never the past; for if the demands of tradition conflicted with the dignity or rights of the individual, tradition would have to be set aside. As in a great crisis, Adam Bede strikes his squire in the face with impunity, so in Jewett's work, there is always absolute equality between commoner and aristocrat on the level of basic human rights.

Other characteristics of the Deephaven rustic and seafarer also reminded Sarah Orne Jewett of the English. Their very "faces were not modern American faces, but belonged rather to the days of the early settlement of the country, the old colonial times." Their language, too, with its traces of Chaucerian vocabulary, as she imagined, had a flavor of the heroic days of the old country.[40] Yet these were superficialities and not at the basis of Jewett's anglophilism. What she most values in New England life is what we sometimes colloquially term "character," meaning an innate solidity and dependability. In her *Story of the Normans* she attempts to show that this "character" is a racial strain going far into the past of the Northern peoples, stronger now in Scandinavia then in her beloved England. "The green mountain-sides and fresh air of old Norway," she writes, "have not yet ceased to inspire simple, unperverted souls, from whose life a better and higher generation seems more than possible."[41] At any rate, in New England the time-honored traits and ways brought over unspoiled from the fields and beaches of England belong to a former age, lingering only in an occasional cove of the Maine coast or in some inaccessible inland valley. With the homesickness that we feel for the scene of a novel that has moved us deeply, Jewett completes her reading of New England's past. As she approaches middle age, she turns to a more important volumne—that of the present.

V. SELF-RELIANCE AND SOLITUDE:

The Country Folk of Sarah Orne Jewett and Helen Hunt Jackson

It is only as a man puts off all foreign support and stands alone that I see him to be strong and to prevail.

EMERSON, *"Self-Reliance"*

1. *"A White Heron" and Other Stories*

In one of her most delicate and poignant tales, "A White Heron," Sarah Orne Jewett tells the story of a little city girl brought to live with her grandmother in a remote, but tidy and cheerful, farmhouse on the coast of Maine. The grandmother and granddaughter have been living there alone for a year, and the child has come to know the woods and fields like a wild animal, and, as to young Wordsworth, nature has become all in all to her.

One day, while driving home their cow, she meets a young ornithologist who has set himself the task of finding a specimen of the almost-extinct white heron. He spends several nights at the farm, in the daytime searching for the bird, with the little girl as a guide. The child is pleased by this relationship, but is vaguely uneasy over the man's purpose. Although she has seen the heron in a nearby swamp, something keeps her from telling him of it.

One morning before dawn she steals out of the house and climbs a white pine of such height that for years it has served as a landmark for ships far out at sea. Her bare feet clinging to the topmost branches, she sees the heron arise into the dawn from its nesting-place in the marshes. The sight is one of the great moments in the child's life.

She works her way down the interminable trunk of the pine and returns to the house, planning to tell the ornithologist what she has seen and to collect the ten-dollar reward he had offered her for such information. But at the last moment "she cannot tell the heron's secret and give its life away."[2] Jewett doesn't consider it necessary to explain this decision. The child had liked—even loved—the man; when he left she missed him bitterly. But when she had to choose between the bird and the man, she chose the bird. Jewett closes the story with a question:

> Were the birds better friends than their hunter might have been,—who
> can tell? Whatever treasures were lost to her, woodlands and summer-
> time, remember! Bring your gifts and graces and tell your secrets to this
> lonely country child![3]

This story is not, as has been thought by some, an indication that Jewett was a man-hater. Rather it is an outgrowth of her belief that the human individuality must be kept inviolate. Independence and self-reliance had long been considered virtues in New England; in celebrating them, writers like Emerson and Thoreau were merely formulating ideas and feelings deeply ingrained into the New England mind. To Jewett, schooled in the time-honored mode of New England thought, the Emersonian maxim, "Be true to yourself," would be in the nature of an intuition. "A White Heron" then may be considered a parable of this belief. The child knew instinctively that her bond with nature was the rich, nurturing soil in which her personality was rooted and would later grow. To betray nature, as symbolized to her in the flight of the heron into the dawn sky, for the sum of ten dollars or even for the friendship of this stranger, would be to betray her own self. This is no sentimental story of a child befriending a bird; no stigma is attached to the collector who would kill the heron. The choice the girl made was the only one by which she could retain her own integrity—by which she could remain true to her own nature.

Such use of symbolism and allegory is not rare in Sarah Orne Jewett, who had faithfully read her Hawthorne. But the message of this story is told more directly, though never more feelingly, in scores of her other stories. One of the most desirable and significant features of New England life to her was the scope it gave to the growth of the individual. Perhaps she interpreted even this as a remnant of older times, of the frontier days when the self-sufficient person alone survived and the rubber-stamp person, the follower of the herd, usually perished. At any rate, this was a more indigenous, a more typically Yankee quality than the English traits she celebrated in her Deephaven folks.

On the rocky New England countryside with its six-week summers and interminable winters there was still much need for self-reliance, greater need, certainly, than in the old country or in other more fertile and clement regions. In the same volume with "A White Heron" is the story of "Farmer Finch," in which the energy, imagination, and initiative of a girl trained to be a schoolteacher prevent the loss of her father's farm. Polly Finch has just been rejected, because of politics, in her application for a desirable teaching position in a local school. Returning home, she finds her father reduced to tears in the face of an inevitable foreclosure. Acceptance of defeat is not a part of Polly's nature. The father enters upon a long and serious spell of illness, but the daughter takes over the farm, studies scientific farming from the agricultural journals, and not only saves the ancestral land but makes it more productive than it has ever been before. Such stories may not appeal to the modern reader of "realism," though Jewett's friend Willa Cather has written successfully on similar themes. Even Jewett is a bit apologetic. "This is only a story," she writes, "of a girl whom fate and fortune seemed to baffle; a glimpse of the way in which she made the best of things, and conquered circumstances, instead of being what cowards call the victim of circumstances."[4] Jewett and Cather had a faith in human beings not popular today. Perhaps they took Emerson's words too seriously: "Thus do all things preach the indifferency of circumstances. The man"—Jewett and many modern readers would add, "and the woman"—"is all."[5]

A hardship in New England as common as the barrenness of the soil and the rigor of the climate was solitude. Many a family in the remote hollows of the hills or on the lonely, granite-rimmed coves along the coast lived entirely unto themselves. But a bitter loneliness was that of the omnipresent New England solitaries—the celibates, both male and female, hanging on like ghosts in their family cottages or mansions. For such solitaries self-sufficiency was as much a matter of life and death as for the pioneer.

It is not surprising that many of Jewett's stories deal with single men and women who have somehow risen against great odds above their surroundings. For example, there is Ann Floyd in the story of "Marsh Rosemary." For many years unmarried, Miss Floyd weds a ne'er-do-well who after living on her earnings for a time deserts for another woman in New Brunswick, Canada. Going to the Provinces in search of him, Miss Floyd finds him living in apparent contentment with a young wife and a baby. Rather than expose him as a polygamist and cause unhappiness to the innocent woman and child, she returns to her celibate life, realizing that the other woman is better fitted for marriage than she is. Her former existence of loneliness and simple service to the community better suits her nature than family life. Again Jewett ends her story with a question:

> Who can laugh at my Marsh Rosemary, or can cry, for that matter? The gray primness of the plant is made up of a hundred colors, if you look close enough to find them. This same Marsh Rosemary stands in her own place, and holds her dry leaves and tiny blossoms steadily toward the same sun that the pink lotus blooms for, and the white rose.[6]

2. "The Country of the Pointed Firs"

Jewett's best-known book, *The Country of the Pointed Firs*, is composed on these themes of self-reliance and solitude. Laid on her beloved coast of Maine, this volume of sketches and stories reflects its author's own visits to Tenant's Harbor near Rockland, and the enduring friendships she made there. Jewett shared Wordsworth's notion that only material that has left its imprint on the memory for years can eventually form itself into effective literature. This is exactly what has happened with the *Pointed Firs* stories; through this aging process their material had become so much a part of her that, as Willa Cather says, they spring up fully alive out of life itself.[7]

The most remarkable character in the book—the finest bit of character-ization that Jewett ever achieved—is Almira Todd, the personification of Yankee self-sufficiency, independence, and practicality. A widow, she maintains her independence by gathering, brewing, and selling herbs, and by taking occasional boarders like Jewett into her cottage that was set so snugly in the herb and flower garden. A woman of massive size, Almira Todd was known for her friendliness, her good humor, her loyalty to her family, and her skill in handling a dory. She worked hand in hand with the local doctor, with whom she was on excellent terms, in aiding the sick of the community. She was a woman of deep feeling. Having been crossed in a youthful love affair, she had never loved her husband, but she had pitied and respected him. Once, when a walk in search of pennyroyal had led her and her boarder to a headland that looked far out to sea, she told in a moment of self-revelation, how she and her husband had come to this very spot when they were courting and had sat here and made their plans, she all the time feeling sorry for him because she didn't return his love. It was in a channel just off this headland that he had later been drowned while trying to get in to shore during a storm. Jewett writes:

> She looked away from me, and presently rose and went on by herself. There was something lonely and solitary about her great determined shape. She might have been Antigone alone on the Theban plain. It is not often given in a noisy world to come to the places of great grief and silence. An absolute, archaic grief possessed this countrywoman: she seemed like a renewal of some historic soul, with her sorrows and the remoteness of a daily life busied with rustic simplicities and the scents of primeval herbs.[8]

So enthusiastic is Jewett over the individualism of her friends the fisherman and farmers of Maine that she frequently mistakes mere oddness, and even insanity, for a commendable self-sufficiency. One of her favorite authors, Matthew Arnold,[9] had repeatedly warned the English that an irresponsible arbitrariness, a proneness to eccentricity, was one of the chief national weaknesses that had grown out of Puritanism. Like New Englanders, the English tended to be too self-reliant and placed too much confidence in their own intuitions and opinions as standards of conduct and thinking. Judging from some of the odd characters that she found worthy of praise rather than pity, one would say that Jewett ignored

Arnold's warnings. Perhaps because she lacked a sense of humor she was simply unable to see the ridiculous as well as commendable side of her eccentrics.

No one will find fault with the self-dependence and initiative of an Almira Todd or a Polly Finch. If the term "rugged individual" ever has a pleasant connotation it is when applied to this sort of character. But the case is different, with dozens of other characters whom Jewett finds admirable; in fact, by sentimentalizing certain neurotics and cranks, by attempting to show in them an excellence that they simply don't possess, she has marred some of her best work.

Three such characters, in an ascending scale of oddness, will illustrate the point. First is Esther Hight, heroine of the chapter entitled "A Dunnet Shepherdess." Esther reminds one in many ways of Polly Finch. Confronted with the almost-insoluble problem of supporting herself and her mother on a farm whose land consists chiefly of granite ledges, she gets the idea from a book that sheep might be successfully grazed among the rocks if one tended them personally and didn't leave their care entirely to dogs. Thus Esther spent her days "far away in the hill pasture with her great flock, like a figure of Millet's, high against the sky."[10] In a modest way, Esther did succeed in revolutionizing the sheep industry in her neighborhood and there is an unquestionable appeal in her lonely shepherding in that "wildest, most Titanic sort of pasture country."[11] But the appeal of the story is spoiled when we find that all this struggle has been totally unnecessary. The invalid mother has been cared for, the mortgage on an almost worthless farm has been paid off. But what then? In the meanwhile, Esther has been in love, since almost before the memory of the oldest inhabitant, with an able fisherman, William Blacket, who already supports a mother and would gladly have supported the mother-in-law as well. But William has had to rest content with seeing his sweetheart for an hour or two just once a year. As a result, he has become neurotic, the victim of shyness so painful that he will not sail his boat past the mouth of Dunnet Harbor for fear of being seen.

The reason assigned for this prolonged celibacy is that each has a widowed mother to care for. Now this may be a legitimate reason for a thirty-year engagement; like situations were all too common in New England. But it is not an ideal arrangement. By ignoring this unhappiness, especially after she had described its painful symptoms in William, Jewett is guilty of sentimentality in its most mawkish form. That particular sketch in *The Country of the Pointed Firs* may thus be spoiled for many modern readers. Yet Jewett's attitude is interesting in that it indicates how far the cult of individualism could carry an intelligent New Englander of the day. Even more significant is her recognition that this individualism is a major source of strength among New England women.

A more painful character is Captain Littlepage, who suffers from delusions and hallucinations. Refined, dignified, and a quoter of *Paradise Lost*, which he has read and reread on his many voyages, Captain Littlepage calls on Jewett one afternoon in a schoolhouse that she has appropriated as a study during the summer vacation. Discussion turns on a funeral recently held in the village. With a sudden but restrained excitement, the Captain makes a mysterious utterance about a "waiting place" where the dead go. He goes on to tell a story he had heard from a crazed Scotsman while marooned by shipwreck at a lonely Arctic mission. According to the Scotsman's story, which Littlepage believed implicitly and repeated with maniacal waving of his arms and pacings up and down, there is situated deep in the polar cap a city of ghosts who have been stranded midway between this and the next world and are awaiting eventual release. The Captain's descriptions have the vividness of a Dante or of a madman. With great difficulty Jewett gets him off this subject and onto such neutral topics as the recent funeral and the decadence of shipping. Later, Almira Todd informs her that Captain Littlepage is given to these "spells."

No one, of course, doubts the existence of such persons; but again Jewett has sentimentalized her character. The Captain is a pitiful, deranged old man. But Jewett sets him up as a typical sea-captain of the old school. His oddity is perhaps regrettable, but it serves, after all, to emphasize his individuality and to add to his old-fashioned quaintness. Jewett is perfectly sincere; she is simply seeing in the Captain more than was ever there. For the moment she has forgotten her father's advice: "Don't try to write *about* people and things; tell of them as they are."[12] Fortunately, in the greater number of these sketches she has managed to follow that advice to the letter.

Well out to sea off Dunnet Landing—the name given Tenant's Harbor in *The Country of the Pointed Firs*—lay Shell-heap Island, a surf-pounded, almost treeless thirty acres of barnacled granite. This desolate spot, the symbol of a primeval loneliness that makes the outer islands of the Maine coast seem like outposts of Antarctica, is the scene of a third story of human oddity. Joanna Todd, a cousin of the sturdy Almira, had been "crossed in love." Constitutionally melancholy, she became convinced, as is common among melancholiacs of Puritan heritage, that she was guilty of unpardonable sin and was thus unfit to live in human society. Having camped on Shell-heap Island with her father a number of times as a child, she now secludes herself there in a tumbled-down clamming shack. She finds enough stunted spruces and driftwood to supply her with fuel; for food she depends on the sea and whatever her garden and the few chickens she maintains on the rock produce. Friends and relatives and even the minister visit her and urge her to leave. But she refuses. Year after year, winter after winter, she drags out her life there. When she dies, she is buried on the island, a fitting place for a recluse's interment.

This story of "Poor Joanna" is marvelous reading. As Jewett says, "there is something in the fact of a hermitage that cannot fail to touch the imagination; the recluses are a sad kindred, but they are never commonplace."[13] The fascination of such stories is greatest when the recluse exists against great odds. We follow breathlessly the itemized lists of Robinson Crusoe's powder, flour, nails, barreled pork, and biscuit, because we know a life depends on what is in those lists. Similarly, as we read of Joanna we estimate the yield of clams of the single mud flat on Shell-heap Island or weigh the possibility of her trapping lobsters off the rocks. We marvel at the self-sufficiency of the woman and at her ability to maintain life unaided in the bosom of the wintry Atlantic. And unquestionably it was this side of Joanna's life that fascinated Jewett—the recluse's utter self-dependence, her refusal to compromise her selfhood by yielding to her friends' plea that she come ashore. Yet the fact remains that Joanna was insane, that a young life was uselessly wasted for itself and for others. But Jewett ignores the dreary, the morbid, the horrible in Joanna's diseased existence. For a third time the accusation of sentimentality must be made. Jewett had once advised Willa Cather to get more outside her stories, not to stand in the middle of them, but to be a looker-on.[14] Excellent advice, but too difficult for even the adviser always to follow.

3. Village Attitudes

"I had been reflecting," Jewett writes in her chapter on Joanna, "upon a state of society which admitted such personal freedom and a voluntary hermitage. There was something mediaeval in the behavior of poor Joanna Todd under a disappointment of the heart."[15] If Jewett was unrealistic in the psychology of her eccentrics and recluses, she was, on the other hand, most realistic in her treatment of the New England villager's reaction toward these people. In fact her own reaction was typical aside from its excessive sentimentality. The people of Dunnet Landing took their Captain Littlepages and Joannas as a matter of course. They might occasionally reflect that it was too bad that people should be so odd. Yet the maxim, live and let live, was taken very seriously in such places. So long as the eccentrics harmed no one, they should be left pretty much to themselves. One might even feel as much pride in them as in the poets, statesmen, or notorious criminals produced by one's town. Frustrated persons might even resort, consciously or unconsciously, to oddness as a way of getting social recognition not otherwise attainable.

The most fascinating case of such eccentricity in New England was that of Emily Dickinson. Yet in all the theorizing as to why Dickinson secluded herself and wore white dresses and in general was queer, one obvious fact has been ignored: the Amherst poet was in no way exceptional in choosing an eccentric way of life. But, some one will object, Dickinson wrote great verse; surely such peculiarity in a great poet is almost unique. Not in the New England of her day. A few miles to the northward, in the almost adjoining town of Greenfield, the recluse Frederick Goddard Tuckerman wrote fine sonnets that were not discovered till after his death. Others, of course, wrote very bad poetry. The neuralgic and neurotic Nancy Luce of Martha's Vineyard spent forty-nine years (1840–1889) in pain-racked solitude writing "primitive"—meaning, in this case, illiterate—verse on such subjects as the death of her hens, who were her only companions. Indeed she named each fowl, and, much to the amusement of the islanders, on every egg she sold would be the name of the bird that laid it.[16]

There are fads in neuroses as well as in physical diseases and clothes. In the late nineteenth century "ladies" had small feet, wore long skirts, and suffered from chronically recurrent syncope; and single women became recluses, particularly if they imagined themselves "crossed in love." The unmarried woman could assert herself by retiring from her fellows and taking up gardening, cats or poetry. In this way she would be following an accepted practice; and so long as she harmed no one she would earn not a little admiration from the townspeople.

It is easy to be facetious about such matters. Yet these solitaries do deserve a certain admiration. In Catholic lands the hermits and nuns have been regarded as highly remarkable persons, deserving and receiving public support and veneration. The anchorites of New England attained no such status as this, of course. Still, in an environment where strength of will and strong assertion of individuality counted for so much they had their niche. Thus widely read writers of the day, like Sarah Orne Jewett and Mary Wilkins Freeman, thickly populated their tales with characters whose lives, often because of love trouble, had gone off on tangents. Emily Dickinson herself, long before any one outside of Amherst suspected she was a poet, was supposedly used as heroine of two such stories by her neighbor Helen Hunt Jackson. In *Mercy Philbrick's Choice* the poet Mercy Philbrick refuses to marry the saintly Parson Dorrance because she is in love with another man. But after Parson Dorrance dies, she transfers her affections to him because her first love has fallen slightly short of the spirit of the Sermon on the Mount in connection with a business deal. As a consequence the perverse Mercy chooses a life of sanctified solitude: "a life lonely, yet full of companionship; sad, yet full of cheer; hard, and yet perpetually uplifted by an inward joy . . ."[17] in short a paradoxical life of the variety that only a Victorian sentimentalist like Jackson or Jewett could dream up. In all fairness to Jackson, however, it must be added that Mercy, unlike her supposed real-life counterpart, Emily Dickinson, lavished her maternal affections on the young folk of the town rather than on her flowers.

In a second story, "Esther Wynn's Love Letters," one of the popular Saxe Holm series, Jackson tells of an affair between Esther Wynn and a mysterious "master," which for unrevealed reasons can never be consummated. Esther stubbornly devotes herself to this impossible love, composing dream allegories and highly original poetry till her health breaks and she is ordered abroad by her physicians, soon to die in the Holy Land. Though we are not told to what extent Esther was a recluse, the peculiar, withdrawn manner of her life is evident. Yet Helen Hunt Jackson had nothing but admiration for this determined adherence to the impossible. Was not Esther, by her dogged celibacy and her refusal to give way to circumstances, living up to the highest dictates of her individuality?[18] Such a performance, to Jackson as to Jewett, seemed so wholly admirable that any discomforts, either mental or physical, suffered by the performer should be carefully expunged from the drama.

The performers themselves, however, often enough attested to the difficulties of their role. Emily Dickinson, for example, told of far different feelings from those of Esther Wynn or Mercy Philbrick. Like St. John of the Cross's *Dark Night of the Soul*, her poetry should be read as the record of a person attempting to live entirely on her own resources. One is inclined to believe she was successful, but the struggle was long and grievous.

> On the bleakness of my lot
>   Bloom I strove to raise.
> Late, my acre of a rock
>   Yielded grape and maize.
>
> Soil of flint if steadfast tilled
>   Will reward the hand;
> Seed of palm by Lybian sun
>   Fructified in sand.[19]

But there were hours of devasting despair—hours not recorded in Helen Hunt Jackson's or Sarah Orne Jewett's accounts of the totally self-reliant:

> I many times thought peace had come,
> When peace was far away;
> As wrecked men deem they sight the land
> At centre of the sea,
>
> And struggle slacker, but to prove,
> As hopelessly as I,
> How many the fictitious shores
> Before the harbor lie.[20]

It is clear then that Jewett in her stories of solitaries and introverts has not been an accurate reporter. Had she been a less timid psychologist, her stories would have been much grimmer—and truer. As it is, she has done these characters more than justice by seeing them with the tolerant eyes of the village. For the days of the New England tithing man, whose function was to bring into line those who in any way overstepped the bounds of Christian living as defined by Calvin, were past. The American principle that within limits set by criminal law one's life is one's own to do with as one likes had come into its own in New England. Villagers might still gossip and disapprove; but the latitude of individual action had become amazingly broad in this region. If, as happens in one of Mary Wilkins Freeman's stories,[21] a woman chose to lock herself in her cottage with fifty cats and never walk down the village street again, she was at liberty to do so. She might be talked about and laughed at, but she would never be interfered with.

Thus Jewett reflected the attitudes of her times, and as a result won the laurels of popularity. New Englanders felt that she presented situations and attitudes of New England village life as it was actually lived. Mary Wilkins Freeman, who occasionally probed into the tragedies of lonely and eccentric lives, was frowned upon. One Boston critic even expressed relief when Mary Wilkins, marrying a Dr. Freeman, moved to New Jersey.[22] She had not allowed her writing to be directed by any theories concerning the sanctity of the individual. Consequently she had seen things that even the villagers, for all their notorious inquisitiveness, had not seen. Still, she is sympathetic towards the eccentrics with whom she fills her stories, even though she sometimes sees the tragic waste of their lives. Regarding village attitudes she is somewhat more analytical than Jewett but arrives at the same conclusions. "Indeed, everything out of the broad common track," she writes in one story, "was a horror to these men and to many of their village fellows." When the deacon and minister in this same story set out to investigate the doings of the solitary Jenny Wrayne, the woman whose queerness offended them, we are reminded that "in actual meaning, although not even in self-acknowledgement, it was a witch-hunt that went up the mountain road that December afternoon."[23] Yet this same deacon and minister realize their mistake and make amends by sending Jenny a fine Christmas turkey. Even in Freeman's stark New England the witch-hunting instinct has burned itself down to a feeble flicker that serves only to light the torch of tolerance—and rather sentimental tolerance at that, since Jenny Wrayne would have been better off if the authorities had retained their purpose sufficiently to commit her to an asylum.

4. "The King of Folly Island and Other People"

Jewett was not an incurable Pollyanna, despite her Victorian—or should we say merely human—tendency to overlook things that she did not wish to see. Although she could rarely refrain from romanticizing her recluses and neurotics, she sometimes rather grudgingly recognized the futility of their lives and, less often, the tragedy of them, particularly where other people involved were being made unhappy. Examples of this will not be found, however, in her best-known books, *Deephaven* and *The Country of the Pointed Firs.* One must turn to a volume composed apparently in a less optimistic frame of mind when Jewett was between forty and fifty years old, *The King of Folly Island and Other People.* Two stories from this volume illustrate their author at her most realistic if not her most artistic.

The title piece is the story of an inhabitant of the fictitious John's Island, twelve miles off the Maine coast, who becomes disgruntled with the meanness of his neighbors and buys the even more remote Folly Island with the purpose of living there in complete isolation. Here he moves with his wife and daughter, swearing never to set foot on any other man's land again. He fulfills his vow. He manages to build a comfortable house and clear an adequate farm; he sets trawls and takes his catch to market, doing his business from his boat at the wharf. One shares with Jewett an admiration for the man's self-sufficiency and steadfastness. We are not surprised to find

> an air of distinction and dignity about this King of Folly Island, and uncommon directness and independence. He was the son and heir of the old Vikings who had sailed that stormy coast and discovered its harborage and its vines five hundred years before Columbus. . . .[24]

But as the story proceeds the King is seen in a slightly less favorable light. For him the life on Folly Island has been rewarding; he has lived up to his vow and gained recognition for doing so, and he has known the satisfaction of wresting out of nature single-handedly a life for himself and his family. But for his wife and daughter the experience has been death. More isolated than he, since in his fishing and business transactions he has human contact, the mother dies early and is laid away in a corner of the fields. The daughter, who minds the loneliness less because she has known nothing else, becomes ill of consumption. But her father, who had driven off and ducked in the water the only suitor she ever had, would sacrifice his daughter to the sanctity of his vow by refusing to take her to a more healthful climate. Here Jewett perceives, but does not utilize, the rudiments of true tragedy—the essentially noble man or woman marred by a fatal flaw in character. "This man, who should be armed and defended by his common-sense, was yet made weak by some prejudice or superstition. What could have warped him in this strange way?" she asks?[25] Because she couldn't or wouldn't probe more deeply for an answer in her own question, "The King of Folly Island" falls short of greatness.

Another story in the same volume, "The Landscape Chambers," puts a similar question. Jewett, who tells the story in the first person, has been riding far into the country. Because of the unexpected lameness of her horse she is forced to put up in a ramshackle Colonial mansion inhabited by an equally dilapidated man and his daughter. The man is kind and expert in his care of the lame horse, and the rider remains for several nights in the home. Gradually the dreary drama being performed by these two forlorn actors reveals itself. The man is not only a miser, but a monomaniac, convinced, like some character in Hawthorne, that he is living under an ancestral curse. Quite correctly Jewett finds the pitiable part of the story to be the daughter's misery as an enforced participant of her father's madness.[26]

The mood of these stories, it will be seen, is very different from that of the sketches of eccentrics in *The Country of the Pointed Firs*. Yet the frequently made criticism that Jewett cannot write tragedy remains just. The necessary psychological insight is always lacking; we are never brought face to face with the agony of these warped minds. Another, perhaps more serious lack is the absence of any great issues in her stories of this type. What she does achieve is largely through atmosphere, and at times this achievement is so great as to approach the mood, if not the profundity and significance, of tragedy. In *The King of Folly Island* a single scene not only sets the atmosphere of dreary isolation but also sounds the solemn, sombre note that is the essence of all tragic writing. The sick girl is standing on the shore with a spyglass watching a "floating funeral" set out from a neighboring island. There was

> the coffin with its black pall in a boat rowed by four men, who had pushed out a little way from the shore, and other boats near it. From the low, gray house near the water came a little group of women stepping down across the rough beach and getting into their boats; then all fell into a rude sort of orderliness, the hearse-boat going first, and the procession went away across the wide bay toward the main-land.[27]

It is such description as this, to be found in even her weakest stories, that lifts Sarah Orne Jewett's writings above the commonplace. One of her chief claims to reputation is her skill in atmosphere.

VI. AN ARMORY OF POWERS:

The Countryside of Sarah Orne Jewett and Alice Brown

Supplanters of the tribe, the farmers dwell.
Traveller, to thee, perchance, a tedious road,
Or, it may be, a picture; to these men,
The landscape is an armory of powers . . . .

EMERSON, "Musketaquid"[1]

1. "A Marsh Island"

Travelers along the coast of southwestern Maine will have seen vast expanses of marsh stretching miles inland from the sea. On a day when the cumulus clouds are marching down from the northwest one experiences on these marshes the same feeling of boundlessness as on the Kansas wheatlands. The saltgrass undulates before the windflows like some strange, olive-green grain, and the cloud shadows glide solemnly from one horizon to another like the shadows that a school of great, lazy-moving fish might cast on the floor of the sea. Netting the flats like irrigation ditches are the tidal channels, now mere trickles between steep, sunbaked banks, now freshets of churning saltwater racing backwards or forwards to the ocean. In the late summer men may be seen on this strange landscape, clusters of tiny workers against the blue-gray band of ocean. These are the farmers, the mowers making the rich hay that flourishes in the briny mud. They do not seem alien to the landscape; they are as much a part of it as the tall supple grass itself.

One wonders where these midget workers come from. But soon one perceives an elevation of land, like the swelling of a prairie, surrounded by the illimitable flatness. This is the marsh island. On it are fields, woods, orchards, pastures, a farmstead, and barns. It is from here that the mowers in the salt meadows come, as islanders go out to take the fish of the sea.

In such a spot Sarah Orne Jewett laid her novel *A Marsh Island*. For her purposes it was an ideal setting. In the discussion of her tales of eccentrics it may have been implied that Jewett dealt mainly with persons at war with their environment. Nothing could be less true. Her Polly Finches, her

Almira Todds far outnumber her Folly Islanders. Rightly or wrongly, she found the vast majority of the New England farmers and fishermen to be at peace with the life to which they had been born. Like the peasants of Hamsun and Björnson, they are an indigenous growth of the soil and sea, living in complete harmony with their surroundings and enjoying the profound, quiet happiness that comes only with such harmony.

No better milieu in which to illustrate this blending of humanity and nature could be found than that of the marsh island. Here Jewett has placed a family on the summit of New England rural happiness. Alone on their little outgrowth of land and entirely proof against jarring influences from outside they are the ultimate personification, the flowering of the ideal of self-sufficiency. Though the mother once wished vaguely for a wider life, she has long since become firmly rooted. The daughter has had her roots in deep from the first. Confronted with the possibility of marrying a rich artist boarder, a representative of the blooded and moneyed city classes, she never seriously considers leaving her marsh island and breaking her engagement to a young yeoman of the region. The father, fashioning his life out of the marsh and the sea as had his forebears for generations before him, knows a fulfillment and peace experienced by few on this earth. Yet these people are in no sense narrow; they represent at their best all the educational, religious, and civic excellencies of New England country life. One might point out that their spheres were limited; so is the sphere of an oak tree or of a mountain. Thoreau would have perfectly understood these people; he realized that it is not the size of one's sphere but the quality of it that matters.

Critics have complained that *A Marsh Island* is a very poor novel. It is not, in fact, a novel at all. It lacks the chief element of fiction—conflict. Where none of the characters are fighting their environment it is difficult and artificial to impose a conflict. Rather than a novel, *A Marsh Island* is a description, an attempt to catch the atmosphere of the marsh and the lives of the people who live so much at peace with it. As such it is a successful book. This is true of all Jewett's most successful work. The less she concerned herself with plot—and the conflict that is the essence of plot —the finer her achievement. Her most impressive productions—*Deephaven*, the larger part of *The Country of the Pointed Firs*, such stories as "The Courting of Sister Wisby" and "Miss Tempy's Watchers"—are description rather than storytelling.

Here then was the summing up of Jewett's vision of New England life. The region had been at its best in the past, before the modern unrest and scramble for money. Yet in many of the living, even in the young people, are perpetuated the best of the past—an unobtrusive self-sufficiency, a love of home, a contentment with durable values, above all a determination to make what one has count for something rather than rush out after easy money, luxury, surface excitements. She realized that many persons could not surmount the difficulties of New England life—the harshness of climate, the barrenness of the soil, the loneliness of poverty—yet she recognized and admired the efforts of such people to mold a way of life out of their own resources rather than to run crying for help to the nearest city. Even where this fierce self-reliance resulted in warped and unhappy lives she was ready to recognize the intrinsic value of the effort, reserving condemnation only for extreme cases where independence became a selfishness that ruined other people's lives. But being optimistic she believed that the vast number of New Englanders who stuck to their old way of life were able to grasp a happiness denied those who clutched after the *ignis fatuus* of easy living elsewhere.

2. Tiverton

In Hampton Falls, New Hampshire, four miles from Exeter and perhaps twenty-five from South Berwick, another local-color writer, Alice Brown, was reaching conclusions similar to Jewett's concerning New England life. Born in 1857 on her family's farm, Brown first was a pupil in the district school that she describes so feelingly in the sketch entitled "Number Five"[2]—as perfect a bit of childhood reminiscence as can be found in American literature—and later attended the Robinson Seminary at Exeter, traveling the four miles to and from her home on foot. An ardent student of Wordsworth, Keats, Milton, and Rossetti, she wrote prose in unconscious iambic meter. For several years she taught school in Boston and in the country, but disliking teaching, went into editorial work, holding positions with the *Christian Register* and later with the *Youth's Companion.* In 1886 she spent almost a year in France, and in 1890 she passed five months in London, Devon, and Cornwall, her experiences in these places being described in a book entitled *By Oak and Thorn.* In 1895 she took a walking trip through Wales and Shropshire with the Boston poet Imogene Guiney. In the same year the two friends published a critical study of Robert Louis Stevenson, whom they inordinately admired and whose purple passages in particular Brown attempted to imitate, much to the detriment of the purity and simplicity of her earlier style.

Alice Brown wrote just two books that are important in a study of rural New England at the end of the century. But these two books—*Meadow Grass* and *Tiverton Tales*—are her best, as well as among her first. She wrote much verse; many novels and short stories on a variety of themes from New England country life to such psychical subjects as transmigration of the soul and communication with the dead; a biography of Guiney; and many plays, including *Children of Earth*, which won a $10,000 Harper's prize, based on the theme of a New England woman's longing for love.

Meadow Grass, her first and perhaps most deserving success, and its companion volume, *Tiverton Tales,* deal with her home town of Hampton Falls, to which she always returned for summer vacations. Like Rowland Robinson, Rose Terry Cooke, and Sarah Orne Jewett, Brown used a single village and its inhabitants as the material for a series of stories and sketches that can be read independently but that when taken together, give an extensive and detailed picture of a locality. Tiverton is essentially the same as the places about which Sarah Orne Jewett, Whittier, and Lucy Larcom wrote so lovingly. Brown's attitude is no exception to theirs. The terrain within a radius of fifty miles of Portsmouth, New Hampshire, must have been remarkably idyllic, for it has invariably fostered contentment in its literary inhabitants, among them Robert Frost.

None of these writers had a greater love of the region than did Alice Brown. The atmosphere of complete harmony between people and their environment, which broods like a guardian angel over the marsh island of Jewett's book, envelops Tiverton with an equally blessed peace. Here again is that highest phase of self-sufficiency—that of a yeomanry rooted deep in a soil that rewards it tillers for their love and work. It is the type of self-sufficiency that Emerson describes in his essay on "Farming" in *Society and Solitude.*

> The farmer times himself to Nature, and acquires that livelong patience which belongs to her. Slow, narrow man, his rule is, that the earth shall feed and clothe him; and he must wait for his crop to grow .... He is permanent, clings to his land as the rocks do. In the town where I live, farms remain in the same families for seven and eight generations; and most of the first settlers (in 1635), should they reappear on the farms today, would find their own blood and names still in possession. And the like fact holds in the surrounding towns.[3]

It is in dealing with this type of farmer in one of the oldest sections of New England that Brown has been most successful. Though in her later books her favorite theme was the thwarted love impulse in women—a frustration typical enough of New England life—in the best pieces in *Meadow Grass* and *Tiverton Tales* the theme is the unbreakable tie between the countryman or -woman and the soil that gave them existence.

In "Number Five" she tells of the influence of Tiverton on a farm-bred child who has later gone elsewhere in search of his fortunes. With a Wordsworthian belief in the influence of childhood scenes on later life, she writes:

> We who are Tiverton born, though false ambition may have ridden us to market, or the world's voice incited us to kindred clamoring, have a way of shutting our eyes, now and then, to present changes, and seeing things as they were once, as they are still, in a certain sleepy yet altogether individual corner of country life.[4]

There follow seventeen pages of fresh and moving variations on that most difficult, because most hackneyed, theme of the little red schoolhouse. That Brown could be original on the subject is proof of the feeling with which she approached it. Her girlhood in Hampton Falls had given her a hold on life—a feeling of belonging—that never deserted her. "For we who have walkd in country ways, walk in them always, and with no divided love, even though brick pavements have been our chosen road this many a year."[5]

Another sketch, "Farmer Eli's Vacation," considered by some to be Brown's finest story, celebrates a farmer's deep attachment to the acres that have given—and taken—his life. The narrowness, the hardship, of Farmer Eli's existence is not glossed over.

> For Eli, though he had lived all his life within easy driving distance of the ocean, had never seen it, and ever since his boyhood he had cherished one darling plan—some day he would go to the shore, and camp out there for a week. This, in his starved imagination, was like a dream of the Acropolis to an artist stricken blind, or as mountain outlines to the dweller in a lonely plain. But the years had flitted past, and the dream never seemed nearer completion.[6]

One day in his old age Eli does break away. Leaving the farm in the care of the hired man, he sets out with his family on the short drive to the seaside. He sees the ocean and spends one sleepless night in his tent on the shore. At dawn his daughter finds him gazing wistfully out on the water. When she asks him what is wrong, he simply says he is going home; he will sneak off before the others awake, leaving a note, so that they can stay out their week without worrying about him. The situation could be treated as a defeat for Farmer Eli—as a lesson in what the grinding life of a farmer can do to character. But Brown prefers, as would Jewett, to treat it as a triumph. Eli's life was full enough without the added experience of seeing the Atlantic Ocean. Thus there is nothing pathetic or tragic in his return in the early morning.

> As he jogged homeward, the dusty roadsides bloomed with flowers of paradise, and the insects' dry chirp thrilled like the song of angels. He drove into the yard just at the turning of the day, when the fragrant smoke of many a crackling fire curls cheerily upward, in promise of the evening meal.[7]

Another character who has found complete happiness is Dilly Joyce, the heroine of several Tiverton tales. An old maid who lives alone and likes it, Dilly has none of the frustrations that Brown's later spinsters suffer from. Explaining why she gave up nursing two years ago, she says:

> I wa'n't havin' no time at all. I couldn't live my proper life. I al'ays knew I should come to that, so I'd raked an' scraped, an' put into the

> bank, till I thought I'd got enough to buy me a mite o' flour while I lived, an' a pine coffin arter I died; an' then; . . . I'd be as free's a bird. Freer, I guess I be, for they have to scratch pretty hard, come cold weather, an' I bake me a 'tater, an' then go clippin' out over the crust, lookin' at the bare twigs. Oh, it's complete! If I could live this way, I guess a thousand years'd be a mighty small dose for me. Look at that goldenrod, over there by the stump! That's the kind that's got the most smell.[8]

There is nothing selfish about Dilly's life. Her mere presence in the community, even if she has given up nursing, is an asset. To discontented souls, to people who are prone to career off after delusive ends, she is an example of what a quiet life can be. A comforter of the bereaved, a straightener out of tangled love affairs, she is more important to Tiverton than its board of selectmen or its beloved minister, Parson True. Though appearing in many stories, Dilly is at her best in "At Sudleigh Fair," in which she circulates among the assembled rustics like the spirit of human understanding and common sense—the central symbol of contentment in a canvas overflowing with bucolic fullness and good cheer. When the serenity of this picture—reminiscent of Hardy's fair scenes in artistry if not in mood—is temporarily ruffled by the troubles of an unhappy couple, an arsonist and his mistress, Dilly is the restorer of tranquility. The arsonist confesses, and feels the first peace he has known in weeks; his sweetheart regains her equilibrium by deciding to wait and work for him while he serves his jail sentence. But the plot is not the important thing in this story, and Brown devotes little attention to it. Dilly and her influence as a personification of the peaceful, soul-healing atmosphere of Tiverton are the main interest.

The hold of this beneficent environment on its inhabitants is attested to everywhere in the literature of the day, and it was as evident along the coast as in the hinterland. Sarah Pratt McLean, the Connecticut author who has written so sympathetically of Cape Cod, puts into the mouth of one of her fishermen an utterance that effectively sums up the Yankee's attitude toward one's birthplace.

> I tell you how 'tis, teacher. Folks that live along this shore are allus talkin' more'n any other sort of folks about going off, and complainin' about the hard livin', and cussin' the stingy sile, but thar's suthin' about it sorter holts to 'em. They allus come a driftin' back in some shape or other, in the course of a year or two at the farderest.[9]

In his story of John Gilley, Charles W. Eliot has given one—and perhaps the most cogent—reason for this strong pull of environment. In describing the Gilley family's island home he writes:

Then, they always had before them some of the most splendid aspects of nature. From their sea-girt dwelling they could see the entire hemisphere of the sky; and to the north lay the grand hills of Mt. Desert, with outline clear and sharp when the northwest wind blew, but dim and soft when southerly winds prevailed. In every storm a magnificent surf dashed up on the rockbound isle. In winter the low sun made the sea toward the south a sheet of shimmering silver; and all the year an endless variety of colors, shades, and textures played over the surfaces of hills and sea. The delight in such visions is often but half-conscious in persons who have not the habit of reflection; but it is nevertheless a real source of happiness, which is soon missed when one brought up amid such pure and noble scenes is set down among the straitened, squalid, ugly sights of a city.[10]

In slightly different words, Henry James, returning to America after a generation abroad, makes the same observation:

[In New England] the touching appeal of nature, ... The "Do something kind for me," is not so much a "Live upon me and thrive by me" as a "Live *with* me, somehow, and let us make out together what we may do for each other—something that is not merely estimable in more or less greasy greenbacks"[11]

VII. WILLFULNESS AND WRONG-HEADEDNESS:

The Hill People of Rose Terry Cooke

> And how, we ask, would New England's rocky soil and icy hills have been made mines of wealth unless there had been human beings born to oppose, delighting to combat and wrestle, and with an unconquerable power of will.
>
> HARRIET BEECHER STOWE, *Poganuc People*[1]

1. Zeph Higgins

One of the most interesting and vivid characters that Harriet Beecher Stowe created is the farmer Zeph Higgins in *Poganuc People*. For plain "sotness" and "cussedness" he has no equal in American literature; yet he is as natural an outcropping of the New England hills as one of the immovable boulders in his own fields. The region around Stowe's native Litchfield in western Connecticut, where the autobiographical *Poganuc People* has its setting, must have been heavily populated with just such gnarled and crotchety characters. Nowhere else in New England, except perhaps in the White Mountains, are there quite so many cobblestones per yard of soil or is the terrain so broken and choppy. A lesser and softer race would soon have languished in this glacier-gutted land.

But for Zeph Higgins the Litchfield hills provided a welcome means of self-expression.

> Zeph had taken a thirteen-acre lot so rocky that a sheep could scare find a nibble there, had dug out and blasted and carted the rocks, wrought them into a circumambient stone fence, plowed and planted, and raised crop after crop of good rye thereon. He did it with heat, with zeal, with dogged determination; he did it all the more because neighbors said he was a fool for trying, and that he could never raise anything on the lot. There was a stern joy in his hand-to-hand fight with nature. He got his bread as Samson did his honeycomb, out of the carcass of the slain lion.[2]

In his obsession with rocks, Zeph resembles Ephraim Cabot in O'Neill's *Desire Under the Elms*, though Zeph lacks Ephraim's sense of God-directed mission.

Having cleared his thirteen-acre lot, Zeph was the type to go up into Vermont and clear another farm. He would have admired Seth Hubbell and rather envied him his four-hundred-mile winter trek by ox-team from Long Island Sound to the northern Green Mountains, followed by a summer of fighting the forest with only an ax and an old hoe. Yet Zeph didn't migrate to Vermont, and for reasons too seldom taken into account in the history of American population movements. Briefly, Zeph had been a success; he didn't have to move. It is true, undoubtedly, that in every great migration of the American people a certain number have gone along for the adventure or the glory, rather than because of necessity. It is equally true that many of those who remained behind did so because they had become so well established where they were that there was no use in moving elsewhere. The old saw that "all the people of any ambition in New England moved out West" is as glib nonsense as the new saw that "American cities are populated by the refuse of Eastern Europe." Two classes of people have always tended to refrain from migrations: the ne'er-do-wells and the extremely competent and successful. A migration is probably made up of rather average people. Only when some burning ideological issue acts as a spur does such a venture attract large numbers of highly superior persons. Thus with every movement northward or westward in American history a large number of energetic, intelligent, successful persons have been left behind as bulwarks of the civilization that all such movements are intented to produce.

When western Connecticut suddenly found itself no longer the frontier but the home country to which the memories of settlers on the Kansas plains or in the forests of Wisconsin would stray wistfully back during winter nights in sod huts and log cabins, many a farmer like Zeph Higgins found himself suddenly transformed from pioneer into yeoman, from fanatical subduer of the wilderness to dignified pillar of the established order. The new clothes often did not fit. The residue of previous migrations, these men and women were of a superior quality. They were the triumphant end-product of seven generations of natural selection in as rigorous an environment as any Darwinian jungle. To expect them suddenly to become genteel and docile burghers would be as foolish as to expect a Viking to adapt himself to Sunday-school teaching. Vast inherited energies hitherto kept in check by the hardships of wilderness life, must be channeled elsewhere; it is small wonder that the decorous rivulets of community life are sometimes glutted and overflowed by sudden outbursts of these dammed up potentialities.

In studying the New England farmer, or the American farmer anywhere, one should keep in mind that what we call crustiness, or stubbornness, or bullheadedness may often be the manifestations of a strong nature that has no adequate outlet for its resources. Such manifestations are always fascinating, and supply the theme for many a story by New England writers. Zeph Higgins having laid the Connecticut fieldstones into walls ten feet broad expends his forces in a ferocious quarrelsomeness. Not withstanding a background of two hundred years of austere meetinghouse religion, he fights with the Poganuc deacon and out of spite joins the newly founded Episcopal church, though his independent nature abhors its formalism. In a vicious controversy as to the site of the district school Zeph without waiting for a town-meeting settles the dispute by hitching up his yoke of oxen, placing the school on runners, and moving it to the spot he considered best. In the election he votes Democratic simply because his new enemies, the Congregationalists, are Federalist, though he himself was a Federalist in principles. As one of his townsmen says:

> That fellow's so contrary that he hates to do the very thing he wants to, if anybody else wants him to do it. If there was any way of voting that would spite both parties and please nobody, he'd take that.[3]

Today, a hundred years later, every town in New England has its Zeph Higgins.

There were as many outlets as there were people of strong character. One life would be devoted to a frantic making and hoarding of money; another would be squandered in litigation over a right-of-way or a disputed boundary; another would become obsessed with religion and a selfish preoccupation with the soul and its chances of salvation; still another would be sacrificed on the altar of a monomaniacal neatness and cleanliness that consecrated the home to the broom and dust mop rather than to human lives. More often these energies would be directed into some movement or crusade. Abolition, prohibition, women's rights, prison reform were powered by the sublimated vitality of those who several generations earlier would have been Indian fighters or pioneer mothers.

Occasionally some crusty hill-farmer would continue his fight against nature even after he had conquered. In Conway, New Hampshire, where the ice age has perpetuated its memory by strewing the hills and forests with house-sized boulders, one such farmer found it impossible to terminate his lifelong feud with granite. Having reduced thirty or forty acres into tillable fields, he carved the boulders into ten and even twenty foot slabs. With these he made a fence around the family burial ground that would bid fair to outlast the pyramids. Then for his own leather and iron carcass he hewed one ponderous chunk into a sarcophagus nicely chiseled to his living measurements. This ultimate token of his enemy's subjugation he kept in a shed against the day of his death. He now lies in it as proof against time as Pharaoh himself.[4]

All over New Hampshire a generation ago one could find old men similarly skilled in the splitting of granite, their box of wedges and drills being as essential equipment to them as an ax and bucksaw. The foundations of their houses and barns are built for the ages out of eight- and ten-foot blocks; the posts of their barnyards have been excavated from the great pasture boulders. In the Cold River section on the Maine and New Hampshire border a whole house has been built of these massive slabs. Seeing it now deserted in its overgrown pasture, with the cliffs of West Royce Mountain hanging a thousand feet above it, one wonders if any one ever lived within its clammy walls. It suggest quick and certain insanity for any occupant, this Stonehenge-like monument to a weird fanaticism.

2. Life of Rose Terry Cooke[5]

Half a generation later than Harriet Beecher Stowe another Connecticut writer, Rose Terry Cooke, found many characters like Zeph Higgins among the hills of her native state. Born on a farm six miles from Hartford, she came of a time-honored strain of Puritan stock. Her father, Henry Wadsworth Terry, who was the son of a Hartford bank president, carried back his lineage to a Wadsworth (the same from whom Longfellow descended) who had come to Cambridge in 1632 and settled in Hartford in 1636. Another ancestor is said to have stolen the Connecticut Charter and hidden it in the famous oak. Her mother, who was the daughter of John Hurlburt, the first New England shipbuilder to sail around the world, was of equally indigo blood. From her father Rose Terry Cooke acquired a love of nature and country life. From her mother, who was morbidly conscientious, she inherited a religious nature that brought about conversion at the age of sixteen and made her an ardent churchwoman for the rest of her life. When she was six years old her family moved to the eighteenth-century house of her grandmother in Hartford, and here she became an efficient housekeeper and made that contact with the past that has meant so much to most New England writers. But being of delicate health, she spent much time with her father driving and walking in the woods and fields of the beautiful Connecticut countryside. Like Celia Thaxter and Sarah Orne Jewett, she developed an early and lifelong passion for flower gardening, as well as for all nature.

If Rose Terry Cooke's childhood was typical of upper-class New England, her youth and womanhood were even more so. Graduating from Hartford Female Seminary at the age of sixteen, she taught school first in Hartford and later in Burlington, New Jersey, and at one time served as governess in a clergyman's family. Later she returned home to care for her dead sister's children. Like Harriet Beecher Stowe, she found time between her household duties for writing. At first her main interest was in verse—the conventional religious and sentimental verse of her day—but she wrote many stories, which were more successful than her poems. Though she was successful in selling to the best magazines—*Putnam's, Graham's,* the *Atlantic*—writing was always secondary in importance to her, her home life taking first place.

She didn't marry till she was forty-six. Her husband was an iron manufacturer, much younger than she, whom she had met in a boarding house in Boston while she was studying art there. With her husband she moved first to Winsted, Connecticut, and later to Pittsfield, Massachusetts, where she died in 1892.

3. Comedy and Tragedy in the Connecticut Hills

The bulk of Rose Terry Cooke's poetry and fiction—including her novel *Steadfast*—has long found its place deep in the trash bin of Victorian sentimentality. The excavation of such material would be unproductive. But scattered through her collections she has left a handful of tales that rank with the best American local-color realism and that recreate in character and setting the little corner of northwestern Connecticut that she grew up in. In modified form she has made use of Rowland Robinson's device of building stories around the same group of characters, like Deacon Flint, the storekeeper who waters his rum and sands his sugar.

Cooke is at her best as a humorist, a side of her art well illustrated by the tale of "Cal Culver and the Devil." Cal Culver, a Yankee loafer and ne'er-do-well highly reminiscent of Stowe's Sam Lawson, marries the town shrew, Polythi Bangs of Squabble Hill, in order to have someone to do his housework after his aged mother has become bedridden. Their married life is a continual brawl. Old Mrs. Culver, having been banished to an upstairs room, finds relief from Polythi by dying. Cal, having been driven to work for Deacon Flint, decides it's time that he, too, broke away. He chooses a most ingenious means of release. There is in the town a certain Parson Robbins, who considers himself God's chief champion against the Enemy. Cal visits the parson with the story that while ploughing he has been tricked into signing his soul away to Satan, and the day of fulfilling the contract is fast approaching. Parson Robbins is so sure of his influence with God that once on a Sunday during a great drought, when he was going to pray for rain, he took his umbrella to church with him, though not a cloud could be seen in the sky. The congregation were much impressed when halfway through the service a drenching thunderstorm came up. To such a servant of the Lord, Cal Culver's little affair with the Enemy offered merely an opportunity for a bit of sparring practice.

On the date stipulated for the delivery of his soul to the Devil, Cal and the rest of the congregation are summoned to the meeting house for all-day prayer. At the entrance two blacksmiths armed with clubs stand guard against any sneak attacks. At the end of the exhortations Cal is escorted by these muscular brethren to his home, and they leave him safely inside. But an hour or two later, when Polythi returns from the village, she does not find her husband. As he is never heard of again, we are left to surmise what happened to him. The people of Basset have very definite suspicions.[6]

This and other humorous pieces are told with a skill and realism that make them valuable recordings of the lighter side of New England life. Another group are colored by a grimmer realism. Such stories as "Grit," "Squire Paine's Conversion," "Mrs. Flint's Married Experience," and "Freedom Wheeler's Controversy with Providence" deal with characters in whom the frontiersman's tenacity has been perverted into a crabbed stubbornness and setness of temperament. What Sarah Orne Jewett saw as examples of a commendable self-reliance Rose Terry Cooke saw as harmful wrongheadedness. Generations of toil on rocky New England hill farms she believed too often hardened the men and broke the women.

The story of "Freedom Wheeler's Controversy with Providence" is typical of this group of stories. Freedom Wheeler, who, as the descendant of five or six generations of Connecticut farmers, is endowed with a character as inflexible as granite, marries the meek and gentle Lowly Mallory and enslaves her on his stony dairy farm. Now life on such a farm, even after it has been long established, is never a prolonged holiday. Yet it need not be a death-in-life unless the farmer chooses to make it such. Freedom Wheeler, however, chooses just that, and for the most futile reasons. His wife has borne him a healthy son, whom he named Shearjasub because the inscriptions in the family burying plot indicate that there has always been a Shearjasub Wheeler. But by the same witness, there has also always been a *Freedom* Wheeler. There is no question as to the name of the next child, which of course will also be a son.

Freedom is infuriated when the next two babies both turn out to be girls. He browbeats his wife worse than ever; and to his neighbors he seems to be flying in the face of Providence, which has decreed he shall have girls. Before she dies of exhaustion, however, his wife bears him two boys, each of whom is baptized on birth by the minister rushed to the scene by Freedom himself. But each boy baby, blighted by its mother's weakness, dies on the day of his birth.

Feuding in earnest against the Providence that won't give him a boy to bear his name, he immediately marries again, this time to a termagant who is more than his match. A boy is soon born, but as Freedom is sick at the time with typhus it is afflicted with the name Tyagustus, after a relative on the mother's side. Freedom's rage on recovering need not be recorded here. Later, when another son is born, he succeeds in getting him christened Freedom, but in carrying the infant back to its mother he trips and kills it outright. At last he breaks down.

> With all his faults, he had a simple faith in the truths of the Bible, and
> a conscientious respect for ordinances; and now there fell upon him a
> deep conviction of heinous sin, a gloom, a despair, that amounted
> almost to insanity. But he asked no counsel, he implored no divine aid:
> with the peculiar sophistry of religious melancholy, he considered that
> his prayers would be an abomination to the Lord.[7]

The Assembly's Catechism, on which all his generation in New England
had been brought up, proved too strong even for his flinty will. Perhaps
the best excuse for that inhumane document is that it could break those
who would not otherwise be broken. Gradually Freedom Wheeler
mellows into a better person. But as Cooke says, ". . . facts are stubborn
things; and if circumstances and the grace of God modify character, they
do not change it."[8] We are therefore spared any sudden and improbable
conversion on the part of Freedom Wheeler. The ending like the beginning
of the story is told with a restraint difficult to maintain where it would be
so easy to slip into either slapstick or sentimentality.

4. Willful Celibacy

All of Rose Terry Cooke's strong-minded characters are not like Freedom
Wheeler. At times, like Sarah Orne Jewett's Almira Todd, they achieved
happy and useful lives of self-sufficiency and service to their neighbors.
Such is the case with the solitary old maid who gives her name to the story
"Polly Mariner, Tailoress." For years Polly had lived alone with an invalid
father in the town of Taunton Hill,

> from whose broad and long crest you can see more of Western
> Connecticut in its development of bare round hills, mulein-stalks, stones,
> and life-everlasting, than is good for the soul of the thrifty, or pleasant
> to the eyes of the discerning.[9]

When Polly is thirty-six her father dies, and the neighbors want her to give
up her lonely state and live with them as a hireling. But Polly has the
independence without the cantankerousness of Zeph Higgins.

> "I a'n't a going into nobody's house that way. . . . I don't be'lieve in't.
> Whilst I live by myself an' take care of myself, I a'n't beholden to
> nobody; and I know when my work's done, and what's to pay for't. I
> kin sing, or laugh, or cry, or fix my hair into a cocked hat, and nobody's
> got right or reason to say, 'Why do ye so?' Fact is, I've got my liberty,
> 'n' I'm going to keep it: it'll be hard work p'rhaps; but it's wuth it."[10]

PICTURE GALLERY

The Isles of Shoals (from Celia Thaxter,
Among the Isles of Shoals, *Boston, 1873)*

T. W. Higginson
(from Winslow, Literary
Boston of Today, Boston,
1903)

Harriet Beecher Stowe
(from Stowe, Life of
Harriet Beecher Stowe,
Boston, 1889)

Elizabeth Stuart Phelps
(from Our Famous Women,
Hartford, 1884)

*Rowland Robinson
and his house in Ferrisburgh, Vermont
(from* New England Magazine, *December 1900)*

Helen Hunt Jackson (from her Poems, Boston, 1892)

Alice Brown (from Harper's Weekly, *October 24, 1903)*

Sarah Orne Jewett
(from New England Magazine,
July 1894)

Celia Thaxter in her island garden (from A.F.&R.L., Letters of Celia Thaxter, *Boston, 1895)*

Lucy Larcom (from Our Famous Women, *Hartford, 1884)*

*Mary Wilkins Freeman
(from* Cosmopolitan,
March 1903)

*Rose Terry Cooke
(from* Our Famous
Women, *Hartford,
1884)*

Emily Dickinson as a child
(from Letters of Emily Dickinson,
ed. Mabel Loomis Todd, Boston, 1894)

Sarah Orne Jewett's house in South Berwick, Maine
(courtesy of the Colby College Library)

Polly carries out her program, becoming a town institution, like the two old single women in *The Pearl of Orr's Island*. When a family needed a nurse, a sempstress, a watcher, or a personal adviser on anything from a cure for rheumatism to the love problems of a willful daughter, Polly was on hand. She prides herself on "speaking her mind." For example, her outspokenness prevents a certain minister being called to the parish, because she dislikes his preaching of kindness and light. She believes a parson should preach sin and devote his efforts to warding off the wickedness that is sure to exist in people as their share of original sin.

People still urge her to come and live with them. The village Quakeress, Rachel Green, quotes the Scripture, "It is not good for man to be alone," and adds that the same applies to women. But Polly feels that she was intended by Providence to be left by herself.

> "I swan to man," she says, "it's enough to crisp one's eyelashes to have sech pesterin' goin' on all the time. Why, in the name o' judgment, I can't be left to do what I darn please, is musical to me. Anyhow, I guess I'll do it, or I'll know why an' wherefore, as true's my name's Polly Mariner."[11]

Only her hired man, Israel Grubb, sees her point. "It allers seemed to me," he says, "the foolishest thing a woman could do't hadn't got no folks, to go 'n' take 'em on."[12]

Yet when Polly dies she admits that Quakeress Green, who is at her deathbed, was right: it is not good for one to live alone. Facing the facts of New England life more squarely than did Sarah Orne Jewett, Cooke realized the dismal plight of the tens of thousands of solitary women scattered through the countryside and the small villages. Partly out of necessity and partly as a regional state of mind celibacy had become a sort of fetish in New England. The single lives or late marriages of the women writers we have been discussing were symptomatic and typical. In their works the attitude is even plainer. The thirty- or forty-year engagement, ending either in sterile marriage or the death of one of the affianced, was a popular theme for their stories. And generally, as in Sarah Orne Jewett's "A Dunnet Shepherdess" they treated the theme with sympathy and approbation. Polly Mariner's admission that her life had been wrong is unusual in New England local-color fiction of the period.

VIII. THE ANATOMY OF THE WILL:
Mary Wilkins Freeman

> There was a resolute vein in their characters; they managed them-
> selves with wrenches, and could be hard even with grief.
>
> MARY WILKINS FREEMAN, "A Gentle Ghost"[1]

1. Shades of Salem

In the 1890's Rudyard Kipling spent several years near Brattleboro,
Vermont. Writing of this neighborhood three decades later in his
autobiography, he says:

> It would be hard to exaggerate the loneliness and sterility of life on
> the farms. The land was denuding itself of its accustomed inhabitants,
> and their places had not yet been taken by the wreckage of Eastern
> Europe or the wealthy city folk who later bought "pleasure farms."
> What might have become characters, powers and attributes perverted
> themselves in that desolation as cankered trees throw out branches
> akimbo, and strange faiths and cruelties, born of solitude to the edge of
> insanity, flourished like lichen on sick bark.[2]

Kipling was witnessing the final wreckage of New England back-
country life. Writing of the same period in a caustic *Atlantic* article entitled
"A New England Hill Town," Rollin Lynde Hartt had come to parallel
conclusions.

> The rural environment is psychically extravagant. It tends to ex-
> tremes. A man carries himself out to his logical conclusions; he becomes
> a concentrated essence of himself.[3]

This process, Hartt found, was helped by the backcountry habit of
inbreeding. In his own town the marriage of Glenns to Glenns over a
period of generations produced Glenns "to the [n]th power." Among the
results of this sorry experiment in eugenics were misers, hermits, a dwarf
standing three feet two and one-half inches with his boots on, a giant seven
feet tall, a family of deaf and dumb, and a family that was "muffle-

chopped," that is, had lips that protruded like a moose's. Hartt strongly recommends that Glenns stop marrying Glenns; but the main trouble, he thinks, is that hill-towns are anachronisms, despite older folks' efforts to keep them alive. They are towns without hope—skimmilk communities. "They consist of the ambitionless. We have contributed our best to the city; the leavings remain."[4] Among the many storytellers of life in these towns, he considers Mary Wilkins Freeman the most realistic.

Freeman had learned of New England country life in Brattleboro during the two decades preceding Kipling's sojourn there. Born in 1852 in Randolph, Massachusetts, a few miles south of Boston, she was of a thoroughly New England background. Her mother, a Holbrook of Holbrook, was of a strain once aristocratic though now faded to ineffectual gentility. Her father, a native of Salem, could trace his lineage back to a Bray Wilkins, who, like one of Hawthorne's ancestors, had been a judge in the witchcraft trials of the seventeenth century. But Mr. Wilkins had broken with the Salem tradition and set himself up in Randolph as an architect-carpenter. We are told that his ancestral Puritanism manifested itself in overconscientiousness, sensitiveness, and impracticality. When Mary was a child the family moved to Brattleboro, where Mr. Wilkins became a storekeeper. To the beauty of that region she attributes her urge to write. What formal education she had was in the Randolph and Brattleboro schools and at the Mount Holyoke Female Seminary, which she attended for a year in 1870–71. But, delicate in health and sensitive in temperament, she was much of the time unable to attend school. As with Sarah Orne Jewett and Rowland Robinson, her real education was in her home. She read extensively in Ossian, Dickens, Thackeray, and Poe, and in Goethe and the Greeks in translation. She was a lover and later a writer of poetry, admiring particularly the Elizabethan lyricists and Rossetti. She became acquainted with the works of the local color writers, like Cable, Mark Twain, Bret Harte, and Sarah Orne Jewett.

On the death of her father in 1883—her only sister and her mother being already dead—Mary Wilkins returned to Randolph to live with her friend Mary Wales. Confronted, like so many New England single women, with the need for supporting herself and a relative, in this case an aunt, she turned to writing as a livelihood; she had already won a $50 prize with one of her stories and had two others—"Two Old Lovers" and "An Honest Soul"—accepted by *Harper's*. Since from the beginning she wrote with the sole purpose of making money, the bulk of her work is run-of-the-market stuff: ghost stories, mysteries, cloak-and-dagger romances, juveniles. But two or three volumes of her early short stories and one or two novels, all written before 1900, form as valuable a study of New England rural and village life as we have. In her later years she not only became more and more commercial in quality but drew away from the New England scene. Marrying Dr. Charles M. Freeman in 1902—another late marriage like that of Rose Terry Cooke—she moved to Metuchen, New Jersey. With her new home came new interests, though till her death in 1930 she remained one of America's most popular writers.[5]

Like Hawthorne, Mary Wilkins Freeman saw New England life through the dusky lenses of Salem Puritanism. For the oddities of New England character she had no such simple explanation as inbreeding, or climate, or the influence of a former frontier life. To her the New England mind was a complex of morbidly sensitive conscience and overdeveloped will. She went farther than either Harriet Beecher Stowe or Rose Terry Cooke in tracing the scars left by over two centuries of Calvinism, and often she found these scars to be still festering. As with Hawthorne, her own interest in matters of conscience and will is a hangover of an ancestral preoccupation with the state of the soul. Long before O'Neill these two authors were subjecting the Puritan psyche to an analysis thorough enough to gladden the heart of Freud himself.

Though Hawthorne dealt primarily with the Puritan soul as it existed in the past, the younger writer adapted his methods to a study of the lingering Puritanism of her own times. There is disagreement as to whether Freeman's characters are indigenous to Brattleboro or to Randolph. But to argue the matter is to misunderstand the author's purposes. Like Hawthorne, she was interested in general aspects of New England life rather than in its shadings from county to county or from state to state. Thus, while the names of the towns in her stories correspond to those around Randolph—Dover, Canton, Pembroke—the descriptions of landscape are no more specific than those in *Twice-Told Tales*. In fact, there is little emphasis at all on description beyond the sketching in of a typical New England setting—a marked divergence from the methods of the other local-color writers, who described their regions with photographic realism down to the last tree or crossroads. The characters, too, are generalized rather than individualized; they are symbols, caricatures, like Hawthorne's Ethan Brand or the Reverend Mr. Hooper in "The Minister's Black Veil," each one representing some quality or bent, rather than being a fully-rounded human being. As in Dante's *Inferno*, even their physical appearance reflects their inner state—a hunched back, for example, signifying a crooked will. A writer with such purposes and methods would not wish to particularize her settings. Freeman's stories could have taken place in the hills of Vermont or the flatlands of eastern Massachusetts, or anywhere else where the influences of a dying Puritanism lingered.

Her style, too, is affected by this Hawthorne-like approach to her subject matter. A highly localized dialect like that of Rowland Robinson, for example, would be out of place. Her characters speak a typical, only slightly colored rural New England speech. One would recognize them as New England country people but could not place them in any one region as one could Jewett's Maine fishermen or Rose Terry Cooke's Connecticut farmers. Freeman's descriptive and narrative style is even less obtrusive than the rather formally impersonal style of Hawthorne. At times she has all the directness and simplicity of Hemingway, without the impression of a forced ease. For example, who wrote the following opening sentences of a story, Hemingway or Freeman?

> The day before there had been a rain and a thaw, then in the night the wind had suddenly blown from the north, and it had grown cold. In the morning it was very clear and cold, and there was the hard glitter of ice, and all the open fields shone and flashed . . . .[6]

2. The New England Conscience

Dr. Morton Prince, the great Boston psychiatrist, is said to have been the first scientifically to study the pathology of the New England conscience. In her stories and novels Mary Wilkins Freeman was busy investigating the same phenomenon at the same time that Prince was collecting data for his famous *The Dissociation of a Personality*. Her analysis of the peculiarities of the New England character had gone one step farther than that of either Rose Terry Cooke or Harriet Beecher Stowe, who had come to the conclusion that the disappearance of frontier conditions forced the vigorous New England will to find an outlet in petty and ignoble ends— squabbling with one's neighbor, pinching pennies, browbeating one's wife and children. To Mary Wilkins Freeman the New England character had been molded by its religion rather than by the frontier. The steady and strenuous development of the conscience and the will among the Puritans had reached its culmination in the settlement of North America. Pioneering and Calvinism went hand in hand, but Calvinism led the way. The spreading of Protestant Christianity would be considered a sacred obligation; in fulfilling that obligation—in fighting and converting the hostile heathen and in wringing a livelihood out of a sterile, frozen land—what greater assets could there be than a will trained in iron self-denial and a conscience, a sense of duty, that dared not flinch before death itself?

Freeman would agree with Stowe and Cooke that the comparative ease of New England farm life after the coming of the railroads released much spiritual energy that for want of better outlets was expended in meanness and "cussedness." If one deprives a spirited horse of the exercise that nature and generations of heredity have fitted it for, one should not be surprised if it kicks down the sides of its stall or bites its owner. But Stowe and Cooke did not take into account the effects brought about by the disappearance of Puritanism itself. By the end of the Civil War old-time Calvinism was a thing of the past in New England; it had been losing ground, in fact, since the days of Jonathan Edwards. Now Calvinism alone provides more than enough scope for the stubbornest of wills and the most meticulous of consciences. A Calvinist can take in stride a wilderness full of bellicose Indians—yet can keep in trim without this additional and rather superfluous exercise. But once the religion weakens the Calvinist is like the unexercised racehorse. The muscles of will and conscience become flabby and then diseased. In her *Poganuc People* Stowe records the weakening of the old orthodoxy; Zeph Higgins even joins the Episcopal Church. Stowe doesn't seem to realize, however, how inadequate the Episcopal Church is for a man like Zeph. Its dogma is even less able to control his colossal cussedness than is the relaxed form of Calvinism preached in the Congregational Church that he "signed out" of. Zeph needed sermons like Jonathan Edwards's "Sinners in the Hands of an Angry God" to keep him in spiritual fettle. Since there was no such preacher to dangle him periodically over the furnace of Hell and thus temper his conscience, his energies simply exploded, bringing misery to himself and his family and consternation to the community.

During the last hundred years the Puritan conscience has become as vestigial an organ in the American mind as is the appendix in the body. But, like the appendix, the vestigial conscience is subject to disease. In Mary Wilkins Freeman's stories this disease usually takes the form of a pitiable worrying over trivialities. One of her earliest and best stories, "An Honest Soul," printed in *Harper's* in 1884, is typical. The heroine is Martha Patch, an unmarried sempstress who is so poor that, though she wishes for a window opening on the street, she can't afford it and has to be content with a view into her backyard. One day two customers each give her bundles of rags to be made into quilts, for which she will receive a dollar apiece. On completing the job she finds that she has used in one customer's quilt a bit of cloth belonging to the other. A normal person would ignore this fact; a meticulously honest person would point it out to the customers, even though realizing it could make no possible difference to them; but Martha Patch tears the quilts apart and resews them. But this second time too she has confused two pieces of rag. Again she rips the quilts and again she sews them together. Much time has now elapsed in which Martha has earned no money; and having earned no money, she hasn't eaten. On the morning she is going to deliver the finally completed quilts, she faints and spends the day on her floor, unable to arise till a neighbor eventually find and resuscitates her.

Sarah Orne Jewett would have considered this woman an example of commendable New England self-reliance and individualism. Freeman is not so sure.

> It is a hard question to decide, whether there were any real merit in
> such finely strained honesty, or whether it were merely a case of morbid
> conscientiousness. Perhaps the old woman, inheriting very likely her

father's scruples, had had them so intensified by age and childishness that they had become a little off the bias of reason.[7]

In "A Taste of Honey,"[8] another story of squeamish conscience, Freeman tells of a girl who postpones her marriage till she has paid off the mortgage on her farm. She feels that she owes this sacrifice to the memory of her dead father, who had devoted his life to the lifting of his debt. Year by year she denies herself and her mother even the luxury of a taste of honey, since all their produce must be sold to meet the payments at the bank. But the lover's conscience is not so highly developed. Tired of the delay, he marries another girl on the very day his finacée makes the last payment and frees the farm.

In both these cases, which are typical of Freeman's stories, the question asked or implied is, "What does it all come to?" Jewett would have answered that these people at least retained their integrity, their self-respect. Freeman would not entirely reject this reply. As we shall see later, she considers self-respect of great importance. She finds compensations even in lives like these. But she would ask one final question: What are we to think of a society in which such potentialities of dedication and self-sacrifice must be expended on such futilities?

3. *The Crooked Will*

In Mary Wilkins Freeman's stories disease of the conscience is usually accompanied by disease of the will. The old woman who remade her patchwork quilts twice was stung by a morbidly sensitive conscience and driven on in her futile task by volition so terrific that it defied starvation itself. But as in this story our attention is focused primarily on the freakish conscience, in other stories it is focused on the workings of the lopsided will. In the selection entitled "A Conflict Ended" the villager Marcus Woodman quarrels with the rest of his parish over the choice of a minister who is not "doctrinal." Though no one ever knew exactly what Marcus meant by the word "doctrinal," he swore that if this man were called he would never go inside the church door as long as he lived. Some one commented that he would have to sit on the steps, then. Marcus answered, "I will set on the steps fifty years before I'll go into this house if that man's settled here."[9] And he is true to his word. Summer and winter Marcus sits on the church steps during meetings. His fiancée Esther breaks with him, but retains enough of her old affection to lend him her parasol during his sitting spells on sunny July Sabbaths. Eventually, after a ten-year interval, the impasse is resolved. The two decide to marry and Marcus after a violent inner conflict succeeds in breaking himself of his habit. "As near as I can make out," Esther says, "you've taken to sitting on the church steps the way other men take to smoking and drinking."[10]

Only a city dweller would find the stubbornness of Marcus Woodman incredible. Villagers and country people the world over can match this tale with others equally fantastic—family feuds dragging on from generation to generation, boundary disputes litigated over periods of time that would do credit to an English chancery suit, molehills daily being converted into mountains to outlast the ages, and a constant cutting off of noses to spite faces. But in New England after the subjugation of the wilderness and the relaxation of old-time Puritanism these vagaries were more rife, one surmises, than in other places and in other times. Every locality has its legendary accounts of Yankee mulishness. Perhaps two brothers living on adjacent farms in a lonely upland valley have had a falling out over the ownership of a tree or a stray calf. Thenceforward for forty years they are not on speaking terms, and each forbids the other to set foot on his land under pain of shooting. Or perhaps a farmer has kept a lunatic relative in a pen in his attic or in his barn, like one of his animals, in obstinate defiance of constituted authority or neighborly advice that would send the sufferer to an asylum.[11] Or an old maid, disappointed in love at the age of seventeen, has refused to budge from her premises for the ensuing fifty years. Marcus Woodman had his peers in every village, and the rural writer need not look far in New England for colorful subject matter. Now, in the days of the radio, television, movies, and automobiles, these or similar deviations from the commonplace are not so numerous, but they can still be found in the remoter communities, where the modern mechanical outlets for energy and emotion have only recently penetrated.

Freeman's most thorough study of the warped will is her novel *Pembroke*, once ranked among the greatest American novels, but now unjustly neglected. The conflict of the story is developed around a typical triviality. Barnabas Thayer loves and is about to marry a neighboring farmer's daughter, Charlotte Barnard, who has already prepared her wedding garments. One Sunday night Barnabas visits his sweetheart, but her father, who is the personification of Yankee balkiness and whim, argues with him concerning the forthcoming election and ends, in a heated moment of controversy, by ordering the young man out of the house never to return. Barnabas is equally stubborn. When Charlotte follows him from her house and calls to him he doesn't answer; and knowing his nature, she realizes he will never return and they will never marry.

But Barney has his mother to reckon with, a woman of iron will, who holds an engagement so binding that she orders her son to go through with his marriage or suffer perpetual banishment from his home. Barney, of course, chooses the banishment, going to live in the house that he had been building nearby for himself and his bride. Here between his own family's farm and that of his former fiancée he lives in silence and isolation.

> It never occurred to him that he could enter Cephas Barnard's house again, ask his pardon, and marry Charlotte. It seemed to him settled and inevitable; he could not grasp any choice in the matter.[12]

Stalemate is thus reached. In the meanwhile the poison generated by these diseased wills infects almost the entire community. Barney's mother, Deborah Thayer, having been thwarted by her son, exerts her terrible volition on weaker members of her family. Her husband, who has long been reduced to a threadbare doormat, is trampled on with redoubled fury. But her youngest son, Ephraim, who is invalided with heart disease, remains somewhat restive. Despite the fact that he is doomed to early and sudden death, he has refused to learn his catechism and by various other ways has jeopardized his chances of salvation. The mother believes that it is her religious duty to "break his will." One day, contrary to the strict orders of the doctor, she beats the boy and he dies on the spot. Though his death was due primarily to overexertion on a coasting party that the boy had taken part in on the sly, the mother doesn't know this. Convinced that she has killed her son, her own will is at last bowed. But meanwhile, her daughter, Rebecca, because of her mother's unreasonable prejudice against her lover, has been driven into a clandestine love affair and an ensuing "shot-gun" marriage.

At Charlotte's home things have been going little better. For a time Cephas, the father, had forbidden Charlotte to enter his house on the grounds that she had run after his enemy Barnabas on the night of the quarrel, but he relents enough to take her back under his roof. He has now sublimated his willpower into a militant vegetarianism and is browbeating his wife into eating sorrel pies baked in unshortened crusts. Charlotte herself has inherited more than she needs of her father's temperament. Though she knows Barnabas will never marry her, she refuses to marry anyone else, turning down the college-bred son of wealthy Squire Payne for no reason at all other than pure contrariness, as she finds the man attractive enough and her family heartily approves of the match.

Other characters on the periphery of the story evince similar symptoms of spiritual warping. Silas Berry, the father of Rebecca Thayer's lover, is a miser whose semiparalysis of body is the outward manifestation of a half-dead soul. Charlotte's aunt, with whom she lived during the parental ban, has also been victimized by a balky lover, who deserts her after twenty years of courting simply because one Sunday night she was unavoidably absent at the time of his customary call. Driven to near insanity (one night she mistakes Barnabas for her own lover), she borrows money on her farm to keep up appearances. Finally she is taken off to the poorhouse. Sitting on the sledge in her best rocking chair, which has been salvaged from her home, she makes a spectacle so pitiable that her lover, retaining more of his humanity than do most of the characters in this novel, rescues her as she passes his house, and soon marries her.

But Barnabas always remains the grimmest exhibit in this display of Puritanism gone to seed. As time goes on and he persists in his contumacy his physical appearance undergoes a Dantesque transfiguration, a weird conforming of the body to the diseased spiritual pattern within. We are first aware of the metamorphosis one day when Barnabas is talking with his would-be rival, Thomas Payne, the Squire's son.

> Thomas stared at Barney; a horror as of something uncanny and abnormal stole over him. Was the man's back curved, or had he by some subtle vision a perception of some terrible spiritual deformity, only symbolized by a curved spine?[13]

On being questioned, Barney says, "I've hurt my soul. . . . It happened that Sunday night years ago. I—can't get over it. I'm bent like this back."[14]

Barney's malady quickly intensifies to a crisis. One very cold winter he frenziedly pours forth his energies into woodchopping in a frozen swamp. It was as if some powerful atavism lured him back to this activity on which his pioneering forefathers had lavished their inexhaustible vigor. Perhaps here he could find a release for the forces that were tearing him to pieces inside.

> Only by fierce contest, as it were, could he keep himself alive, but he had a certain delight in working in the swamp during those awful arctic days. The sense that he could still fight and conquer something, were it only the simple destructive force of nature, aroused in him new self-respect.[15]

During a thaw, however, he is stricken with rheumatic fever. Writhing for weeks in his bed, he is bent double when he gets up, the ultimate symbol of his inner state. During his agony he is nursed by Charlotte, who appears without being asked and stays, in her stubborn manner, despite his wishes or the opinion of the townspeople. Finally Barnabas is suddenly and unconvincingly converted to reasonableness, as is Charlotte, and the two are married. This unrealistic ending—of the sort eschewed by Rose Terry Cooke—is the weakest part of what is otherwise a powerful and moving novel.

Yet the ending alone is not the reason for the complete neglect of *Pembroke* in the present day. The cause lies much deeper. Like many of Freeman's works, *Pembroke* is tragedy. The fierce wills of these descendants from the Puritans correspond to the *hubris*, the overweening pride, that in Greek tragic drama brings about the downfall of otherwise noble and admirable characters and thus produces the pity and fear that, according to Aristotle, are necessary if the function of tragedy is to be fulfilled. The modern reader does not take to tragedy of this sort, unless it is the very greatest—that of Sophocles, Goethe, or perhaps O'Neill. In our local-color reading we want a smattering of the sordid and grotesque, which Freeman amply supplies, but we don't want indifferently successful attempts to achieve the tragic catharsis. Even Faulkner, the most sombre of all regionalists, creates his effects by a macabre irony rather than by tragedy. *As I Lay Dying* and *The Sound and the Fury,* for all their morbidity, twist the face into a sardonic smile rather than into the torque of awe and fear.

Another reason for the neglect of this novel, which Conan Doyle considered the best written in America since *The Scarlet Letter* and which impressed E. A. Robinson with its echoings of life in his own Gardiner, Maine,[16] is its underlying tone of moral seriousness. One must not forget T. W. Higginson's plea for a Puritan earnestness of purpose in American literature.[17] Freeman, as a New Englander and an admirer of Hawthorne, did not need this advice. Whether she read Higginson's article or not—and there is no way of answering this question—she would have naturally infused even her lightest writing with some sense of purpose other than that of mere entertainment. Thus her humorous novel *The Jamesons,* though it is almost a slapstick treatment of the clash between summer boarders and New England villagers, embodies a good-humored plea for a better understanding between these two antagonistic groups. Of Mrs. Jameson, the chief offender among the summer folk, she writes:

> . . . She still tries to improve us at times, not always with our full concurrence, and her ways are still not altogether our ways, provoking mirth, or calling for charity. Yet I must say we have nowadays a better understanding of her good motives, having had possibly our spheres enlarged a little by her, after all, and having gained broader views from the points of views of people outside our narrow lives. I think we most of us are really fond of Mrs. H. Boardman Jameson, and are very glad that the Jamesons came to our village.[18]

Yet the teaching is never obtrusive. In her serious work, like *Pembroke,* she was able to fuse the moral with the story. As a consequence her stories, like Hawthorne's, frequently border on allegory; yet allegory is a legitimate genre, and an effective one for the New Englander to write. Art entirely for art's sake is perhaps too much to expect from a people whose ancestors for three hundred years had had only a limited acquaintance with literary forms other than the sermon.

4. Darkest New England Days

Harold Fisher Wilson in his book *The Hill Country of Northern New England,* a model of its kind, treats the period from 1870 to 1900 under the suggestive heading "Winter." During these years, he found, the economy and culture of the rural districts of Vermont, New Hampshire, and Maine were at their lowest ebb. What was true in these states would be true in the other three New England states as well. The decadence and despair that oppressed Kipling near Brattleboro were cancerous taints in the very bloodstream of the region, consuming the tissue of its old life from the slenderest capillaries among the mountains down through the veins and arteries of the great river valleys and coastal plains. Everything from a pork-and-potatoes diet and drunkenness to tariffs and immigration has been suggested as the cause of this blighting disease. But the writers of the period were interested in effects rather than in causes. Many of these effects have already been discussed—the passing of the old village ways, the disintegration of the Puritan character into balkiness and eccentricity, the gnawing loneliness of life on the farms. One very terrible effect, however, has been only touched on. Sarah Orne Jewett, in a moment of extreme realism in *Deephaven,* described the appalling poverty to be found among the islands and inlets of the Maine coast. Such poverty was more widespread than she ever hinted. Perhaps she herself was blind to it; she has admitted her "organic aversion to all that is ugly, or coarse, or discordant, . . . the mire of life."[19] Her New England contemporaries—Rowland Robinson, Howells, Rose Terry Cooke—were likewise overanxious, in their Victorian way, to keep the mud off their shoes.

Mary Wilkins Freeman has been the victim of no such daintiness. The stock condition surrounding her characters' lives is poverty—sometimes a poverty as grim as that of *Tobacco Road* or *As I Lay Dying;* sometimes that even more grinding poverty of a decayed gentry trying to keep up appearances, such as we find in *The Sound and the Fury.* In painting the economic and cultural bankruptcy of the New England village she uses the somber pigments of a merciless realism; the rosy tints of sentiment are applied sparingly and then only when reality calls for them, as it sometimes does.

In an article in the *Revue des Deux Mondes* in 1896 Mme. Thérèse Blanc, a French reviewer of Freeman's work (and a friend of Jewett, whom she visited in South Berwick), found in her *une âme* as strange as that of a Russian or a Scandinavian. The comparison is startling. Certainly a countrywoman of Zola and Balzac could find nothing strange either in her realism or in that of the Russians or Scandinavians. Blanc accounts for her response by saying that in Freeman's work the spirit of seventeenth-century Puritanism survives; the "reign of the Bible," she calls it.[20] It is this spirit superimposed on a rigid physical realism that strikes the modern, materialistic Frenchwoman as strange. It comes not only from the characters of the stories themselves, but also from the author, who is so much a part of what she is describing. But, at any rate, it is an element of moral earnestness, to use Higginson's phrase again, that is lacking in the scientific detachment of French realism, even in Balzac, but which is amply present in the Scandinavians and particularly the Russians. To make a comparison among novels of peasant life, we find that Hamsun's *Growth of the Soil* and Tolstoy's *Anna Karenina,* though among the world's greatest works of realism, are suffused with a religious feeling, at times a mysticism, totally absent, for example, from Balzac's systematic, unemotional study of French rural life in *A Country Doctor.* Yet all three of these writers were true to the life and the spirit of their own nations. What Blanc would find strange in Hamsun and Tolstoy is strange only in comparison with Balzac or Zola.

It is exactly this spiritual overtone that strikes her as odd in Mary Wilkins Freeman. Although the latter no more has the spiritual insight of Tolstoy or Hamsun than she has their artistic genius, by heritage alone she read life in terms of spirit, just as did Hawthorne. To read life solely in terms of economics would be impossible for one with her background. The economics are always present in her work, but quite rightly she does not make them the main thing. The chief question to her is not how many cows or silk dresses one of her characters may have, but how much peace of mind, self-expression, feeling of oneness with God and humanity. If New England life were bankrupt in these commodities of the soul, then it was bankrupt indeed. If there were an abundance of such goods, then the stony soil, the one best dress for the wear of a lifetime, the diet of beans and potatoes were irrelevant.

More often than not Freeman found a hopeless spiritual bankruptcy. Sometimes, as we have seen, the conscience and will were diseased beyond expectation of recovery. At other times the New England soul was too feeble to be stimulated even by disease into any activity whatsoever. It simply lay in the stream of life like a rotted log, refusing to stir till disintegrated by complete decay. Such is the case in the story of "Sister Liddy," which is laid in a poorhouse. One would be tempted to lump this story with the dozens of others of similar setting by the various authors of New England. But Freeman's treatment of the theme is uniquely grim for the times. A story without a plot, it is reminiscent of the naturalism of Chekhov or Gorky. The characters are a half-dozen female derelicts living in the dreary bareness of a New England poor farm. A tall old woman, evidently insane, predicts the imminent end of the world. A fat old woman, a malicious gossip, constantly taunts and victimizes a pretty old woman who lives on her reputation of handsomeness but is too spineless and weak-minded to answer the jeers of her persecutor. An ugly, pathetic pauper, Polly Moss, escapes the company of her compeers by playing ball with the children in the hall. A maniacal woman, confined to her room, tears her bed apart, or periodically breaks out to run screaming up and down the corridors.

We are introduced to these exhibits of despair in a late autumn rainstorm. The paupers and lunatics wander in and out of the story, dragging their bleak lives as drearily and monotonously as the scudding rain clouds drag their tatters across the ploughed fields where the inmates work in summer. The women are always talking and boasting of their pasts—the people they knew, the places they had been to, the one fine dress they had owned. But Polly Moss, the dreariest of the lot, has never had anything; her life has never been less drab and hopeless than at present. Aroused by the bragging of the others, she invents a sister named Liddy who had known glories, luxuries, and honors, unsurpassable by the pitiful realities of the others' former lives. In the fictitious radiance of Sister Liddy's splendors Polly has her single brief hour in the sun. But being old and broken in health, she is soon on her deathbed, where she confesses her subterfuge. Her final words are spoken for the others as well as for herself:

> I s'pose I've been dretful wicked, but I ain't never had nothin' in my whole life. I—s'pose the Lord orter have been enough, but it's dretful hard sometimes to keep holt of him, an' not look anywheres else, when you see other folks a-clawin' an' gettin' other things, an' actin' as if they was wuth havin'. I ain't never had nothin' as fur as them other things go; I don't want nothin' else now. I've—got past 'em. I see I don' want nothin' but the Lord. But I used to feel dretful bad an' wicked when I heerd you all talkin' 'bout things you'd had, an' I hadn't never had nothin' so—.[21]

Two types of poverty are described here—material and spiritual; both are presented with unflinching regard for facts. But by emphasizing the spiritual poverty above the material Mary Wilkins Freeman has added an element of horror to the bleakness of these lives. It was her reading of the situation in terms of spiritual values rather than simply in dollars and cents that puzzled the French reviewer. The empty purse, the empty larder, the empty stomach are objects of compassion to the materialist. But the empty soul is an object of infinitely greater compassion, even of terror, to the idealist.

This spiritual or psychological probing distinguishes Freeman among her New England contemporaries. Of all the stories about almshouses, for example, none in this period has quite caught the mood of such places, the state of mind of the inmates, so convincingly as the story of "Sister Liddy." Freeman was able to detach herself more fully from her subject and see it as it was rather than as she would like it to be according to her theories. One of Sarah Orne Jewett's poorhouse stories, "The Flight of Betsy Lane,"[22] tells how Betsy, who has unexpectedly received a hundred dollars from a rich friend, goes to Philadelphia to see the Centennial. Sneaking out of the poorhouse at dawn one morning, she rides on a freight train to the nearest station, where she can catch a passenger express. When she arrives in Philadelphia she sees all the sights and makes many acquaintances. Only when her money is gone does she return to the poor farm, where she has long since been given up as having drowned herself in the lily pond. She at once settles back into the old life, at peace with herself and her drab environment. Such a pauper, of course, is a possibility, but she is not convincing. One wonders how she escaped losing the capability of decisive action or even of enjoyment during her years in such an environment. Life on a poor farm doesn't foster self-reliance like Betsy's; rather it breaks the spirit and stultifies the will. The state of mind of Freeman's broken-down old women in "Sister Liddy" seems truer to the laws of life. Sarah Orne Jewett didn't realize that the capacity for living can atrophy from disuse just as muscle can. After a number of years of vegetation, very few paupers would be able to uproot themselves on the spur of the moment and like Betsy Lane face the world with such athletic confidence. The same disregard for psychological reality can be found in Rowland Robinson's "Fourth of July at Highfield Poorhouse,"[23] where despite the meanness of the keeper the inmates are all possessed of an irrepressible gaiety. Neither writer realized the deadly effects of prolonged spiritual drought.

Freeman found that the void of the soul extended into economic levels higher than the poorhouse. In her famous story "A New England Nun" a thrifty woman who has waited fifteen years for her fiancé to return from Australia realizes, when he finally does return, that she is no longer capable of going through with the marriage. During all the barren time a large part of her humanity has parched out of her. She is only able to continue her limited life, "like an uncloistered nun," finding in it a vegetable content-ment. "Serenity and placid narrowness had become to her as the birthright itself."[24] So far had she lost her femininity that she welcomes her lover's breaking their engagement in favor of a young and very womanly schoolteacher.

In a higher social sphere, Freeman shows us Caroline Munson, the elderly and genteel heroine of "A Symphony in Lavender," contenting herself with a similar half-life. A dream that Caroline had concerning the man who later proposed to her caused her to turn him down. But the dream is a rationalization of an inner lack—a psychological rather than sexual sterility—that makes her incapable of a full life. Henceforward she lives alone with an old servant in her ancestral mansion, satisfied with an insipid guardianship of the family silks and teacups.

5. E. A. Robinson

Freeman was almost the sole writer of her time who was willing to face the complete insolvency of the older order in New England life. Only E. A. Robinson, who in 1897 published *The Children of the Night*, has wandered with her in the draughty corridors lately abandoned by Puritanism. The spiritual void inhabited by such characters as Richard

Cory and Tasker Norcross is the same as that in Freeman's more somber stories. Indeed Robinson was an ardent admirer of the psychological realism of Freeman's *Pembroke*. "To one who knows anything about Puritanism the book will be interesting and impressive," he wrote to his friend Harry DeForest Smith. ". . . I rather admire Miss Wilkins' frankness and nerve."[25] It was to escape this emptiness, which blighted his town of Gardiner, Maine, like an ancestral curse, that Robinson fled to New York. But much of his finer poetry is based on his knowledge of thwarted, bankrupt character in the spiritually arid home of his childhood and youth. He devoted a lifetime to the task—among others—of probing the psychological wreckage of Calvinism—a task at which Freeman made a promising beginning but which she soon gave up for more lucrative enterprises. Like so many of the local-color writers of the time, Robinson has even created a mythical community for his characters to live in; but Tilbury Town is the exact opposite of the lesser Robinson's Danvis or of Jewett's Deephaven or even of Rose Terry Cooke's Bassett. It is a community where the solitaries, far from enjoying a sense of self-sufficiency, sometimes shoot themselves like Richard Cory because their lives, vacant despite material wealth and outer culture, offer no reason for continuance, or like Tasker Norcross drag out a life-in-death in huge drafty mansions beneath the centennial elms. There is less bucolic or small-town cosiness, built on the enduring Yankee qualities of humor and self-dependence, than in Jewett or Frost, though other of Robinson's poems, such as "Captain Craig," present a less dismal picture. The farmers and villagers of Tilbury frequently become warped, like the miser Aaron Stark with his "eyes like little dollars"; or drown their loneliness in drink, as does Mr. Flood; or like John Evereldown live and die enslaved to an obsession. So vividly has Robinson drawn the plight of all these characters that the names of some of them have become synonyms for various forms of frustration.

Most powerful of all Robinson's poems of frustration is "Mr. Flood's Party." Years ago I remember seeing in the New Hampshire home of Joseph Nesmith, the artist, a color-print entitled "An Old Man's Winter Night." (Or am I thinking of Frost's poem of that title?) Bent forward in his rickety straight-backed chair, a jug beside him, an old farmer sips his hard cider. On a table a lamp seems to be running out of oil. The only other furnishing in the room is a stove that the patch of snow drifted under the door shows to have been long since extinguished. I have never looked this picture up, and it may be very poor art—a possibility that in no way distresses me. The picture said much to Nesmith, a sensitive and lifelong observer of his native New England. What it said—though less subtly—was exactly what E. A. Robinson was saying in his poem about Mr. Flood, who on the lonely road homeward one winter night finds no other drinking companion than the moon and no toast other than his own precarious health. Here is complete spiritual bankruptcy of an individual—perhaps of a region and its way of life.

Other signs also were not lacking to Robinson. The collapse of the old economy—the real free enterprise that once actually did exist in rural America and was not merely the figment of the imaginations of newspaper editors—is grimly etched in "The Mill," the story of a miller and his wife who kill themselves because "there are no millers any more." The wholesale abandonment of Maine farmhouses is described in the funereal triolet "The House on the Hill." And the deserted community—a sight still to be seen in New England—is presented in all its dreariness in the sonnet "The Dead Village," beginning with the terse sentence:

> Here there is death.

It is the exception in Robinson's early work to find a character living harmoniously. But these exceptions—like Cliff Klingenhagen, whose life is lived according to the Sermon on the Mount, and Flammonde, who gets outside his own frustration by devoting his life to the welfare of his neighbors—are notable. Their existence would seem to reflect Robinson's own philosophy—his "desperate optimism"—that would not permit him to give way entirely to hopelessness.

6. Compensations

E. A. Robinson's vision of his native region was of course somewhat too pessimistic. As he himself implies in his poem "New England," the wind is not always north-north-east and conscience doesn't always have the rocking chair. His Tilbury Town was as much as symbol of his own state of mind, as it was a true representation of Gardiner, Maine. To interpret late-nineteenth-century New England life by his poems would be a great mistake; genius too often colors reality with its own hues. Lesser writers are apt to give a more liberal picture of their times, since they tend to be more in harmony with them. Freeman does not give us as unified a picture of her region as does Robinson, but she gives in her greater diversity a more realistic one.

Emerson in his essay "Compensation" has written:

> As no man had ever a point of pride that was not injurious to him, so no man had ever a defect that was not somewhere made useful to him. . . . Has he a defect of temper that unfits him to live in society? Thereby he is driven to entertain himself alone, and acqure habits of self-help; and thus, like the wounded oyster, he mends his shell with pearl.[26]

In her Puritanic preoccupation with the soul—or, since modern readers like the Greek word better, the psyche—Freeman was always seeking for some spiritual compensation in the barren and arid lives that her characters so often lived. Frequently her search was unsuccessful, as in *Pembroke* or stories like "Sister Liddy." But sometimes in the case of even the gauntest old maid she would find moments of spiritual elevation that went far to balance the lopsided budget of empty days. This compensation came generally as a brief upsurge of long dormant vitality—an hour's triumphal reassertion of the personality, sweeping all pettiness and frustrations before it.

In the famous story "The Revolt of Mother," which Theodore Roosevelt recommended American mothers to read for "the strong moral lesson" in it, [27] a farm woman has grown tired of waiting for years for her inconsiderate husband to fulfill his promise of enlarging their cramped dwelling. The climax comes when he starts work on an enormous and luxurious barn. One day, while the husband is away, his wife simply moves her family into the barn, setting up her housekeeping in the stables, which she correctly considers much more commodious than the farmhouse. After decades of being browbeaten it is the woman's moment of triumph. Public opinion is shocked; the minister attempts to mediate; but she holds her ground. When her husband, Adoniram, returns he is

> like a fortress whose walls had no active resistance, and went down the instant the right besieging tools were used. "Why, mother," he said hoarsely, "I hadn't no idee you was so set on't as all this comes to." [28]

This is a typical example of the triumphal moment that comes to the lives of so many of even the drabbest of Freeman's characters. But she herself did not consider "The Revolt of Mother" realistic—and she was a firm believer in realism. The act described in the story she considered too daring and too imaginative for a New England woman. [29] Another of her characters, Candace Whitcomb, heroine of "A Village Singer," is perhaps more lifelike. For forty years Candace has been the paid soprano in the village choir. When her voice begins to crack, she is given a surprise party at which she is presented with a photograph album. Enclosed in the album is a note announcing the church's purpose of relieving her of the strain of her musical duties. The first Sunday on which her successor, Alma Way, sings, Candace, who lives next door to the church, plays her organ as boisterously as she can and sings at the top of her cracked vocal chords. Needless to say, Alma's performance is spoiled and the service is ruined. When Mr. Pollard, the minister, calls to expostulate with Candace he finds a raging Medea rather than the mousy choir singer he had known so long.

> He was aghast and bewildered at this outbreak, which was tropical,

and more than tropical, for a New England nature has a floodgate, and the power which it releases is an accumulation. Candace Whitcomb had been a quiet woman, so delicately resolute that the quality had been scarcely noticed in her, and her ambition had been unsuspected. Now the resolution and the ambition appeared raging over her whole self.[30]

Wilson Ford, Candace's nephew, who has been engaged to Alma Way for ten years but can't marry her because he is poor and his mother is such a termagant that he wouldn't have his wife live with her, also attempts expostulation. Candace orders him away with threats of disinheritance. A lifetime of outraged self is at last finding expression, and one cannot condemn her. Her abrupt towering over her frustration is heroic; one feels the same admiration as for a caged animal suddenly set free. But the triumph is evanescent. When her nephew has left, she realizes suddenly that she is very ill. Her head throbs and her body shakes. Before going to bed she stands a moment in the back door and sees the glare of a nearby forest fire—symbolic of her own inner conflagration.

> Candace locked the door and went in. The trees with their delicate garlands of new leaves, with the new nests of songbirds, might fall, she was in the roar of an intenser fire: the growths of all her springs and the delicate wontedness of her whole life were going down in it. Candace went to bed in her little room. . . .[31]

It is her deathbed. In the morning she awakes, her fires burnt out, but she has had her moment. After making her peace with her nephew and the village, there is nothing left for her to do but die. In her few hours of fierce revolt there has been a compensation, a justification, for the humdrum years of her restrained and frustrated life.

A somewhat different working of Emerson's principle of compensation is found in the life of Joseph Lynn, the old man in the story "The White Birch." In his old age Joseph, desiccated through years of celibacy, falls in love with shallow but pretty young Sarah Benton, who consents to marry him for his money and thus jilts her youthful lover Harry Wyman. Sarah's friend, Marcia, upbraids her in round terms and gets her to admit to Harry that she loves him more than she does the old man. Harry then goes to Joseph and explains the situation to him. Joseph, who is good-hearted, accepts the inevitable gracefully. Workers have already been preparing to move his house nearer the road, since he feared its seclusion far back in a grove of birches would be displeasing to his young bride. Now he rescinds the orders for moving and settles back into his customary life. But his disappointment is not overwhelming. During his years of loneliness he has known compensations that still remain—in his case the quiet joys that come from close kinship with nature. When he has made his decision to give up the girl, he goes out into his birch grove.

> ... All at once the dearness of that which is always left in the treasure-house of nature for those who are robbed came over him and satisfied him. ... He sat a long time leaning against the white birch-tree through whose boughs a soft wind came at intervals, and made a gentle, musical rustle of twinkling leaves, ... and the man's love and sense of primeval comfort were so great that he was still filled with the peace of possession.[32]

To conclude, Freeman's contribution has been a psychological insight hitherto unknown in New England literature with the exception of Hawthorne. The volume of her important work, as has been already said, was slight—consisting of the two or three collections of short stories and the one or two novels discussed in this chapter. The general level of her work is far below that of Sarah Orne Jewett, for example, who maintained her high literary standards through more than a dozen books. But at her best, Freeman has seen more deeply into the life of her region than has Jewett. Of a less well-to-do family, she experienced New England life on a drabber level, and she was much more critical of it than any of the writers thus far considered. In the impressive line of analysts of the New England mind—beginning with Jonathan Edwards and continuing through Frost—Freeman occupies a secure position. More adept than Hawthorne, Emily Dickinson, or Robinson in standing outside her environment, she was able to bring to her work an objectivity that in part compensates for her obvious artistic inferiority to these other writers. One must turn to Frost to find the equal of her calm, dispassionate probing.

IX. CONTROVERSY WITH NATURE:
Celia Thaxter

> At about ten o'clock, Mr. Titcomb and myself took leave; and
> emerging into the open air, out of that room of song and pretty
> youthfulness of woman, and gay young men, there was the sky, and the
> three-quarters waning moon, and the old sea moaning all round about
> the island.
>
> HAWTHORNE, *The American Notebooks*[1]

One of the first actions of General A.W. Greely on arriving in his rescue
ship at Portsmouth, New Hampshire, was to get out to the Isles of Shoals
nine miles offshore and thank the Island poet, Celia Thaxter, for the
pleasure he and his men found in her verse during their two-year
abandonment in the Arctic.

"It tided over many a weary hour of our solitude," he is reported as
saying. "My companions especially like your poem called 'Tryst,' which I
read to them again and again."[2]

Now, General Greely is better known as an explorer than as a critic of
poetry. Yet his high opinion of Celia Thaxter's poems, considering the
grim circumstances in which he read them, is provocative. Who would
suspect a minor poet of Victorian New England to have anything to say to
a group of starving castaways in the polar night? In fact, what poet at all
could bring "great pleasure" to such men in such a predicament? One
would hesitate to name the Solomon of Ecclesiastes, or the author of Job,
or Homer—some poet who took as a theme fate and the despair that
consciousness of adverse fate wreaks in the human heart.

But a reading of Celia Thaxter's poems explains much. Some of them
are based on a concept of nature bound to have meaning for men at the
mercy of the Arctic. The poem "A Tryst," which Greely praised so highly,
is reminiscent in mood of many of the later realists, of such works for
example, as Crane's "Open Boat" or London's "To Build a Fire."

The first stanza of the ballad tells of an iceberg starting from the North
on its southward journey.

At whose command? Who bade it sail the deep
  With that resistless force?
Who made the dread appointment it must keep?
  Who traced its awful course?

The appointment, of course, is with a passenger steamer sailing from some
southern port with its cargo of "brave men, sweet women, little children
bright." Gradually the poem traces the inevitable convergence on the
trysting place.

Was not the weltering waste of water wide
  Enough for both to sail?
What drew the two together o'er the tide,
  Fair ship and iceberg pale?

No God sent a warning. Nature did not bestir herself to save her children.
It was in the unspeakable heart of things that the ship be doomed.

She rushed upon her ruin. Not a flash
  Broke up the waiting dark;
Dully through wind and sea one awful crash
  Sounded, with none to mark.[3]

The poem, though flabby in prosody, is not flabby in sentiment. It does
not whine: it does not curse "whatever brute and blackguard made the
world." It states a fact: nature is indifferent. To people, like Greely's men,
who have been ignored by nature in their most desperate need this
thought necessarily strikes home, however imperfect its expression.

This, moreover, is the tone of the majority of Celia Thaxter's poems.
The meaningless destruction of birds and flowers, shipwreck, drownings,
the bereavement of women whose men have been lost at sea, all appear to
her as evidence of an unfeeling, mechanistic nature. Often she sharpens the
feeling by pointing the inexplicable contrast between benignant and
malignant moods of nature: the sea in a flat calm of an August afternoon
and the sea in the midst of a January blizzard; the sea that forms a carpet
for the gentlest of dancing moonbeams in mid-July and the sea that bathes
in freezing brine the golden hair of a boy tangled head downmost on the
bowsprit of a schooner aground in a March gale; the sea that would lie like
a mirror all night while a murderer rows nine miles and back again to beat
out the brains of two women with an ax; and the sea that in a single day
would carry the frozen corpse of a young fisherman two hundred miles out
to sea in his dory; the sea in winter and the sea in summer, two distinct
and equally inexplicable worlds; the island in late spring, when the head
of every cove is gay with wild roses and beach peas bowing in the offshore
breeze, and the island in early winter, when the granite rocks themselves

crack in briny frost. These are the symbols—simple and old as humanity —that Celia Thaxter uses in her verse. The remarkable thing is that she used them impartially. Though she realized the ugliness and cuelty of nature, she never overlooked its beauty and kindliness.

This nicely balanced dualism was unusual in the America, and especially the urban New England, of her day. The tendency was to regard nature either as entirely beneficent or intentionally hostile. Not till our own time have those who make their opinions known generally acquiesced in the notion that humanity is neither nature's favored child nor the butt of her inveterate enmity.

The idea that nature, if unspoiled by civilization, is kind to all her creatures was an aspect of the Romantic movement in Europe. Writers like Bryant and Jonathan Edwards first took up the idea in America, but it reached its fullest development here in the Transcendentalists. Emerson saw nature as more than a symbol of God's goodness; it was God. It was the metaphor of spirit; and spirit, which is God, was infinitely good. The Concord landscape, the snowstorm, the sky, all manifested the beauty of the spirit that pervades the universe and of which the material universe is indeed the unessential, though lovely, garment. Thoreau, the surveyor, woodsman, and naturalist, who had come into as close contact with nature as anyone of his time, found her overwhelmingly kind to those who could atune their spirit to her influence. If nature under certain aspects occasionally seemed unaware of humanity, the fact only enhanced her grandeur, and in no way depressed him, as it did Celia Thaxter. A true romantic, he liked a spicing of bleakness in his natural scenery. In his *Cape Cod* he congratulates himself on first seeing the ocean in a storm. On inspecting the wreck of the *St. John,* in which a hundred and forty-five Irish immigrants were drowned in this same storm, he calmly—and transcendentally—states:

> On the whole it was not so impressive a scene as I might have expected. . . . If this was the law of Nature, why waste time in awe and pity? . . . Infants by the score dashed on the rocks by the enraged Atlantic Ocean! No, No! If the St. John did not make port here, she has been telegraphed there [in the other world]. The strongest wind cannot stagger a Spirit; it is a Spirit's breath. A just man's purpose cannot be split on any Grampus or material rock, but itself will split rocks till it succeed.[4]

The optimism of these Concordians was staggering. Alcott, even when threatened by starvation at Fruitlands, refused to admit that nature is not altogether friendly. To acknowledge any ill will in nature would, indeed, undermine the most basic principles of Transcendentalism and Unitarianism. There was no room for a devil in the cosmos of these mid-century thinkers. God is good; nature is God; nature is good.

Melville, perhaps, was the most notable American writer before the "naturalists" to question nature's universal benevolence. Nature, in his view, could at times be outright hostile; yet this hostility could be fought against. Thus in her most vicious mood, nature was unable to humble the spirit of Captain Ahab. But this is far from the fatalistic belief that nature is indifferent and that natural law is inexpugnable—the attitude of Celia Thaxter and, later, of the so-called naturalists, such as Stephen Crane and Jack London.

There was nothing new, of course, in Celia Thaxter's recognition that an angry sea acts according to other laws than human convenience; but, to repeat, the attitude was unique in the America of her day. Not so in England. For example, we find Wordsworth, a devout nature worshiper, lapsing into infidelity as he arraigns the whimsical treachery of the "smiling sea" in which his brother has been drowned. With this tragedy poisoning his faith, he observes approvingly Sir George Beaumont's picture of Peele Castle done against a background of stormy ocean.

> Not for a moment could I now behold
> A smiling sea, and be what I have been;
> The feeling of my loss will ne'er be old;
> This, which I know, I speak with mind serene.
>
> Then, Beaumont, Friend! who would have been the Friend,
> If he had lived, of Him whom I deplore,
> This work of thine I blame not, but commend;
> This sea in anger and the dismal shore.
>
> O 'tis a passionate Work!—yet wise and well,
> Well chosen is the spirit that is here;
> That Hulk which labors in the deadly swell,
> The rueful sky, this pageantry of fear!

Similarly, Cowper, the greatest glorifier of the English countryside, found the ocean to be an appropriate emblem of the God by whom, in his melancholic insanity, he imagined himself to be deserted. In his magnificent poem "The Castaway" he compares his own lot to that of the man overboard in stormy weather.

> No voice divine the storm allayed,
>   No light propitious shone,
> When snatched from all effectual aid,
>   We perished, each alone:
> But I, beneath a rougher sea,
> And whelmed in deeper gulfs than he.

In fact the sea has vied with the Lisbon earthquake in shaking the faith of nature worshipers, pantheists, and those greatest of optimists, the deists, who find everything to be for the best in the best of all possible worlds. Unable to accept old Bishop Burnett's theory that the imperfections of nature were God's way of punishing humanity for the fall of Adam—the predeluge world having been as smooth and perfect as a fine apple—these people could only despair whenever the earth appeared to be something other than a model nursery for human beings.

The mood was more common, and blacker, a generation later in England. To Tennyson and Arnold—Celia Thaxter's favorite contemporary poets—the neutrality of nature in human affairs was a patent, though disheartening, fact. Arnold uses the ocean as the symbol of all nature.

> Nature with equal mind,
> Sees all her sons at play;
> Sees man control the wind,
> The wind sweep man away;
> Allows the proudly riding and the foundering bark.[5]

But long before she had heard of Wordsworth, Tennyson, and Arnold —before she could have spelled out their lines—Celia Thaxter knew the ways of nature. From her earliest childhood, as we shall see later, her point of observation had been an island lighthouse. Her attitudes were thrust upon her by the fickle, boisterous Atlantic itself. As with the other rural and coastal New Englanders we have been discussing, she was first a product of New England—its harsh winters and brilliant summers; its glacier-blasted soil and its beachless, granite coast; above all, its rugged realism, which could form its own opinions on nature and other matters without consulting the latest philosophy of Concord, London, or Paris. Wordsworth and Arnold had no more taught Celia Thaxter her early and lifelong love and terror of the sea than did Emerson and Thoreau. Her view of nature was no more governed by these men than Mary Wilkins Freeman's knowledge of the Vermont hill-farmer came from Tolstoy's description of the Russian peasant. But it is an interesting coincidence—if nothing more—that both these writers happened to fall in with wider streams of attitude.

No one, of course would consider Celia Thaxter in any sense comparable as an artist with such authors as Emerson, Melville, or Arnold. Nor would one attempt to show that she was an appreciable influence on the "naturalistic" school of Crane and London. Although she shared the belief of these latter writers that nature's whim and law ignore human feelings and hopes, her views were less sombre, better balanced, then theirs; she was readier to see the occasional kindliness as well as the grimness of nature. Unlike them she realized that there is such a thing as a June day, even in New England. Nor, lastly, would one make the claim that Celia Thaxter was ahead of her times; if popularity means anything, she was decidedly of them. The point is that, aside from her religious unorthodoxy, she represents an attitude which is eminently typical of her group of provincial writers and which has been perhaps neglected in our admiration for the more brilliant achievements of the Emersons and Hawthornes. Indeed, she represented in many ways an approach to life that we condemn in comparison both with our own and with that of the Golden Age of New England. Yet this mode of life had much in it that is enduring and worthy of study.

One must begin with Celia Thaxter's upbringing on the Isles of Shoals. Her own prose account of her life—*Among the Isles of Shoals,* a work written on the insistence of her friend Whittier—is her only first-rate literary production; but concerning herself and her family it omits information that contributes to an understanding of her as a writer and a person. The fact is that a legend, based on a rickety foundation of fact, developed concerning the circumstances of her family's removal from Portsmouth, New Hampshire, to the Isles of Shoals. The legend is as follows: When Celia was four years old her father Thomas Laighton, ran for governor of the state, was defeated in what he thought was an unfair election, and in his chagrin got an appointment as keeper of the lighthouse on White Island at the Shoals, whither he repaired with his wife, three children, and a hired man under the self-imposed vow never to set foot on the mainland again. The legend becomes vague as to how closely he abided by this vow, but the story serves as a parable illustrative of New England "setness" of character and self-sufficiency.

The facts are quite different from the legend. Thomas Laighton, who had been the editor of a Portsmouth newspaper, had in 1839 actually run for political office—that of selectman of Portsmouth—and, as he thought, had been unfairly defeated. Deciding to redirect the course of his life, he bought with his brother three of the Isles of Shoals with the intention of setting up a fish-buying business there. At about the same time the position at White Island Lighthouse fell vacant and Laighton obtained an appointment to it, thus placing himself on the scene of his projected fish business. If he had made a vow never to return to the mainland, he soon broke it; for several years later he was elected to the state legislature, the sessions of which in Concord he had to attend each spring and fall. Yet for the most part the family lived pretty much unto themselves, first at the lighthouse and, in the summers and while Laighton was in Concord, on nearby Smutty-nose, one of the three islands Laighton had bought, where they kept a small inn that catered to excursionists and sportsmen from the mainland. Indeed the situation of the family in the early years and later, during all but the summer season, on Appledore Island, on which Laighton had erected one of the first large summer hotels in New England, would have gladdened the heart of Rousseau or of Bernadin St. Pierre. Judging from the magnificent devotion of her childen, the mother must have been a woman of extraordinary resource and depth of feeling. To her more than any one else belongs undoubtedly the success of the venture. Yet in the nature of things the children were cast upon their own resources; environment and the self were their greatest educators.

The environment—the bleak little archipelago of the Isles of Shoals, where the children grew up—is best presented in Celia's own words. Comparing the islands to the Galapagos group as described by Melville, she writes:

> Very sad they look, stern, bleak, and unpromising, yet they are enchanted islands. . . . Landing for the first time, the stranger is struck only by the sadness of the place—the vast loneliness; for there are not even trees to whisper with familiar voices,—nothing but sky and sea and rocks. But the very wildness and desolation reveal a strange beauty to him . . . . For the world is like a new-blown rose, and in the heart of it he stands, with only the caressing music of the water to break the utter silence. . . .[6]

Thus to Celia Thaxter, as to Sarah Orne Jewett in her *Country of the Pointed Firs* and to Hawthorne in his *American Notebooks,* the rocky outer islands of the New England coast become a symbol of loneliness. Yet, like her brother, Cedric, who on his first visit to Portsmouth, at the age of thirteen, moped in a cellar till he returned to the Shoals, Celia Thaxter never felt fully at ease elsewhere. While living in Newtonville she wrote in her first published poem, "Land-Locked":

> O Earth! thy summer song of joy may soar
> Ringing to heaven in triumph. I but crave
> The sad, caressing murmur of the wave
> That breaks in tender music on the shore.[7]

The chief realities in the lives of these island children were the sea and the seasons. Always in winter the sea was a source of mystery and terror.

> The driftwood is always full of suggestions:—a broken oar. . . . a section of mast hurriedly chopped, telling of a tragedy too well known on the awful sea. . . . As a child I was never without apprehension when examining the drift, for I feared to find some too dreadful token of disaster.[8]

One incident, told in Elizabeth Stuart Phelp's *Chapters from a Life,* is sufficient reason for Celia Thaxter's hatred of the island winters. During a storm the two watched a vessel break up on the rocks just offshore. Unable to carry help through the surf, the spectators for five hours beheld the crew, who clung to a ledge, drop one by one into the breakers. "Fools to cling!" the agnostic Thaxter said to evangelical, sentimental Phelps. "They were fools—*fools* to cling!"[9] The idea of shipwreck indeed early became an obsession with her. Some of her best poems are about wrecks that she witnessed or heard about: "The Wreck of the Pocahantos," "The Spaniards' Graves," "A Tryst," "The Cruise of the Mystery." In her letters she dwells with obsessive insistence upon the wrecks that occurred during the bitter island winters.

But the summers were a brief sojourn in heaven. At the lighthouse the children cultivated minuscule gardens among the rocks and explored the teeming life of the tidal puddles. Later, at the hotel on Appledore, Celia had one of the most remarkable flower gardens in New England, for salt air and the rocky soil are inexplicably friendly to flowers. And always during these short summers was the smiling sea.

> The waves are full of whispers wild and sweet;
> They call to me—incessantly they beat
> Along the boat from stern to curved prow.
>
> Comes the careering wind, blows back my hair,
> All damp with dew, to kiss me unaware,
> Murmuring "Thee I love," and passes on.[10]

Never, though, was the memory of winter fully absent. The basic symbolism was embedded in the very marrow of this island girl. She writes in *Among the Isles of Shoals*:

> And all the pictures over which I dream are set in this framework of the sea, that sparkled and sang, or frowned and threatened, in all the ages that are gone as it does to-day, and will continue to smile and threaten when we who listen to it and love it and fear it now are dust and ashes in our turn.[11]

And in her verse:

> The barren island dreams in flowers, while blow
>   The south winds, drawing haze o'er sea and land;
> Yet the great heart of ocean, throbbing slow,
>   Makes the frail blossoms vibrate where they stand;
>
> And hints of heavier pulses soon to shake
>   Its mighty breast when summer is no more,
> And devastating waves sweep on and break,
>   And clasp with girdle white the iron shore.[12]

Outwardly, Celia Thaxter's life was rather uneventful. Except for a short trip to Europe with a sick brother and a few years' residence in Newtonville after her marriage, she always remained within the little triangle of the Isles of Shoals, Portsmouth and Kittery Point—like so many New Englanders never visiting even New York. Owing to a temperamental incompatability, her married life was not happy. She had met her husband, Levi Thaxter, who was eleven years older than she, when he came to the Isles of Shoals on the recommendation of his Harvard classmate T.W. Higginson to practice elocution by declaiming like Demosthenes to the waves. According to Hawthorne, Celia was the first to fall in love; but as Levi had fallen in love with the place—he eventually became Laighton's partner in the hotel venture on Appledore—the two were much together. For several winters Thaxter remained on the islands as tutor to the children; later, when married, he served as pastor on Star Island, another of the Shoals group. The wedding, Higginson tells us, had been decided on, the pastor sent for, and the ceremony performed all in one day, when Celia was sixteen years old.[13]

One year later—in the autumn of 1852—Hawthorne made the visit to the Shoals that he describes in his *American Notebooks*. Stopping at the Laighton hotel, where he was later joined by Franklin Pierce, he struck up an acquaintance with the Thaxters, whose cottage was nearby, and spent at least one evening with them drinking apple toddy and singing. Levi he found to be intelligent, frank, and gentlemanly; Celia pretty, musical, ladylike, free and easy, not at all prim and precise. The evening left a lasting impression on him—"this room of song and pretty youthfulness of woman" with "the old sea moaning all round about." Hawthorne, too, like so many visitors to the Shoals felt the peculiar spell of the islands. While there he added many pages to his notebooks: the story of "Old Bob," the ghost of one of Captain Kidd's men, who was slain so that he could not divulge the whereabouts of treasure he had helped to bury on the islands, and who now haunted the scene of his death; the story of the romantic schoolteacher who sat on the rocks till she was washed away by the waves; the account of a woman among the early settlers—the English were established there as early as 1645—who hid from the Indians in a cave and killed her children when their crying threatened to reveal the hiding place. Of the landmarks on the islands he describes the cleft rock, supposedly split at the time of the crucifixion, and the cairn built by Captain John Smith ("The tradition is as good as truth," he says). Above all he was impressed by the sea and the loneliness of the islands; with a Thoreau-like gusto for the sublimely dreary he avows that he never saw a more dismal place in a storm. Yet one feels that in part at least he is seeing the place as a sort of backdrop for the lives of the young couple whose apple toddy he drank. It is they who give the islands human significance. Thus he is struck by the idea that the Thaxters' son, Karl, was the first baby born on Appledore since the Revolution.

As it affected her writing, her marriage was probably fortunate for Celia Thaxter. Thaxter was of a cultured old New England family—was related, in fact, to James Russell Lowell, who published Celia's first poem in the

Atlantic—had studied elocution under Charles Kean, and was an admirer and accomplished public reader and interpreter of Browning. When he married his pupil with the shell necklace and bracelets he did not terminate her education. An able critic of verse, he helped and encouraged her in her own writing. But perhaps more important, he brought to their home many stimulating friends—men of the world and the intellect, like John Weiss, the popular preacher, and William Morris Hunt, the painter. As time went on, this circle of acquaintance—many of whom, like Hawthorne, the Thaxters first knew as visitors to the Laighton hotel—grew till it constituted a splendid representation of the nation's cultural leaders: such authors as Hawthorne, Whittier, Thomas Wentworth Higginson, James Russell Lowell, James Whitcomb Riley; such painters as J. Appleton Brown, Childe Hassam, and Ross Turner; and such musicians as Ole Bull, Julius Eichberg, the cellist, and John K. Paine, the composer.[14] The child brought up in a lighthouse with only the company of her two brothers thus became, in the summers at least, the center of a salon the equal of any that America has had.

With some of these persons she was on terms of intimate friendship both in winter and summer. Between her and Whittier, for whom she had great admiration, there was a constant interchange of visits. In fact the two were almost neighbors, for Po Hill in Amesbury is plainly visible from the Shoals. Thus in a correspondence of thirty years' duration Whittier would begin his letters: "Po Hill sends Appledore good-morning." To Whittier, Thaxter wrote not only of personal problems, but also of her literary problems. He in turn constantly encouraged her in her writing, even revising her poems when he thought it necessary; thus the influence of Whittier is frequently apparent in Celia Thaxter's work. To him, moreover, she owes the idea of her best prose work, *Among the Isles of Shoals;* for it was his suggestion that she write for the *Atlantic* the sketches on the history and life of the islands that were later published in book form under that title.[15] With the inseparable Sarah Orne Jewett and Annie Fields she was also most intimate. Her correspondence with Fields—which alone constitutes a frank and moving autobiography—forms the bulk of her published letters; and after her death Jewett with a kindred love of the New England coast and its people edited her poems and juvenile writings.

With many of her husband's friends, such as William Morris Hunt, T.W. Higginson, James Russell Lowell, and John Weiss, Celia Thaxter was also on friendly terms. Some of these, like Weiss, came to the Shoals year after year for long visits. Hunt, when suffering a nervous breakdown brought on by family troubles and the ordeal of painting his famous murals in the Capitol at Albany—supposedly the finest painted in America up to that time—chose Appledore as a spot to try to recuperate in. It was Celia Thaxter who that same summer found him drowned, probably a suicide, in the lily pond. The streams of life as well as the ocean, were sometimes storm-darkened at the Isles of Shoals.

During a summer vacation durable friendships can be built up without any previous foundation. From the stream of "paying guests" that flowed through the Laighton hotel—Thaxter had her pick of interesting persons. And her charm, as well as her growing literary fame, made her friendship acceptable to most. Those whom she liked she would invite to gatherings in her cottage, and thus for her musical evenings she could command such talents as Ole Bull's and Julius Eichberg's. In fact many people visited the Shoals for the sake of Celia Thaxter's salon. The natural result was that many of these friendships were perpetuated by correspondence in the winters.

Summer salons have long been common in New England. At Shelburne, New Hampshire, Paul Elmer More was the central figure of a distinguished group. Another was associated with Weir Mitchell at Mt. Desert. Also, many of the so-called summer "colonies," such as Silvermine, Dorset, and Provincetown, inevitably come to mind. The influence of these intellectual and artistic nuclei on the national culture has undoubtedly been great, though there is no way of estimating how great. With all such groups, the one at Appledore had much in common. Yet it had its distinctive features, too. It was under the unusually strict domination of one person, Celia Thaxter; and because she was a native of the locality, as were other mainstays of the group, such as Whittier, it partook more of the *genius loci*—was not so much an alien excrescence on the landscape. If the indigenous culture of rural and coastal New England had anything to offer, here was a channel through which it could flow into the nation's life.

But the effect of all this brilliant company on Celia Thaxter, aside from any superficial social maturation, was at first surprisingly small. Though she was constantly under the influence of the thought of the day, though she read and admired Emerson and Huxley and could later correspond with Weiss on the significance of Tyndall's "Belfast Address",[16] her outlook on life changed not at all. Surrounded by Transcendentalists and Unitarians and steeped in all the classics of their school, she was never herself a Transcendentalist. On the other hand, she was in no sense either an orthodox Christian or an agnostic. Her belief defies any classification other than that of a varying theism. She apparently had her father's independence of mind without his stubbornness.

It is doubtful if Celia Thaxter felt any compelling need for a religion during this early part of her life. As a child she tells us that she occasionally had a feeling of oneness with nature:

> I was fain to mingle my voice with her myriad voices, only aspiring to be in accord with the Infinite harmony, however feeble and broken the notes might be.[17]

This "natural religion," however, did not suffice for middle life. The two-faced quality of nature—the treachery whereby she wantonly destroys the loveliest of her creations—could not be explained, and the result for Thaxter was a deepening intellectual despair. Thus she writes how she exclaimed over the coffin of a dead child: "Sleep well! Be thankful you are spared so much that I see humanity endure, fixed here forever where I stand!"[18] And in a letter to Annie Fields apropos of a wreck in which two men drowned, she marvels at the Browningesque optimism of a certain Mrs. Greene (who is "sure that all that is *must* be for the best") and adds:

> I am too much alone, and get sadder than death with brooding over this riddle of life; and Nature is so placid; and the sea and the rocks have ground the life out of those two to whom life was so sweet.[19]

Although her husband was one of the leading admirers of Browning and promoters of Browning Clubs in America, so that the great poet out of gratitude supplied the epitaph inscribed on his headstone at Kittery Point, Maine, Celia Thaxter found the perturbed and less optimistic Tennyson much more congenial to her own vision of life.[20]

Yet in this sensitive island woman whose personality had not been pre-empted by any religious orthodoxy one would expect to find a fertile ground for Transcendentalism to take root in, especially with Emersonians like Weiss and Albee on hand to inculcate it. But perhaps even Emerson would not have been a Transcendentalist had he been reared on a rock in the North Atlantic. In Concord, as in most of inland New England, nature is generally in a kindly mood. The summers, though short, are brilliant; the autumns are a rollicking symphony of variegated color and weather; the winters, aside from a few days of fog and thaw, are a wholesome excitement; only the interminable mud of spring is disheartening. Never need one feel that God has forsaken one. Even a blizzard has its attractions, revealing to an Emerson the Oversoul's expression of itself in the matchless curves of a snowdrift; and providing a Whittier an opportunity to enjoy the coziness of family life on the farm. But Amesbury and Concord are at some distance from the sea. A blizzard at the Isles of Shoals means a gale that blows out the fires in the stoves and that like as not will toss a schooner onto the rocks and drown its crew. The few pantheistic moments that Celia Thaxter did enjoy always occurred in mid-summer.

There was a latter-day realism in the attitude of Celia Thaxter—a realism much more typical of her region than the mysticism of Emerson or the coziness of Whittier. Those who live next to nature by compulsion have a different outlook than those who live next to her by choice. Another coastal writer, Sarah Orne Jewett, realized that her country of the pointed firs was pleasant only six months of the year; and Mary Wilkins Freeman found little evidence of the Oversoul on the hill-farms of northern New

England. A true closeness to the soil is apt to preclude belief in any philosophy based upon the Godhead of nature. As a matter of fact, Celia Thaxter, like Jewett and Freeman, believed that "it is not good for men to live. . . . in remote and solitary places."[21] Though she particularly decries the effect of isolated life on women, she tells of a man brought up on Boone Island, more remote even than the Shoals, who "spoke with bitterness of life in that terrible solitude, and of the loneliness which had pursued him ever since."[22] People in these circumstances must find other, perhaps more realistic, ways of life than the transcendental. That these writers of the soil and sea did find such ways is the chief reason they are worth our attention today.

Thus Celia Thaxter, though she esteemed both Emerson and her friend Whittier,[23] found in neither writer the answer to her doubts. In Tennyson, whom she admired above all poets, she had at least the comfort of finding similar questionings to hers, but still no answers. The discoveries of science interested her intellectually but left her cold devotionally. The over-developed religious faculty that sooner or later afflicts so many descendants of the Puritans was still to be satisfied. It is perhaps a commentary on the inadequacy of Unitarianism and Transcendentalism for the un-complex mind that Celia Thaxter—intelligent, but essentially simple by nature—dabbled first in spiritualism and later espoused the more questionable variety of theosophy, only in her final years developing a geniunely thoughtful religious outlook and reconciling the callousness of nature with the idea of God the father.

In the late nineteenth century finer intellects than Celia Thaxter's played with ouija boards and levitation. In Europe Elizabeth Barrett Browning, Harriet Martineau, and George Sand were ardent spiritualists. In America the movement, which had received impetus from the "rappings" of the notorious Fox sisters of Rochester, New York, was described by one detached writer as mass hysteria. New England seemed particularly afflicted immediately after the Civil War. Frank Preston Stearns in his *Sketches from Concord and Appledore* attributes this fad—along with antivivisectionism, teetotalism, and anti-capital punishment agitation—to the need in New England for some crusade to absorb the emotional energy formerly poured into abolitionism. But in America as a whole perhaps the chief appeal of spiritualism was that it offered to bereaved persons a hope of contacting the spirits of their kinfolk killed in the War. Thus Elizabeth Stuart Phelps's *Gates Ajar*, though not spiritualistic, sold hundreds of thousands of copies because its theme was the possibility of a mystical union with the souls of the dead. At any rate mediums, both professional and amateur, well-meaning and fraudulent, could be had at a dime a dozen. Browning, who had to cope with the tendency in his wife, attacked the movement in his "Mr. Sludge, the Medium" and incidentally made as keen an analysis of this particular instance of the human craving to be duped as any of the more scientific investigators.[24]

In all events, when Celia Thaxter was eighteen Hawthorne noticed on her table a book on spiritualism.[25] Later David Wasson reported being present at a friend's house in Newburyport where she was acting as an amateur medium, and Frank Preston Stearns witnessed a session with a planchette in which she believed she had established contact with her father, dead for two years.[26]

At first these aberrations were of no great moment, for Thaxter enjoyed a sound nervous and physical constitution. But she had had a bitter trouble. Her elder son, Karl, was retarded and was under her constant care till her death. In addition there was the usual run of vexations, such as straitened finances and the delicate health of her husband. Life was exacting its tribute, but Thaxter's funds of vitality were not yet exhausted. She could take these misfortunes in her stride, with only an occasional halting step.

Then in 1877 her mother died. The unhinging impact of this blow is best described in a letter to Annie Fields:

> There is no comfort for us anywhere except by the gradual hand of time. The "consolations of religion" I cannot bear. I can bear my anguish better than their emptiness, though I am crushed breathless by my sorrow. It seems as if I could never fill my lungs with air again, as if I never wished to look upon the light of day.[27]

The scar remained till death. But the event had one constructive effect; it forced her to face the problem of death and in the end brought her a stability that she had not previously known.

The pagan-like grief of Celia Thaxter for her mother is not to be simply explained. Elizabeth Laighton was, we are told, a most remarkable woman; it was mainly she who not only made the early life at White Island Light bearable for the family but actually converted it into a beautiful experience. She must have been an authentic New England matriarch—almost the pioneer woman in her inexhaustible capacity to take on her own shoulders most of the vexations of family life. Yet such persons may be domineering, and in their too-successful efforts to shield their families from all unpleasantness they create an unwholesome dependency upon themselves. Quite likely the desperate homesickness that all the children felt when away from the Shoals was for the mother more than for the place. For religionless people, parents like Elizabeth Laighton can serve emotionally as a faith; they become the sole unifying force in life, connecting one's days from childhood to old age. When such persons die their dependents suffer the same effects as from sudden disillusionment in religion.

When Celia Thaxter, having laid out her mother with her own hands, dropped into the grave on Appledore an anchor of flowers as the symbol of hope and said, "I *hope* all things, I believe nothing,"[28] she was as helplessly adrift as the storm driven schooners she describes in her ballads. At any rate she had lost the firmest hold she had on life, and now she was casting desperately about for another. The spectacle was not pleasant. She first attempted spiritualistically to call back her mother's soul. When she failed she was aware for the first time of the true nature of death. The horrible, but somewhat fascinating, phantom that had haunted the winter seas had now become very real and familiar.

What she eventually did was exactly what she had sworn not to do: she fled to the "comforts of religion." But not to Christianity, or Unitarianism, or Transcendentalism, or any other form of New England orthodoxy; these creeds were apparently no longer alive enough to attract one in need. Instead she took up with Theosophy, which, under the leadership of Mme. Blavatsky, was just beginning to make a stir on this side of the Atlantic and was, with many people, serving as a new religion. One of Blavatsky's followers, a certain Mohini Chattergi, was at the time in America and somehow Thaxter got to know him personally. Under his guidance she read the *Bhagavad-Gita* and the New Testament. According to the sentimental Annie Fields, "The Bible was born anew for her."[29] The conglomerate belief that was actually born to her is best described in a letter that she wrote to Whittier.

> So, dear friend, I am become a most humble and devoted follower of Christ, our Christ, for all races have their own Christs to save and help them. . . . I understand it all now, and feel as if all my life I had been looking through a window black with smoke; suddenly it is cleared, and I see a glorious prospect, a glorious hope. . . . Salvation . . . means being saved from further earthly lives, and of reaching God and the supreme joy, the continual wheel of rebirth and pain and death being the hell, the fire of passions that burns forever, the worm of desires that never die. . . .[30]

It would be interesting to know the effect that the announcement of this credo had on the orthodox Whittier, who once said to Celia Thaxter when she announced that she did not say her prayers: "I am sure thee does without knowing it."[31] One thing is certain, however; her new faith was no recognizable form of Christianity; and in point of fact Thaxter could never bring herself to join any church, though her brother reports that toward the end she frequently attended Unitarian services at Portsmouth. Nor was it in any sense even a well-considered form of Hinduism or Buddhism. Thaxter had been duped. Admiration and study of Oriental religion were, certainly, most common in New England; she was not the only one who read her *Bhagavad-Gita* and derived comfort from it. But the difference between, say, Thoreau's thoughtful approach to the Vedas and Thaxter's outbursts is painfully obvious.

For Theosophy as it then existed in America was in some respects absurd. Although its general doctrine was high-sounding and harmless, its authority was based in part on Mme. Blavatsky's claimed contact with some probably nonexistent Tibetan Mahatmas who supposedly communicated with her by means of letters precipitated out of mid-air. The kindest thing modern commentators can say of her and her lieutenants is that in their zeal they succeeded in deceiving themselves. No more fantastic story can be imagined than that of Mme. Blavatsky, an ex-medium, who wandered about Asia, Europe and America purveying her continuously changing oriental mysticism to anyone willing to listen. The personal life of Mohini, Celia Thaxter's mentor, is particularly unsavory. Yet along with the dupes some intelligent persons were brought into the movement—among them, for a time, Thomas Edison.[32] As it exists today, the supposed magic practiced by Mme. Blavatsky has been more or less forgotten, and the ethical side—admirable enough in itself—alone has been emphasized. It was this element, as well as the Oriental explanation of existence—Karma and reincarnation—that appealed to Celia Thaxter.

Henceforward Thaxter believed quite literally in metempsychosis. She refers to life as "this particular phase of existence"[33] and to death as "the change of state."[34] She now asserts that she enjoys a funeral more than a wedding, and she recommends to a friend the reading of E.D. Walker's theosophical work *Reincarnation.* She speaks of Karma and attends Mohini Chattergi's lectures on "The Song of Solomon." The simplicity of her faith alone saves it from vulgarity. To her fellow ornithologist Bradford Torrey, whose essay "Behind the Eye" she read with pleasure, she writes:

> Have you noticed, when people go out of this world, they pass from behind their eyes, precisely as when a face looks from a window and then leaves it?—there is the window, but the person is gone. Not extinguished, never!—but simply passed away from behind the windows from which all their lives they have looked.[35]

One service, however, Mohini Chattergi did do for Celia Thaxter. He pointed out to her the error of attempting to establish contact with departed spirits.

But despite her adherence to the doctrine of reincarnation, this belief was not the chief, nor even a very important, component in her outlook. It assuaged the wound inflicted by her mother's death, but long before this event and to an even greater degree after it, she had arrived at a way of life that served for her day-to-day happiness and that of her family. And herein she was in part living a doctrine preached by the Unitarians and Transcendentalists. It was simply the conviction that the only worthwhile thing in this world—the only Godlike thing—is love; God in fact is love. This basic principle of living, by which she was according to all accounts eminently successful in conducting her life, occasionally expressed itself in orthodox Christian phraseology, as in the hymn-like "Love Shall Save Us All."

> There is no hope but this to see
>   Through tears that gather fast and fall;
> Too great to perish Love must be,
>   And Love shall save us all.[36]

But this example of revivalistic flamboyancy is no more typical of Celia Thaxter than the pantheistic poem:

> For the spirit of God is in everything; and the
>   life of all is one,
> From the wing of the gnat and the breath of the
>   rose to the central fires of the sun.[37]

If she failed to bolster her belief with the subtleties of Emersonian argument, she was still immune, even in the case of Theosophy, to prolonged religious hysteria. Much more typical is a poem, first published in *St. Nicholas,* called "The Heavenly Guest." This piece, which is a verse rendition of Tolstoy's parable, "Where Love Is, There God Is Also," is perhaps the only excellent poem she ever wrote.[38] The truest—and the only necessary—thing to be said of it is that it catches the spirit of Tolstoy's story as no other rendition of it has, for it perfectly expressed in simple terms the very simple belief that Celia Thaxter had always lived by. Undoubtedly she would not have believed in the minutiae of Tolstoy's theology, but his postconversion spirit she recognized at once as kindred to her own, as did so many other American writers—Howells is notable among them—of this time.

Yet even in her old age Thaxter never closed her eyes to the other side of God, the cruel side, as did the Unitarians. If Love is the only God, or aspect of God, that she will regulate her life by, she is all too conscious of the existence of a mysterious evil. The following verses are typical.

> Vainly we weep and wrestle with our sorrow—
>   We cannot see his roads, they lie so broad:
> But his eternal day knows no tomorrow,
>   And life and death are all the same with God.[39]

> And fruitless prayers pierce heaven from trusting souls,
>   Trampled defenceless the wild waves beneath.[40]

Being born too late to blame all evil on the devil and being too honest to dismiss by sophistry the evidence of her own eyes she came to a conclusion that in T.S. Eliot has been acclaimed as a mark of profound intellectuality. She gave up the struggle of comprehension and decided with Dante, whom she had first dipped into while peeling squash as a young housewife in Newtonville, that in *"la sua volontade e nostra pace."*[41] But unlike Eliot or Longfellow she accepted this one inevitable conclusion of Dante without becoming Anglo-Catholic or immersing herself in the Middle Ages. Evil appeared to be God's will. What else could one do but accept it?

Let us repeat that Celia Thaxter was a woman of great simplicity, at times shallowness, of mind. Were she otherwise her life would be of little interest to us, for her achievement was small. But being uncomplex, she was typical. Though lacking the brilliance of genius, she had much common sense. And having arrived at certain conclusions, she ordered her ways thereby and went on with the business of existence.

We have seen her rather pathetic solution to the carking problem of death. But her solution to the problem of living is a different matter. It is easy to say that Love should be the cardinal principle of our lives and the application of the principle seems clear enough. One should love one's fellow beings. This Thaxter did; her devotion to her family, particularly to her handicapped son, was magnificent; her faithfulness to her friends was unflinching. But what of her love of the beautiful part of nature, of flowers for example? What of her love for fine music? Great painting? Brilliant conversation? If love is to be a guiding principle in life, it must be applied to all aspects of life: to the regulating of one's physical environment, of one's entertainment, of one's reading, as well as to one's family and social relationships.

Most remarkable, perhaps, was her devotion to flower gardening. In a notably readable book, *An Island Garden*, somewhat garishly illustrated by her friend Childe Hassam, Thaxter describes in detail her lifelong efforts to establish on the granite ledges of Appledore Island a flower garden of surpassing beauty. She tells of her year-round toil—how she planted and nurtured the seedlings in the house in mid-winter, how she imported toads from the "main" to combat the slugs that infested the island and devastated the tenderer plants, how she struggled against blight, drought, and deluge—till at last she had converted one corner of her Atlantic rock into a spot of beauty, where several hundreds of varieties of flowers scented the salt air. The garden symbolized to her the duality of nature, the constant encroachment of evil and cruelty upon goodness and beauty. Over this spot of nature she had control. If she fought hard enough, the forces of evil could be beaten back from this square of ground. In time the garden became the great passion of her life—greater even than literature. Her brother tells us that she would talk to her hollyhocks. She herself speculates as to the possibility of consciousness in plants, and she quotes the French scientist Flammerion in support of her speculations. Not satisfied with cultivating and writing about flowers, she later took to painting them on china and in copies of her books.

And this was common in New England. The same feelings that compelled Thaxter to make lovely with flowers the rocks on which innumerable mariners had lost their lives in shipwreck compelled many a hill-wife and fisherman's wife to cultivate her bit of yard. One need only travel through the New England countryside today to see what is meant, but the writing of the time also amply proves the point. The most outstanding literary horticulturist was, of course, Emily Dickinson, who, rejecting this world, fashioned her own private universe of poetry and flowers. But Sarah Orne Jewett's villages and islands are also sprinkled with flower gardens; and even the bleak terrain of Mary Wilkins Freeman is frequently bedizened by the gardens of her spinsters and solitaries. Indeed, Jewett and Freeman consciously used the flower garden as a symbol of one of their basic themes: the determination of rural New Englanders, no matter how limited their opportunities, to make the best of what little nature has given them and to make meaningful their own life. If there is a more worthwhile determination, it has not yet been revealed to humanity.

This determination to nurture the good and beautiful and starve out the bad and ugly affected other phases of life and in its exaggerated form became stigmatized as Victorianism. And the stigma is in many cases deserved. When it caused one to close one's eyes to social evils, to refuse to admit the existence of squalor and vice, and in short to view life from behind blinkers and through a set of rose-colored spectacles, the results were, of course, ludicrous, unless downright disastrous. Sarah Orne Jewett records a trivial—yet rather pathetic—instance of this Victorian myopia, which was unfortunately all too common. In her story of "The Dulham Ladies," two elderly women descended from an illustrious family but unaware that they no longer counted in the life of their town, frimped themselves up with false hair and, much to the amusement of the younger generation, attempted to assert their old authority in the local sewing circles. But when a person, as did Celia Thaxter, recognized evil and then methodically strove to overcome it, no accusation of purblindness can be made. The modern criticism of this approach arises from the fact that we prefer to fight solely an agressive, and frequently losing, warfare against the forces of darkness, whereas the Victorians in addition to offense, employ the defensive method of erecting a citadel of sweetness and light and then devoting their efforts to warding off any encroachment on it by the enemy—the tactics that strike us as so amusing in the life of George Apley in John Marquand's novel, *The Late George Apley.*

In addition to her gardening, painting, and writing, Thaxter found other areas in which to arraign herself against the evil side of nature. All her life, for example, she had an inordinate love of birds, since, as to many poets, they symbolized all that is most beautiful in the external world. Following here in the great American tradition of naturalism—which in New England had produced such figures as Thoreau, Gray, and Agassiz—she not only wrote about birds but studied and recorded their habits, furnishing data to the naturalist Bradford Torrey on the ornithology of the Isles of Shoals. Also she became a vice-president of the Audubon Society, and thus threw her prestige—which was remarkably strong—into the fight against the decimation of songbirds for the decorating of women's millinery. Such matters are, perhaps, trivial; yet they indicate a state of mind. Celia Thaxter's attitude toward birds was typical of New England, like that of the young bride in Frost's exquisite poem, "The Hill Wife," in which he describes a woman's longing for the return of the birds after her long winter's isolation on a back-country farm.

Other enthusiasms of Celia Thaxter—denied to most country people—were good music and good conversation, both of which abounded in summer in the famous flower-decked livingroom at Appledore. Her days, she tells us, were systematically divided between these two pleasures—conversation in the mornings and afternoons, while she painted, and music in the evenings. The composers about whom she wrote poems were Mozart, Schubert, Chopin, and Beethoven. Her favorite was apparently Beethoven, on whom she wrote the sonnet beginning

> If God speaks anywhere, in any voice,
> To us, his creatures, surely here and now
> We hear Him, while the great chords seem to bow
> Our heads, and all the symphony's breathless noise
> Breaks over us with challenge to our souls![42]

In her *Letters* she tells us that the first break in the depression brought on by her mother's death came while she listened to Paine playing Beethoven, and Annie Fields writes that it was under the same influence that Thaxter's "spirit came to a conscious sense of its own independent, disengaged existence."[43]

Celia Thaxter's personal relationships on levels profounder than that of the purely social were of the happiest sort, since she chose her friends for their human worth not for their social position or wealth. To most rural New Englanders of the time any other basis of esteem would be unthinkable; the Puritan conscience—which is said to linger like an old stain—made hypocrisy too uncomfortable. Thus Sarah Orne Jewett, the daughter of a Brahmin, wrote admiringly and without condescension of Irish immigrants[44] and counted the wives of fishermen, as well as Annie Fields, among her bosom friends; and Whittier, himself a farmer, was the friend of the humblest inhabitants of Amesbury. Similarly Celia Thaxter was most friendly with the native Shoalers and later with the immigrants newly arrived from Norway, who reminded her of the magnificent peasants in Björnson's *Arne*.

Nor was this the result of any sentimentality concerning the inevitable goodness of those living next to nature. Celia Thaxter knew that the evil side of nature manifests itself as readily in humanity of any class as in the angry sea. Her story "A Memorable Murder,"[45] is based on the almost Calvinistic theme of infinite potential for evil. The story—a truly powerful bit of prose—recites with Dostoevskian realism the true account of the ax murder on lonely Star Island, one of the Isles of Shoals, of two Norwegian women by a degenerate German who rowed out the nine miles from Portsmouth in the moonlight to commit his crime. As she describes the dory's undisturbed, moonlit progress over the unseasonably calm March sea—another instance of nature's indifference to human conception of right and wrong—one feels that here in this brutish seaman is the ultimate symbol of natural cruelty. One is reminded of Melville's characterization in *Billy Budd* of the depraved master-at-arms "in whom was the mania of an evil nature, not engendered by vicious training or corrupting books or licentious living, but born with him, in short, a 'depravity according to nature' ".[46] To Melville the existence of this "natural depravity" was a source of wonder, but to Celia Thaxter it was no more remarkable than a peculiarly destructive equinoctial gale. Thus she was able to follow with a degree of scientific detachment unknown in Melville the course of the murderer across the moonlit sound between Portsmouth and the Shoals—though not without a certain horror, such as a physician might feel on tracing the course of a cancer through a beautiful human body.

Her contemporaries, of course, wondered why she told this revolting story; the answer should have been obvious. The facing of such a phenomenon in its utter nakedness is the prerequisite to coming to any real terms with life. When one had sufficiently pondered over this nadir of human depravity, then only would one value and love fervently enough the kindness, the devotion, the love that are the summer side of human nature. Is it not proper to shudder at sadistic madness and to smile upon loving kindness?

To complete the pattern were her love of children and her success as a juvenile writer. Perhaps the most compelling tribute that can be paid the literature of this period in New England is to call attention to the great body of good children's stories that it produced. Louisa May Alcott, Sarah Orne Jewett, T.B. Aldrich, and Laura Richards are but a few of the writers in this genre, many of whom came out in and were encouraged by Mary Mapes Dodge's deservedly famous *St. Nicholas*.[47] Celia Thaxter's juvenile poems are by far the best verse she wrote. Many individual poems, like "The Sandpiper," are almost as universal as Mother Goose, and a large body of her poetry finds its way into children's anthologies and is taught in the lower grades in school. Her children's stories, too, as Van Wyck Brooks points out,[48] are exquisite, with a genuinely Andersen-like quality of wonder about them.

The state of mind is by now clear: acceptance of such evil as was inevitable and a careful nurturing of the good. Children, the friendship of agreeable people, music, birds, good reading, and good conversation—these made life worthwhile. The winter storms at sea, the depravity of a degenerate human mind, ugliness, sterility, senseless destruction of nature's beauties—these were to be avoided at all costs. Moreover, if one did not avoid them, one could not cling to life. Had not Celia Thaxter herself discovered in a fresh water pool the body of William Morris Hunt, drowned by suicide resulting from nervous depression?[49] Hunt had not bound himself strongly enough to life; he had not strongly enough loved the good, and only love can hold one to life. Life is love; and death is evil and hate.

Various derogatory epithets have been attached to the type of life led by Celia Thaxter and her contemporaries: it has been called "the genteel tradition," "Victorianism," "escapism." But one should not judge too harshly. In choosing a way of life one should be pragmatical. This Thaxter was to an eminent degree. If her fighting for the preservation of songbirds, painting china, and illustrating in watercolor copies of their own poems seem old-maidish to us, at least they are as worthwhile as such modern pastimes as reading detective stories and drinking cocktails.

Just what has been Celia Thaxter's contribution to literature? As has already been mentioned, her adult verse, widely read, was definitely second or third rate. Her popularity resulted from the fact that she represented to average Americans, particularly New Englanders, what they considered a practical and sane viewpoint and that she tussled with problems and doubts that were filling all literate minds. This adult verse —vastly overestimated by Van Wyck Brooks—will last only as an indication of the New England state of mind in her period.[50] Her children's verse and stories are, on the other hand, charming. Her long prose works, *An Island Garden* and *Among the Isles of Shoals*, are of a different caliber from her poetry. *An Island Garden*, as the name implies, is primarily a gardener's book; yet, though technical in its discussion of horticulture, its style is strong and its digressions are of interest to the general reader.

Among the Isles of Shoals is undoubtedly her most lasting work. This book—which records the history and legends of the Isles, describes their physical aspect, their atmosphere, and their inhabitants, and tells the story of Thaxter's life there—still makes fascinating reading. Originally published serially in 1869 and 1870 in the *Atlantic*, it was an instantaneous hit. Dickens, reading it on his visit to America, praised it highly, adding however, his conviction "that these Islanders must be dreadfully bored with their islands."[51] Horace Greely considered it the best piece of prose he had read in a long time,[52] and Annie Fields, somewhat over-enthusiastic, compared it to *Walden, The Natural History of Selborne,* and Jefferies's *The Story of My Heart.*

A more intelligent comparison than any of these would be with Melville's *Encantadas,* which she quotes and which her friend Lowell, who thought it contained the finest stroke of genius he had ever read in prose, may have recommended to her as a model. The plan of *Among the Isles of Shoals,* at any rate, is almost identical with that of Melville's work. Each is a description of a group of islands, with sections of flora and fauna, geographical and geological data, history, folklore, and legends, and human-interest stories. And each purposes to rise above the level of a guidebook by catching the atmosphere and mood of the places described.

And in accomplishing its purpose—the catching of the spirit of a tiny but typical corner of New England life—Celia Thaxter's book is completely successful, as any one acquainted with the New England seacoast will immediately recognize. Whittier in one of his letters to Thaxter tells how a storekeeper and his wife in Amesbury who had once lived on Matinicus Island off Rockland, Maine, were reminded by this book of their former island life. They had felt the poetry of their surroundings but had never before seen it "written out."[53] The comment of these simple people is the best that can be said of the book; and though it has not been republished in many years, it is still far from dead. Written on the urgent requests of persons who, like Whittier, had been affected by the strange, lonely beauty of the islands, it was the first and perhaps the best of the descriptions and studies of life on the New England coast. It answers realistically—with an undertone of perhaps unconscious poetry—all the questions the stranger would want to know: How does the climate affect life here? What is the history of the place? How are the people different from others? How do they earn a living? And, most important of all to mortals, what makes life here worth living?

X. MILLS AND MILL HANDS:
Lucy Larcom and Others

> Did you ever think what those sleepers are that underlie the railroad?
> Each one is a man, an Irishman, or a Yankee man. The rails are laid on
> them, and they are covered with sand, and the cars run smoothly over
> them. They are sound sleepers I assure you. And every few years a new
> lot is laid down and run over; so that, if some have the pleasure of riding
> on a rail, others have the misfortunes to be ridden upon.
>
> THOREAU, *Walden*[1]

1. Work as a Puritan Virtue

In the Puritan way of life hard work had been a virtue of equal standing
with piety and duty. Idleness, like luxury, was spawned of the devil. In the
colonizing of a wilderness no one could deny the appropriateness of this
attitude; one must either work or perish of starvation and exposure. But by
the middle of the nineteenth century, when Thoreau in *Walden* had
already questioned whether his fellow citizens were living like baboons or
like human beings, thoughtful New Englanders were modifying their
views on the sacredness of all labor. It was one thing—doubtless a highly
ennobling thing—to toil fourteen hours a day, as did the Pilgrims, to
wring a subsistence out of a barren and inclement land. It was another
thing, however, to enslave oneself for the same number of hours daily in
a factory for the purpose of enriching the manufacturer. Granted that the
manufactured product—usually textiles and shoes in New England—did
much toward fully clothing a world that under the handicraft system had
been half naked, there was still the question of profits—profits gained
from others' labor and used for a luxurious living proscribed by all
Christian and Puritan dogma.

The abolition movement first set New Englanders thinking about labor
and profits. Southerners were not the only ones to point out that
conditions in a Merrimack textile mill were not so different from those in
a Mississippi cotton field. Yet most New Englanders did not take this
extreme view; in fact the majority were not even wholeheartedly in favor
of abolition. Only a militant and noisy few questioned the conditions of

work either in the South or in the new industrial cities of the North. Thoreau in his Walden experiment proved to himself, though to very few others, that all work beyond that necessary for the essentials of life was stultifying. The noise and hurry of the new era, typified by the recently built railroad that cut across the south end of Walden Pond, seemed pure fatuity to him.

The Brook Farm and Fruitlands experiments were somewhat different attempts to solve the same problem. The founders of these communal colonies retained the Puritan ideal of manual labor as essential to character building, but they believed it should be shared by all and varied with intellectual activity. Those who worked solely with their hands would become brutish and lose contact with the life of the mind. Those who devoted themselves wholly to the mind would lose contact with important material realities. The theory was essentially the same as Tolstoy's belief that every man should do his "bread work," and had much in common with the social systems blueprinted by Fourier, Ruskin, Morris, and others dissatisfied with the conditions of industrial labor.

The collectivism of Brook Farm and the extreme individualism of Thoreau were equally distasteful to most New Englanders. The general opinion regarding the new industrialism and the accompanying degradation of labor is less easily stated than the succinct theories of the idealists. Yet there was a fairly uniform reaction, particularly in the rural districts, where the Yankee outlook was still unmixed with the alien views introduced by the immigrants. This reaction grew out of the centuries-old conditions of New England country life itself and not out of the books of political theorists, unless the Bible be considered such a book. As we have seen in an earlier chapter, the New England village, after the hardships of the first settling had been overcome, approached complete political, social, intellectual, and economic democracy. Most of the male population were voters, having voice in the town meeting and in the equally important church government. The Revolutionary ideal that all are created equal was taken so literally that even a domestic servant class as we know it today was nonexistent; the hired "help" ate and sat with their employers and felt in every way equal to them. The schools, the church, and in many instances the public libraries—in other words, the spiritual and intellectual parts of village life—were open to all and used by all who felt the desire to do so. Though there were some landless people, most families owned their farms; tramps and millionaires were both rare on the New England countryside; children thought "rich" and "poor" were storybook words, describing things as unreal as fairies or giants.[2]

In such a Jeffersonian democracy of yeomen everybody worked and took work as a matter of course. Work was the basis of family life, as family life was the basis of the community. From one's work came all the benefits that made the home enjoyable and meaningful—the bounteous family meals cooked over the hickory-fired kitchen hearth; the cattle and horse and poultry that were like lesser members of the family; the leisure for church-going, reading, and family prayer; for the community husking, apple-paring, moving, and woodcutting bees; for Fourth of July celebrations and for training days: all these were the result of work evenly divided among the members of the family and the community. It is little wonder that work was universally thought of as ennobling and pleasing to God, who rewarded it so liberally.

The rural writers of the time in New England—Rowland Robinson, Sarah Orne Jewett, Mary Wilkins Freeman, Lucy Larcom—looked at the laboring conditions of the new era from this point of view. During their childhood in their native villages the nearest thing to a modern proletariat had been the specialized artisans—a cobbler, some sempstresses, a blacksmith, possibly a carpenter or carriage maker. Lke the sturdy, lovable Uncle Lisha in Rowland Robinson's stories of pre-railroad Vermont, these skilled craftsmen no more resembled the later mill operative than the farmers did the Russian moujiks; they were generally prosperous, prominent villagers, looked up to by their neighbors and accepted on terms of equality.

2. *From Beverly to Lowell*

One writer, Lucy Larcom, made the ethics of work her special province. In her two most ambitious volumes—*A New England Girlhood* and *An Idyl of Work*—she records her experiences and thoughts as a typical Yankee mill girl in Lowell, Massachusetts. Born in 1824 in the little North Shore seaport of Beverly, she had a thoroughly New England background and upbringing. Her father, a retired shipmaster, was a respected shopkeeper dealing in West Indian imports, the first member of his family having come to Beverly in 1655. Her mother, partly of French ancestry, had a buoyancy of temperament that must have pleasantly spiced the otherwise Puritan atmosphere of the household.

"It is strange that the spot of earth where we were born should make such a difference to us,"[3] Larcom says at the beginning of *A New England Girlhood*. The difference that it made to her is the subject of some of the finest chapters of reminiscence in American literature. In this book, written for girls but delightful for persons of all ages, we are given a detailed picture of life in a Massachusetts village in the first half of the nineteenth century. Similar in purpose to that other account of a New England girlhood, Stowe's *Poganuc People*, it is vastly superior to it; told in a simpler and purer style, it lacks those characteristic blights of Stowe's writing—mawkishness, "love interest," overcomplicated plot. Like Mark Twain and like T. B. Aldrich in his *Story of a Bad Boy*, Larcom has stuck to simple facts of her childhood, without any attempt at literary embellishment.

Beverly when she lived there was a flourishing little seaport with an atmosphere like that which a generation later lingered in dilution over Jewett's Deephaven.

> Men talked about a voyage to Calcutta, or Hong-Kong, or "up the Straits",—meaning Gibraltar and the Mediterranean,—as if it were not much more than going to the next village. It seemed as if our nearest neighbors lived over there across the water; we breathed the air of foreign countries, curiously interblended with our own. . . . For part of our currency was the old-fashioned "ninepence",—twelve and a half cents, and the "four pence ha'penny",—six cents and a quarter. There was a good deal of Old England about us still. . . . Our Sabbath-school library books were nearly all English reprints.[4]

The Puritan atmosphere, too, was strong. The old Calvinistic religion held despotic sway. The Sabbath—it was still considered heathenish to use the word Sunday—began on Saturday afternoon; Christmas was ignored as a holiday, the Fourth of July and Thanksgiving alone being celebrated; the children's first reading lessons were from the Bible; and at meetings the imminent coming of the millennium was preached in sermons that dragged themselves out to "ninthlies" and "tenthlies" before the pastor pronounced the sweet-sounding "finally." As with so many of the children of old New England, Lucy's mind was early blighted with fears of Hell and death, and her overdeveloped religious faculty afflicted her all her life. She tells of childhood attempts on Sabbaths to take an interest in the more pious volumes in the family library—Scott's Commentaries on the Bible, Harvey's *Meditations Among the Tombs,* Young's *Night Thoughts,* "Edwards on the Affections," though on weekdays Walter Scott, Bunyan, and even poets like Byron, Wordsworth, and Coleridge were permissible reading. Rather pathetically, her earliest pleasure as a small child was in singing hymns, of which she memorized hundreds and the metrics of which spoiled almost every poem she ever wrote, since, unlike Emily Dickinson, she did not have the genius to transform their crude prosody into great verse.

At the age of thirteen, when living in Lowell, she underwent conversion, and, subscribing to the theology of the Westminster Assembly, became a member of the Orthodox Church. In later life she regretted this youthful haste. She found that she could not conscientiously believe in many of the pivotal doctrines of her church, among them the Atonement, Predestination, and the verbal inspiration of the Bible. Above all, she disliked the Calvinists' preoccupation with doctrinal quibbles rather than with the fundamentals of Christianity. Like most thinking New Englanders after the Civil War, she rejected the Hebraic God of wrath for the God of love preached by Christ. The emphasis in Christianity in New England had shifted from the Old Testament to the New. After much agony of conscience Lucy Larcom in her old age found peace in Phillips Brooks's Trinity Church and its religion based on the Beatitudes rather than on the Decalogue. A lifetime and the ministrations of one of the world's greatest physicians of the soul had been needed to heal the spiritual lacerations inflicted in her childhood in the Old South Church of Beverly.

But there had been antidotes to this religious poison of her childhood. One of nine children, she knew the security as well as the companionship of a large family. The great kitchen with its open fireplace, its brick ovens, its settle—for this was before the era of stoves—she always remembered as a symbol of domestic happiness. The beauty of the sea and landscape around Beverly—then completely rural—became an early passion with her. Looking at the stars as a child, she had an ecstatic intuition of a pre-existence like that described in Wordsworth's great "Ode."

> I did firmly believe that I came from some other country to this; I had a vague notion that we were all here on a journey,—that this was not the place where we really belonged.[5]

All her life she had a Wordsworthian love of nature as a manifestation of deity; her yearly trips to the White Mountains after middle age were virtually religious pilgrimages.

Although her family were "indifferent and ignorant as to questions of pedigree,"[6] her growing consciousness of the part her ancestors played in the two-hundred-year-old history of Beverly gave her that same fortifying sense of belonging to a great tradition that was so important in Sarah Orne Jewett's life. Living elsewhere during the greater part of her adulthood, she always retained her allegiance to her birthplace. During a bribery investigation involving Beverly she wrote both to the newspapers and to the governor in defense of her native town. When George Woodberry, the Beverly-born poet, published his first verses she went out of her way to write him a congratulatory letter. After comparing him favorably with Clough and even Milton, she adds: "I am proud, too, that you are a Beverly boy, as I am a Beverly woman."[7] It is fashionable to sneer at this sort of local patriotism; yet the sense of having roots, of belonging to something worthy of pride, is all too scarce in America for the happiness of its citizens. With Larcom love of home must be placed with her love of family and her love of nature as a stabilizing force in a lonely, wandering life.

In 1835, when Lucy was eleven years old, the death of her father forced the family to move to Lowell in search of a livelihood. The new city on the Merrimack had become known throughout the world as a sociological and mechanical marvel. Its system of canals for the utilization of waterpower was the last word in hydraulic engineering. Its labor policy was equally extraordinary, especially to Europeans used to a degraded proletariat. Charles Dickens, who visited the city while Lucy Larcom was still a mill hand there, gives in his *American Notes* a famous, if somewhat sketchy, picture of the "Lowell System." It was the policy of the corporations to recruit their "help," which by the nature of the work was primarily female, from the farming communities of Maine, New Hampshire, Vermont, and western Massachusetts. Most of the girls, of thrifty, God-fearing families like Lucy Larcom's, were instilled with all the ideals and inhibitions of old-fashioned Puritanism. As a rule they came to Lowell only for temporary work. One girl might wish to earn money to further her brother's education or her own; another might be helping to pay off the mortgage on the family farm; another might wish to lay aside a dowry for future housekeeping. Contrasting these workers with the grimy, undernourished hordes of Manchester or Birmingham, Dickens writes:

> I cannot recall or separate one young face that gave me a painful impression; not one young girl whom, assuming it to be a matter of necessity that she should gain her daily bread by the labour of her hands, I would have removed from those works if I had had the power.[8]

The founders of the mills, Francis Cabot and Nathan Appleton, had purposely attempted not to duplicate in the great new Merrimack city the conditions of the Old World. The lives of the operatives were made as pleasant and wholesome as possible. In accordance with the concepts of the day, each girl was required to attend some church; there were a free Grammar School and many night schools; there was a well-equipped operatives' hospital; strict curfews were enforced; and the operatives' boarding houses, one of which the widow Larcom kept after coming to Lowell, were run only by the most respectable matrons and had to measure up to rigid standards set by the corporations.

For relaxation many of these earnest country girls cultivated an interest in reading and writing. Lucy Larcom tells how she and her fellow workers smuggled pages torn out of books into the mills to read in their spare time, thus circumventing a regulation against reading books (interpreted as *whole* books by the girls) during working hours. On the walls of the window alcoves, which were enlivened with potted plants, they pasted clippings of poems to be read during stray moments of leisure. Next to theology, that subject perennially dear to the New England mind, the chief topic of conversation among the girls was the reading they had done outside of work. Some of the girls subscribed to the outstanding British and American periodicals—*Blackwood's Magazine, The Westminster Review, The North American Review.* Carlyle's *Heroes and Hero-Worship*, lent to Lucy Larcom by a Dartmouth student, brought them "a startling and keen enjoyment."[9] Their reading lists included Locke's *Essay on Human Understanding,* Milton's *Paradise Lost,* Cotton Mather's *Magnalia,* Pope, Dryden, Jeremy Taylor, Shakespeare, and many standard contemporary authors like Dickens, Lowell, and Tennyson. No wonder that the night schools flourished and lyceum-lecturers like Emerson would find the Lowell halls crowded with an attentive audience drawn largely from the mill workers.

Some of the girls found time from their reading, studying, Sunday-school teaching, and walks in the surrounding countryside, to establish their own literary magazines. Out of several ventures of this kind crystalized the famous *Lowell Offering,* which achieved a national circulation of four thousand and was favorably commented on and quoted by other journals. The merit of the magazine, to which Lucy Larcom contributed many pieces, has undoubtedly been exaggerated; probably it would not have surpassed most college literary magazines and would have won little recognition if the public imagination had not been stimulated by the fact that it had been written by mill girls. Yet Dickens's enthusiastic estimate of it is interesting:

> Of the merits of the *Lowell Offering* as a literay production, I will only observe, putting entirely out of sight the fact of the aricles having been written by these girls after the arduous labours of the day, that it will compare advantageously with a great many English Annuals. It is pleasant to find that many of its Tales are of the Mills and of those who work in them; that they inculcate habits of self-denial and contentment, and teach good doctrines of enlarged benevolence. A strong feeling for the beauties of nature, as displayed in the solitudes the writers have left at home, breathes through its pages like wholesome village air; and though a circulating library is a favourable school for the study of such topics, it has very scanty allusion to fine clothes, fine marriages, fine houses, or fine life.[10]

3. The Yankee Girl

When we consider the high standards of womanhood in New England at this time, there was nothing remarkable in these Lowell mill girls and the humane treatment accorded them. The Yankee Girl had become an ideal and she had taken her idealization seriously enough to try to live up to it. The idealization of the New England woman had begun at least as far back as 1723, when Jonathan Edwards wrote his famous purple passage about his future wife, Sarah Pierrepont, whom he had hardly seen:

> They say there is a young lady in [New Haven] who is beloved of that Great Being, who made and rules the world, and that there are

certain seasons in which this Great Being, in some way or other invisible, comes to her and fills her mind with exceeding sweet delight, and that she hardly cares for anything, except to meditate on him—that she expects after a while to be received up where he is; being assured that he loves her too well to let her remain at a distance from him always . . . Therefore, if you present all the world before her, with the richest of its treasures, she disregards it. . . . She has a strange sweetness in her mind, and singular purity in her affections; . . . and you could not persuade her to do any thing wrong or sinful, if you would give her all the world. . . . She is of a wonderful sweetness, calmness and universal benevolence of mind; especially after this Great God has manifested himself to her mind. She will sometimes go about from place to place singing sweetly; and seems to be always full of joy and pleasure; and no one knows for what. She loves to be alone, walking in the fields and groves, and seems to have some one invisible always conversing with her.[11]

This passage has been given so fully because it sets the style for so many women characters in later American literature. Harriet Beecher Stowe quotes it in her *Minister's Wooing,* with the implication that her heroine, Mary Scudder, beloved by Edwards's great disciple, Samuel Hopkins, measures up to its specifications.[12] But in most cases there was no conscious reference to Edwards. Veneration of womanhood—particularly rural and small-town womanhood—was part of the spirit of the age. Timothy Dwight, in his *Travels in New England and New York,* adulates the women he met, finding them everywhere to be orderly and energetic in mind, quiet in disposition, and physically handsome.[13] Thomas Wentworth Higginson in his novel *Malbone* selected his high-minded heroine from among "the daughters of old ministers and well-to-do shopkeepers in small New England towns,"[14] and these were the best-educated and most capable girls in America. William Dean Howells used the type over and over again as heroines for his novels. Lydia Blood in *The Lady of the Aroostock,* for example, is at first regarded by her shipmates as a rather pitiable provincial. After all, she is only a schoolteacher from a backwoods town who in the enforced intimacy of a European voyage has been temporarily cast in with a group of Boston sophisticates. But before the Atlantic is half crossed one of the Bostonians is in love with her and the other recognizes her for the fine-spirited, self-reliant person she is. The American Girl had, in fact, become a stereotype in her country's literature in the nineteenth century, and she was by no means confined to the New England countryside, though her original habitat seems to have been there. She is omnipresent in Henry James's novels—appearing as Verena Tarrant in *The Bostonians,* as Daisy Miller in the novel that bears her name, and as Bessie Alden in *An International Incident.* Like Howells's Lydia Blood, these young women astound American or European society with their guileless disregard of convention. Yet they invariably end by winning the admiration of even the most blasé. With their "sweetness, calmness, and universal benevolence of mind," to use Edwards's phrase, they carry millionaires and dukes before them, and in the gleaming armor of their innocence and self-sufficiency they stand a triumphant symbol of the superiority of American democracy over the effete aristocracy of Europe or the Europeanized American *haut monde*.

4. An Idyl of Work

The mill owners of Lowell had a similar idea of American womanhood when they took such care in creating the proper environment for the girls who left their respectable farm and village homes to work for them.[15] But the girls themselves had very definite notions as to what was their due. The most complete expression of these notions is found in two books of Lucy Larcom—*A New England Girlhood* and *An Idyl of Work*.

In *A New England Girlhood* Larcom tells how at the age of eleven she got a job changing bobbins on the spinning frames in one of the Lowell mills. Her working hours were from five in the morning to seven at night, and her wages were one dollar a day plus a dollar and a quarter allowance for board. Modern labor unions would certainly disapprove of these conditions. Yet Larcom records no permanent damage done her by the experience. With the exception of the three months yearly that every child worker was required to spend in school, she worked steadily at one job or another for eleven years, after which she migrated to the Illinois prairies with her sister. In fact, writing of these days fifty years later—after a lifetime as a teacher and author—she finds them in many ways rewarding. If one didn't wish to make more than two or three dollars a week, one could do work that left much leisure time for reading or talking on the job. Many interests could be cultivated and lasting friendships formed. Larcom especially liked the sturdy girls from the hills of northern New England, and from them she learned to love the mountains long before she had ever seen anything higher than the pastoral slopes of northeastern Massachusetts.

There is no doubt that the atmosphere of comradeship and serious intellectual endeavor that these mill girls lived in during the early days of Lowell went far to alleviate the inhumane working hours and the miserable wages. But neither the girls nor the operators would have seen anything wrong or unusual in a fourteen-hour day or even in child labor, so long as time was provided for schooling. The Puritan tradition among all economic classes must again be reckoned with. As Larcom writes,

> We learned no theories about "the dignity of labor", but we were
> taught to work almost as if it were a religion; to keep at work, expecting

nothing else. It was our inheritance, handed down from the outcasts of Eden. And for us, as for them, there was a blessing hidden in the curse.[16]

On a New Hampshire hill farm or in a Maine coast fisherman's cottage work would begin even before five in the morning and end well after seven in the evening. Girls brought up to believe that such toil is the primary condition of life could not be expected to rebel at similar conditions in the mills.

On one thing they did insist: work can place no stigma on the individual; persons must be judged by what they are, not by the work they do, provided it be honest. Lucy Larcom ardently subscribed to this credo. She writes in her preface to *An Idyl of Work:*

> That any work by which mankind is benefited can degrade the workers seems an absurd idea to be met with in a Christian republic, and whatever shadow of it lingers among us is due to the influence of that feudal half civilization from which we have only partially emerged, and to which, through a morbid desire for wealth, show, and luxury, we are in danger of returning.
>
> Labor, in itself, is neither elevating nor otherwise. It is the laborer's privilege to ennoble his work by the aim with which he undertakes it. . . .[17]

The significance of Larcom's *An Idyl of Work* and the chapters on Lowell in *A New England Girlhood* stems from the fact that she wrote these in a generation after the experiences narrated in them. In that generation, which included the Civil War, New England had undergone a transformation from an agricultural region to an area devoted primarily to manufacturing. Under the stimulus of war factories had sprung up along every river, from its mouth to its headwaters high in the northern hill country.[18] Larcom during this time had spent a number of years with her sister in Illinois, where she had finally received, at Monticello Seminary, the education she had dreamt about while changing bobbins in the Lowell mills. Returning to the East, she served long as a professor of literature at Wheaton, all the time writing poetry and juveniles for current magazines. An inner religious conflict born of the divergence of Puritanism from what she considered the true spirit of the New Testament was perhaps her main preoccupation during these years. But she was also pondering the question of labor—the philosophy of work and the place of the working people in the modern world.

Her most extensive treatment of this subject was *An Idyl of Work,* a blank-verse epic of twelve "books" erected on the flimsy framework of a sentimental love story. Written by a woman who as a child had read

Cowper's *The Task* and Young's *Night Thoughts* as religious literature, this ambitious poem is the dying gasp of that tradition of eighteenth-century didacticism that at its worst produced such dreary abortions as James Grainger's *The Sugar-Cane* and John Dyer's *The Fleece*, poetic treatises on the West Indian sugar industry and British wool-raising respectively. But Larcom had the Puritan's sense of duty in writing this work, which was dedicated to working women "by one of their sisterhood." Her digressive passages, which as in all such works are multitudinous and protracted, contain her reactions to the insistent problems introduced by the machine age.

There can be no doubt that Larcom's reactions were typical—much more so, for example, than Edward Bellamy's. Village people like her are everywhere bound by tradition; but in New England villages "the social lag" sometimes amounted to almost a standstill. Eighteenth-century thinking had so indelibly impressed Larcom as a child in Beverly, that she was a century behind the times even in her versification. In reading *An Idyl of Work* we must not expect to find any startling solutions to industrial problems. But we will find the reaffirmation of some eighteenth-century Puritan ideas, some of which the twentieth century would do well not to ignore.

What were some of the propositions that Larcom and others of the post–Civil War generation believed in? To begin with, she believed in equality. Discrimination based on wealth, color, work, or sex was untenable. The poem opens with a definition of the word "lady."

> " 'Lady' or 'girl' or 'woman',
> Whichever word you choose", said Esther, "each
> Means excellence and sweetness. 'Lady', though
> Can slip its true sense, leaving an outside
> Easy to imitate. At first it meant
> 'Giver of loaves'. . . ."[19]

While Larcom ridiculed the fatuous use of the word "lady" in such compounds as "saleslady," "chamberlady," and "washerlady," she did very firmly believe that its earlier connotation of sympathy and service was better exemplified by these factory-*girls*—certainly they were not foolish enough to wish to be called "factory-ladies"—than by those females of merely external elegance who claimed sole right to the title.[20] The relation between employer and employee should be that found on New England farms of an early era.

> . . . The Old-time 'help',—
> In our Republic, service means just that,
> And all house-masters and house-mistresses

Should hold to that idea,—'help', that came
Into a family of ample wealth
And not luxurious tastes, or into one
Less favored, bringing kindness, conscience, strength,
Would be given leisure, would find sympathy,
Also abundant freedom. This has been,—
May be once more—in the millennium![21]

With the increased stratification of social life in New England, particularly in the cities, the "hired help" became "servants." As a result the independent farm girls refused that sort of service and welcomed the chance to work in the mills, where their self-respect would be less likely to be bruised[22]—until "factory help" degenerated into "hands."

It was also necessary for the self-respect of these mill girls that they consider their work of benefit to humanity. Aiding the rich to live in idle luxury would be even more degrading than accepting the status of a servant. Working in a factory—weaving cloth, making shoes, sewing clothes—was beneficial to humankind; this was the sort of toil to which Adam had been condemned by God, and, though toil, must be pleasing to the condemner. Larcom writes:

> That the manufacture of cloth should, as a branch of feminine industry, ever have suffered a shadow of discredit, will doubtless appear to future generations a most ridiculous barbarism. To prepare the clothing of the world seems to have been regarded as womanly work in all ages. The spindle and the distaff, the picturesque accompaniments of many an ancient legend—of Penelope, of Lucretia, of the Fatal Sisters themselves—have, to be sure, changed somewhat in their modern adaptation to the machinery which robes the human millions; but they are, in effect, the same instruments, used to supply the same need, at whatever period of the world's history.[23]

Those who question whether mere textile workers have ever reasoned thus about their work do not have the slightest conception of the Puritan character. As Harriet Beecher Stowe says in *The Minister's Wooing*, "in no other country" but New England "were the soul and the spiritual life ever such intense realities, and everything contemplated so much (to use a current New England phrase) 'in reference to eternity.' "[24] That the spiritual touchstone should not be applied to a part of life so important as one's work would be unthinkable, even in the days of relaxed Puritanism in which Lucy Larcom writes. As time went on the Lowell mill girls did begin to question the spiritual implications of their work, as many a page in Larcom's writings testifies.

5. Questionings

The first questionings were stimulated by the abolition movement, which
swept up the New England conscience like a whirlwind. Even the most
lethargic conscience might have been pricked by the situation the textile
workers of antislavery sentiment found themselves in. In *An Idyl of Work*
Larcom writes:

> . . . Labor is not always beautiful.
> To much that is distasteful we're compelled
> By circumstances. For our daily bread,
> We, who must earn it, have to suffocate
> The cry of conscience, sometimes.
> When I've thought,
> . . . what soil the cotton-plant
> We weave, is rooted in, what waters it,—
> The blood of souls in bondage,—I have felt
> That I was sinning against light, to stay
> And turn the accursed fibre into cloth
> For human wearing. I have hailed one name,
> You know it—"Garrison"—as a slave might hail
> His soul's deliverer. Am not I enslaved
> In finishing what slavery has begun?[25]

So ardent an abolitionist was Larcom that she broke permanently with the
one serious lover she ever had, because their opinions on slavery differed.
Out of this experience came the poem "A Loyal Woman's No," in which,
as in Whittier's "The Yankee Girl," an abolitionist maiden proclaims to
her pro-slavery suitor:

> Not yours,—because you are not man enough
> To grasp your country's measure of a man.
> If such as you, when Freedom's ways are rough,
> Cannot walk in them, learn that women can![26]

It was not the physical conditions of work but the spiritual condition of
the worker that concerned New Englanders like Larcom. Child labor, a
fourteen-hour day, and three-dollars-a-week wages did not concern these
latter-day Puritans so long as the workers retained their freedom and their
full measure of dignity as individuals. But once let these two conditions—
so primary in a religion in which individuals' relation with their creator,
rather than with society, is emphasized—be jeopardized and there is
violent protest. The stifling of a human soul so that it could not work out
is own fulfillment on earth and later in heaven was thought of as a terrible
sin. Harriet Beecher Stowe repeats over and over again that it is the

spiritual implications of slavery that are most regrettable. Slaves with the kindest master still must have their freedom if they are to have full human stature.

When shortly after the Civil War New Englanders discovered that the factory system was dehumanizing workers more subtly perhaps than chattel slavery had done, but as inevitably, they were no less outspoken than in regard to the older evil. Gradually they began to realize that fourteen hours of drudgery in a factory were different from fourteen hours of toil on one's own farm or in one's own home; the relations of the physical with the spiritual conditions of work were more clearly understood. Yet the spiritual effects—the human waste of the factory system—were most deplored. In *An Idyl of Work* Miriam, a wealthy friend of the girls who figure in the poem, ponders the question thus:

> She asked herself if she, in girlhood's dawn,
> Would have striven through such hindrances, if she
> Would not have yielded to despair, and drudged,
> And only drudged, her daily fourteen hours,—
> Their work-day's length, nor ever touched a book,
> Or nursed an aspiration.
>   Miriam shared
> With all New-Englanders an honest pride
> In the provincial energy and sense;
> But this was waste,—this woman-faculty
> Tied to machinery, part of the machine
> That wove cloth, when it might be clothing hearts
> And minds with queenly raiment. She foresaw
> The time must come when mind itself would yield
> To the machine, or leave the work to hands
> Which were hands only.
>   Just to think of it!
> Minta, so full of health, ability,
> And right aspirings; Esther, whom she felt
> At least an intellectual equal; and—
> This most unfit of all—sweet Eleanor,
> A flower of delicate birth and saintly-pure;—
> These counted but as "hands!" named such!
>   No! No!
> It must not be at all, or else their toil
> Must be made easier, larger its reward!
> These girls, too, from their talk, were not so far
> Above the rest. Here was a problem, then
> For the political theorist: how to save
> Mind from machinery's clutches.[27]

It must be remembered that Lucy Larcom wrote this poem in 1875, thirty years after her own experiences in the Lowell mills. During that time she had become less Calvinistic and more humanitarian, without losing the Puritan's intensity of feeling or moral earnestness. The change was reflected in a concern with material conditions of work, which, according to her own accounts, she did not have while actually working under them. She had also read such English social critics as Morris and Ruskin, who were deeply concerned over the dehumanizing effects of mass production and division of labor on the modern worker, as compared with the spiritual fulfillment that the medieval artisan experienced in work. The result was that by the age of fifty she had a social philosophy that was greatly broadened by experience and reading but that was still deeply grounded in the religious and moral training of her New England girlhood. One can sneer at the slowness of Larcom's apprehension of evils that lay under her nose. Certainly Thoreau at the age of twenty had advanced far beyond her. But many writers were equally laggard. For example, Howells was in his fifties before, as recorded in *Annie Kilburn,* he could look into a textile mill and realize that the machines were as alive as the workers.[28]

Lucy Larcom's alarm over the new social dispensation was as grave as that of the later Howells or of Bellamy. With her Puritan fearlessness of the truth she contrasts the lot of the modern permanent proletariat with that of the mill girls with whom she worked as a child in Lowell. Like Howells, she seemed to come to the conclusion that "no one was meant to work in a mill all his life."[29] On the concluding pages of *An Idyl of Work* she writes:

> Like the sea
> Must the work-populations ebb and flow,
> So only fresh with healthful New-World life.
> If high rewards no longer stimulate toil,
> And mill-folk settle to a stagnant class,
> As in old civilizations, then farewell
> To the Republic's hope! What differ we
> From other feudalisms? Like ocean-waves
> Work-populations change. No rich, no poor,
> No learned, and no ignorant class or caste
> The true Republic tolerates; interfused,
> Like the sea's salt, the life of each through all.
>
> In that third decade past, thoughts grave as these
> Could scarcely visit the young toiler's mind,
> Who knew her labor transient; who at will
> Took up or dropped her shuttle, well assured
> That life had various need of her two hands.
> Mill-work meant then a fresh society
> Of eager, active youth, long held apart
> In rustic hamlets; that, like flint and steel,
> Meeting, struck light from faculties unknown.

* * * * *

That hour
Can never be repeated. Whoso toils
To-day toils in a different atmosphere.
The chariot-wheels of Progress fill the air
With dust.—Yes, it was something to be born
While this gray Mother Century was young.[30]

6. Remedies

Though the most respectable of the mill girls in Lowell occasionally helped
in organizing and successfully carrying out strikes,[31] Lucy Larcom, like
others of her time, felt that striking was an instance of making the better
cause the worse.

> ... There had been
> Meetings, conventions; now and then a girl
> Spoke on the rostrum for herself, and such
> As felt aggrieved. Ruth did not like that course,
> Nor "strikes", that ever threatened. "Why should we,
> Battling oppression, tyrants be ourselves,
> Forcing mere brief concession to our wish?
> Are not employers human as employed?
> Are not our interests common? If they grind
> And cheat as brethren should not, let us go
> Back to the music of the spinning-wheel,
> And clothe ourselves at hand-looms of our own,
> As did our grandmothers. The very name
> Of 'strike' has so unwomanly a sound,
> If not inhuman, savoring of old feuds
> And savage conflicts! If indeed there is
> Injustice,—if the rule of selfishness
> Must be, invariably, mill-owners' law,
> As the dissatisfied say,—if evermore
> The laborer's hire tends downward, then we all
> Must elsewhere turn; for nobody should moil
> Just to add wealth to men already rich.
> Only a drudge will toil on, with no hope
> Widening from well-paid labor".[32]

Liberals like Professor Parrington[33] have scoffed at the spineless means
by which these New England woman writers would combat the social
injustice they sometimes describe so fearlessly. For example, Elizabeth
Stuart Phelps of Andover, the author of such mawkish religious works as
Gates Ajar and *Hedged In*, had lamely recommended a return to true
Christian principles as a remedy for the evils of industrialism as she
described them in her book *The Silent Partner*. But if Phelps derived her

social thinking from the New Testament, another writer on the labor question, Mary Wilkins Freeman, went back to the Old Testament for hers. Freeman's *The Portion of Labor* was as realistic and outspoken a book on its subject as had yet appeared. Writing at the turn of the century, she found Lucy Larcom's forebodings justified; the mill-folk, Yankee and immigrant alike, had already settled into a "stagnant class," out of which there was no hope of arising, as there had been in Larcom's Lowell days. All the wretchedness associated with such a class is presented: a bitter strike in which two men are shot, starvation, suicides, family feuds, broken homes, insanity—the prolific brood of poverty married to despair. Yet at the end she can only have one of her chief characters, Andrew, quote Solomon:

> To-day, ever since he had heard of his good fortune, his mind had dwelt upon certain verses of Ecclesiastes. Now he quoted from them. "Live joyfully with the wife whom thou lovest all the days of the life of thy vanity, which He hath given thee under the sun, all the days of thy vanity, for that is thy portion in this life and in thy labor which thou takest under the sun. . . . I withheld not my heart from any joy, for my heart rejoiced in all my labor, and that was my portion of labor". Then Andrew thought of the hard winter which had passed, as all hard things must pass, of the toilsome lives of those beside him, of all the work which they had done with their poor, knotted hands, of the tracks which they had worn on the earth towards their graves, with their weary feet, and suddenly he seemed to grasp a new and further meaning for that verse of Ecclesiastes.
>
> He seemed to see that labor is not alone for itself, not for what it accomplishes of the tasks of the world, not for its equivalent in silver and gold, not even for the end of human happiness and love, but for the growth in character of the laborer.[34]

Such a conclusion might have validity for a person with a Puritan background like that of Freeman. The notion that the earth is a testing-ground of character has its roots deep in the Calvinistic past. But the modern sociologist like Parrington can find small comfort in the thought that "God works in mysterious ways his wonders to perform." The dreary round of miseries that afflicts the laborers in Freeman's book strikes him as representing human stupidity or pigheadedness rather than the will of God.

None of the rural New England writers of the time offered any detailed or very practical remedy for the industrial cancer that was consuming their green and pleasant land. Any sort of collective living was unthinkable to them. Like Hawthorne, Emerson, and Thoreau, they rejected the Brook Farm experiment on the grounds that it sacrificed spiritual individuality for material security. They approved of the Brook Farmers' belief in the dignity of manual labor, but they disliked the communal conditions in which the workers lived. In a conversation in Larcom's *An Idyl of Work* the New England attitude is summed up. A girl has just asked:

> "Is there no way to give each a fair chance?"
> "Why, yes", said Miriam. "Have you never heard
> Of the Brook Farm experiment, now being tried?
> A well-born friend of mine was there, for weeks,
> Doing her share of menial work, to give
> Others free hours for study: and she learned,
> In that community, to reverence hands
> Hardened by useful toil, no less than brows
> Bent with the weight of thought."
>   "But there's no home
> For any one, in everybody's home;
> And home's the very best of selfish things
> In all this selfish world," said Eleanor.
> " 'In families He sets the solitary';
> 'In phalansteries', Fourier would say.
> Esther, and our one little room, is more
> To me than ten Brook Farms".
>   "And, on the whole,
> Miss Willoughby, I'd rather struggle on,
> And puzzle out my problem by myself",
> Said Minta; " 'tis the simplest thing to do;
> I will ask no man's help or blessing. Laugh!
> And laugh you will. . . ."[35]

The mill girl Minta was not the last New Englander to be reluctant to hand over her personal problems to the state to solve. Perhaps this atavistic individualism, inherited from six generations of lonely struggle with one's own individual soul, is retarding New England and America in what some consider an evolutionary tendency toward a wholesome collectivism. In this problem as in all others the New Englander turns to the past for a solution rather than to the future. It is in this respect that Lucy Larcom is so typical. Observing the progressive degradation of labor over a period of fifty years, she can only lament the more favorable conditions of her youth. New approaches seem superfluous. The three-century–old "spiritual reference" of New England should still be valid. Equality and inviolability of the individual, the dignity of all useful work, the teachings of the Bible, would appear to these persons as sufficient foundations for the good life. And they were right, except that they did not have the vision to apply these principles to the industrial era. Larcom's recommendation that we go back to weaving our own cloth if the mill owners oppress their employees is, of course, pathetically naive. Yet Edward Bellamy, with the same New England "moral earnestness" as Larcom, and with much the same small-town, Calvinistic background, was able to envisage a system in which both the machine and the essentials of Christianity were retained. That Bellamy's Utopia was utopian, no one will deny; but its chances of realization are far greater than the chances that we will scrap our machines and return to the handicraft age. But Bellamy was not a typical New Englander or American, as recent history exemplifies. The typical attitude is that of the Larcoms and the Phelpses. It is an attiutde of the conscience rather than the reason and imagination, as with Bellamy. In New England, when the rift between timeworn principles and present actualities grows too wide, the conscience steps in and attempts to narrow the rift. The pull is from two directions: the old principles are stretched forward to meet the new conditions and the new conditions are pushed backwards to meet the old principles. The rift is never wholly closed; it is simply narrowed to bridgeable dimensions.

XI. FOREIGNERS

> In the distinctions of the genius of the American race it is to be considered that it is not indiscriminate masses of Europe that are shipped hitherward, but the Atlantic is a sieve through which only or chiefly the liberal, adventurous, sensitive, *American-loving* part of each city, clan, family are brought.
>
> EMERSON, Journals[1]

The Genteel Tradition, as George Santayana termed the upper-class smugness that afflicted America from the end of the Civil War to the turn of the century, was in general unfriendly to "foreigners," as all immigrants and first- or second-generation descendants of non-Protestant immigrants were called. Professor Parrington in *The Beginnings of Critical Realism in America* has justly castigated this attitude toward the class that more than any other did the dirty work in building the railroads and staffing the factories that gave the nation a hitherto-unknown prosperity. Particularly does he frown upon that archbishop of the Genteel and editor of the *Atlantic Monthly*, Thomas Bailey Aldrich, who wrote against immigration with all the fanaticism of a Ku Klux Klanner or a Christian Frontist. The best known statement of his bigotry is found in the versified monstrosity called "Unguarded Gates," in which he recommends closing the door in the face of all those underprivileged Europeans who took the Declaration of Independence and the broadsides of the Carnegie Steel Company seriously enough to want to try their fortunes on this side of the Atlantic. But compared with his letters, "Unguarded Gates" is a model of restraint.

> I believe in America for the Americans; I believe in the widest freedom and the narrowest license, and I hold that jail-birds, professional murderers, amateur lepers . . . and human gorillas generally should be closely questioned at our Gates.[2]

He believes that one can apply to every city government in the nation Kipling's description of New York's government as "a despotism of the alien, by the alien, for the alien, tempered with occasional insurrections of decent folk!"[3] Carrying his hackneyed train of thought out to the last stereotype, he predicts that "we shall have bloody work in this country . . .

147

when the lazy *canaille* get organized. They are the spawn of Santerre and Fouquier-Tinville."[4]

Was the attitude of New Englanders in general accurately reflected by the editor of its chief literary organ? The descendant of an ancient and honored New England family, Aldrich had been born and spent part of his boyhood in Portsmouth, New Hampshire, a typical habitat, according to Dr. Holmes, of the Brahmin class. But during his formative years and later he had also lived in New Orleans and New York. When at the age of thirty he resumed permanent residence in New England it was in Boston. Despite the wholesome boyhood described in that likable book, *The Story of a Bad Boy*, he was subjected more to the genteel refinements of upper-class city life, whether in the South, New York, or New England, than to the intensely free, democratic life of the New England countryside or village. He was the child of the rather snobbish tradition of which he was later to be chief champion.

In evaluating Aldrich it is helpful to differentiate between rural and urban America; between the New England of small villages and isolated farms and the New England of Beacon Hill, Boston, or Hillhouse Avenue in New Haven. These are two different worlds living in two different traditions. On the countryside in New England and in the two-thirds of the nation settled by New Englanders the old village democracy still prevailed; regardless of wealth or occupation the people mingled freely in school, church, town meeting, and, to a great extent, in each other's homes. The social dispensation described in books like Harriet Beecher Stowe's *Poganuc People* and Rowland Robinson's *Uncle Lisha's Shop* was yet extant in Aldrich's lifetime. But in the great cities the aristocratic tradition, never dead since Colonial times, was receiving a new lease on life. The wealthy old-time Americans carefully isolated themselves from their shirt-sleeved fellows, whether of Yankee or immigrant stock; they established or appropriated their own schools and colleges (Groton, St. George's, Amherst, Yale) and their own churches (usually Episcopal), and, being unable to create a political as well as a theological and educational aristocracy, they withdrew from both national and local government, leaving it to the *canaille*, whom they later cursed for doing a bad job. To justify their exclusiveness, these people dreamed up a tradition—the Genteel Tradition—which in Parrington's words "had become the refuge of a stale mentality, emptied of all ideals save beauty, and that beauty become cold and anemic. Its taboos were no more than cushions for tired or lazy minds."[5]

In the nature of things this tradition was representative of a very small portion of the urban and of virtually none of the rural population of America. In New England Aldrich was the only major writer who was wholeheartedly of the Genteel. He was also the only one of the new generation of writers who was so closely identified with Boston—that is, with the Back Bay and Beacon Hill. The others—Sarah Orne Jewett, Lucy Larcom, Rowland Robinson, Mary Wilkins Freeman, Rose Terry Cooke— were country or village bred and as a consequence less exclusive. To be sure, literary people are always affected by the ways of thought in the cities. With the *Atlantic* under the guidance of Aldrich—and all of these authors wrote for the *Atlantic*—one could not reasonably expect to find even in the most remote corner of the northern mountains the hard-boiled "realism" of a James Farrell or a William Faulkner. Yet the up-country writers wrote with a healthful willingness to see life as it is rather than it was dreamt to be in the salons of Boston and New York, or Bar Harbor and Newport. Only when they had the opportunity of becoming infected with "respectable" city thought did they give way to the mawkish and the goody-goody. Thus Sarah Orne Jewett frequently forgot the lessons she had learned while going the rounds with her country-doctor father down in Maine, and stooped to writing "nice" stories for her Boston acquaintances. On the other hand, Rowland Robinson, who would have been as much a stranger in Boston as in Calcutta, never permitted his earthy Vermont tang to be absent from his stories.

But the inferiority of the Genteel Tradition of the cities to the enduring vitality of the countryside and villages is best illustrated in the attitude toward "foreigners," or immigrants. T. B. Aldrich's attitudes have already been noted. Contrary to general opinion, the attitude of the rural writers was much more tolerant—a fact that even so keen and influential an observer as Parrington has failed to record.[6]

The two chief immigrant groups in rural and small-city New England in the generation following the Civil War were the Irish and the French Canadians. A few of these settled on farms, replacing Yankees who had either gone west or degenerated into an ineffectual dry-rot; but the majority were drawn to the mill towns, where work was readily available. Although the manufacturers and the states themselves encouraged immigration, it would be wrong to think the indigenous Yankee laborers and farmers invariably received the newcomers with open arms.[7] Kipling, who had lived for several years in the Connecticut Valley, writes of the native American's scorn of "foreign trash" that was insinuating itself into the government and economy of the nation.[8] This attitude is known to all Americans; it is found in New England—country and city—in no less virulent form than in other parts of the country. What is more significant is not the immemorial first reaction of the insider to the outsider; the laws of sociology could have foretold that the immigrant would have often been greeted by the average hill-farmer with exactly the same initial inhospitality as by the average Back Bayer. The tests are: How general and how long-lived is this prejudice? And how do the cultured, the educated, the so-called leaders of thought and opinion, feel about the newcomer of different race, language, or religion? The New England countryside stands a better chance of passing these tests of human decency than do most other sections of the nation, including the cities of New England itself.

The chief writer on the French Canadian was Rowland Robinson. During the time that Robinson was writing there were approximately fifteen thousand *habitants* in his native state, and he was thus afforded ample opportunity both for observation and prejudice. Robinson's reaction was certainly not that of the Good Samaritan. In his *Vermont: A Study of Independence*, he writes apropos of the western emigration from Vermont:

> To fill the place left by this drain on its population, the State has for the most part received a foreign element, which, though it keeps her numbers good, poorly compensates for her loss.
>
> Invasions of Vermont from Canada did not cease with the War of the Revolution. . . . On the contrary, an insidious and continuous invasion began. . . .[9]

At first, Robinson continues, these invaders were largely itinerant laborers who would flock over the border with their families during haying time, most of them returning to their own country after the hay was in. Robinson's keen sense of the picturesque rather than his racial bias was piqued by these mowers, who not only fulfilled a useful function but added color and spirit to Yankee farm life as they sang their ancient, rollicking peasant songs to the rhythm of their swinging scythes. But with the invention of the mowing machine, the quaint mowers gave way to hordes of French beggars, of whom Robinson writes with a pen dipped deep in the well of prejudice. "They were an abdominable crew of vagabonds, robust, lazy men and boys, slatternly women with litters of filthy brats, and all as detestable as they were uninteresting."[10]

What is the difference between Robinson's tirade against the French and Aldrich's against all foreigners? The difference, though not so pronounced as it ought to be, is just this: Robinson is ready to see—even without reluctance—any good that may be found in the French Canadians. He does not condemn all immigrants as a class and blame them for the evils that befell his state. As a matter of fact, he blames other, truer causes—the western exodus, the railroads, industry, and mechanization of farming. The Canadian influx was an effect rather than a cause. Though he was too much a Yankee not to regret the substitution of an alien race for the Vermonters who had moved away, he was always willing to recognize the excellence of the French when they deserved it. The hordes of beggars from the north must have been every bit as objectionable as human degradation everywhere can be. The fact that the *habitants* who settled in Vermont gave up their culture and religion so readily, even changing their noble French names to insipid English equivalents, also lowered them in his opinion; one would not find a Vermonter, he thought, treating his heritage so lightly.

In judging Robinson's tolerance of the French Canadian one has to rely on the preponderance of evidence. If his history of Vermont evinces a considerable degree of Aldrich-like bigotry, his other works are imbued with the humanity and broadmindedness of his Quaker ancestors. As has already been pointed out, one of the most lovable citizens of Danvis—the mythical Vermont village that furnished the characters and background for most of Robinson's stories—is the French Canadian Antoine (pronounced Ann Twine by his Yankee friends) Bissette. Next to the humorous cobbler Uncle Lisha, Ann Twine is obviously Robinson's favorite citizen of Danvis. More important, he is pictured as a favorite among his fellow villagers. Not a single Danvisite ever holds his nationality against him. On the contrary, he is accepted into the inner sanctum of Uncle Lisha's shop as one of the best of good fellows and tallest yarn-spinners. Furthermore, he conspires with his Yankee friends—in the book *Uncle Lisha's Outing*—in helping a fugitive slave on his way along the Underground Railway—a test of true humanity which by no means every native Vermonter in Robinson's books is permitted to pass. In other words, Antoine Bissette who figures prominently in a half-dozen books, is a living refutation of whatever charges of bigotry can be brought against Robinson on the basis of the few brief passages quoted from *Vermont: A Study of Independence.*

As a matter of fact, the idea so common to popular thought that the French Canadian is still despised by the general run of New Englanders is not born out by fact. Any prejudice that once existed is now almost extinct. Robinson's attitude toward Antoine was typical rather than exceptional. In the northern states, where there has been the most immigration, cooperation and neighborliness between the two groups has been the rule rather than the exception. They mingle freely in the schools, in the general-store bull sessions, in town meetings, and in many village social gatherings. Despite the barriers of religion, intermarriage is so common as hardly to excite comment from the most diehard Protestant Yankee. Thrifty, industrious, and efficient farmers, the French Canadians have proved themselves economic assets to many a decadent northern New England town. By being good citizens and good neighbors as well they have won complete acceptance and have had their share of civic honors. In Maine, New Hampshire, or Vermont, a selectman named Coté or Pelletier is as common as one named Brown or Smith.

This tolerance of immigrant groups is reflected in the works of other rural New England writers. Celia Thaxter made lifelong friends among the Norwegians who settled on her Isles of Shoals after most of the Yankees had left for less rigorous climes.[11] Of one of the immigrant women she is reported to have said, "I hope she will be with me when I die."[12]Nor was Thaxter's attitude one of condescension; it was a feeling of fellowship and respect born of many a winter of isolation together, when each person was compelled to be his or her neighbor's comforter, midwife, nurse, or undertaker. Only the most sincere friendships could survive that sort of test.

Oddly enough, the most wholehearted champion of the immigrant in New England was Sarah Orne Jewett. Though she was born in the Brahmin town of South Berwick, only a few miles from Aldrich's Portsmouth, and though for forty years she was steeped in the atmosphere of Boston, where she made months-long visits at the home of Annie Fields, no New Englander has ever treated the lives of the Irish and French Canadian immigrants more sympathetically than she. It is superfluous to say that her Boston visits could not have contributed to this humane view. Rather her thoroughly democratic feelings, nurtured throughout a childhood and girlhood as the daughter of a country doctor to whom all human beings were alike in their capabilities of both suffering and kindness, survived and overrode the bitterness that her circle of Boston acquaintance felt toward these "foreigners" who were outbreeding, outvoting, and in many ways "outsmarting" the old population. Scattered through Jewett's volumes are a half-dozen or more tales that treat with sympathy and respect the more praiseworthy qualities of the Irish: their warmth of heart, their buoyancy, their family solidarity, their willingness to work, their initiative, the depth and sincerity of their religion. In these simple human qualities Jewett believed the newcomers outshone the descendants of original settlers, who might learn a lesson from them. Like her protégée, Willa Cather, who made a similar comparison between the Central European immigrants and the Yankee homesteaders and villagers in Nebraska, she felt that the transplanting of these simple people into the materialism and ugliness of New England manufacturing towns only spoiled them and made them more miserable than they had been in the home country, despite any accumulation of money they might make. Americanization, both to Jewett and to Cather (despite her later xenophobia), was too often a process of deterioration, a substitution of artificialities for the far more worthwhile traditional values frequently brought over from the old country. Theodore Roosevelt's frenetic exhortations to all immigrants to toss overboard at Ellis Island their old-world ways of life and thought would have struck these two women as very short-sighted. Certain spiritual commodities might be imported from abroad, as well as such material things as nitrates and cheap labor.

Among Jewett's tales of the Irish are "The Luck of the Bogans,"[13] in which Dan Bogan, the son of two kindly and thrifty immigrants, is spoiled by the new environment and, taking to drink, is killed in a brawl; "Between Mass and Vespers,"[14] the story of scholarly, warm-hearted Father Ryan, who befriends another Irish youth gone bad in the new country; "A Little Captive Maid,"[15] a sentimental adaptation of the Biblical story in II Kings 5, the last days of a dying Yankee grandee being made happy by the youth and charm of a gay-hearted Irish lass who works in his house as a servant (a situation reminiscent of that in Tolstoy's *Death of Ivan Ilytch*); and "Where's Nora?,"[16] in which Irish Nora, starting with nothing, makes her way on her own initiative to a successful business career and a happy marriage, much as do some of Jewett's self-reliant farm girls in such stories as "A Dunnet Shepherdess" and "Farmer Finch." In all of these stories the Catholic Church and her conscientious, hardworking priests are praised as being the true friends of her sons and daughters and the sole guardians of the older values against the inroads of the new-world materialism. When an Irishman does go bad Jewett does not attribute the downfall to inferior blood and culture—as some would have done—but rather to the new environment. "Who of us," she writes, "have made enough kindly allowance for the homesick quick-witted ambitious Irish men and women, who have landed every year with such high hopes on our shores?"[17] She may well ask the question. It is mainly in the rural districts and from the rural writers of New England that the Catholic immigrant has achieved social place and recognition. Gladys Hasty Carroll's sympathetic and realistic treatment of the Polish farmers in a Maine community in *As the Earth Turns* is a typical present-day survival of Jewett's attitude.

One further story of Jewett's should be discussed in refutation of remarks like Parrington's that the New England rural writers of this time were down on the foreigners and were concerned solely with lamenting the vanishing grandeur of their region.[18] According to common concepts —which are usually wrong—the story "The Gray Mills of Farley" couldn't possibly have been written by a New England Brahmin. And probably it could not be written by a Bostonian New England Brahmin, if Marquand's delineation of that class in *The Late George Apley* is correct. Yet it could be—and was—written by a Brahmin from a small Maine village, where human values were still held as dear as monetary or esthetic values. "The Gray Mills of Farley," written in 1898, is laid in a small milltown in which the run-down tenements, as well as the factories, are owned by the corporation—one of those modern corporate baronies, still very common in the South, but fortunately becoming extinct in the North. In a single paragraph Jewett sums up the sociology of such towns.

> The Corporation had followed the usual fortunes of New England manufacturing villages. Its operatives were at first eager young men and women from farms near by [cf. Lucy Larcom's childhood days in Lowell], these being joined quickly by pale English weavers and spinners, with their hearty-looking wives and rosy children; then came the flock of Irish families, poorer and simpler than the others but learning the work sooner, and gayer-hearted; now the French-Canadian contingent furnished all the new help, and stood in long rows before the noisy looms and chattered in their odd, excited fashion. They were quicker-fingered, and were willing to work cheaper than any other workpeople yet.[19]

Lacking a formal plot, the piece is a sketch of this typical mill village in hard times. The plant has closed and the workers are thrown out of work. Since the French are able to return to their homes in Canada, most of the unemployed are the Irish. The way in which the people get through the depression is as inspiring in its way as the parts of *The Grapes of Wrath* in which the poor survive only through mutual assistance and neighborliness. Like Steinbeck, Jewett perceives that the greatest weapon of the poor against want and oppression is their own solidarity; and in cooperation and self-aid these impoverished mill workers are the equals of the Okies. As one of the characters says, "I don't think Ireland has ever sent us over any misers; Saint Patrick must have banished them all with the snakes."[20] But the people are not left entirely to their own resources. The fine old Catholic priest Father Daley starts a one-man public-works project by pushing the building of a new church that had long been planned for. In this way he keeps up the hope and spirits of his parishioners, at the same time returning to them in the form of wages the contributions they had made during flusher times. The mill agent also is a humanitarian, doling out seed potatoes, making personal loans to the more desperate workers, and constantly striving to reopen the mills.

In contradistinction to the people and their pastor are the avaricious mill owners. The agent had wished to declare only a six-percent dividend during the year previous to the shutdown, but the chief director and stockholder insisted on nine percent. His motives for so doing became clear when he sold out his shares during the temporary boom of the company's stocks after this generous dividend had been declared. When the inevitable collapse came the workers and lesser stockholders were left holding the bag. Being a decent person, Jewett disapproved of this sort of business. The agent's plan of cutting down on the dividends during slack periods so as to keep the men at work seemed to her a sensible and humane way of avoiding mass calamities like that which befell Farley on the closing of its only industry. Yet the agent himself was only an underling controlled by absentee directors in State and Wall Streets. Though Jewett gives no hint of any more drastic remedy than that suggested by the agent—she is not a socialist—she permits her characters to lash out against the system in most vigorous terms—and terms expressive of her own views. One outspoken but kindly Irishwoman scolds:

> "Sure the likes of us has a right to earn more than our living, ourselves being so willing-hearted. 'Tis a long time now that Mike's been steady. We always had the pride to hope we'd own a house ourselves, and a pieceen o'land, but I'm thankful now—'tis as well for us; we'd have no chances to pay taxes now."[21]

Referring to company ownership of the tenements, another woman rants:

> " 'Tis all the company cares about is to get a good rent out of the pay. They're asked every little while by honest folks 'on't they build a trifle o' small houses beyond the church up there, but no, they'd rather the money and kape us like bees in them old hives. Sure in winter we're better for having the more fires, but summer is the pinance!"[22]

In this story Jewett's habit of not seeing unpleasant things is in abeyance. She omits none of the hardships of the New England textile workers. She points out that then, as today, one wage earner in such towns is unable to keep a family. All members of the family have to work to make ends meet, and if there is an invalid to be cared for—"that heaviest of burdens to the poor"[23] ends usually don't meet. Of the little girl Maggie, whom she uses as a symbol of the evils of child labor, she incisively remarks:

> When Mrs. Kilpatrick spoke to her she answered in a hoarse voice that appealed to one's sympathy. You felt that the hot room and dry cotton were to blame for such hoarseness; it had nothing to do with the weather.[24]

One likes to think that the humanity of a Celia Thaxter, a Sarah Orne Jewett, or a Rowland Robinson is typical of the Yankee spirit. In condemning New England for intolerance, one thinks too readily of the Salem Witchcraft Delusion and the Sacco and Vanzetti case. One is too impressed perhaps by the fact that in both these cruel instances of New World bigotry two Brahmins of the Brahmins—two presidents of Harvard University—figured largely on the side of darkness. President Increase Mather and President Lowell, sincere and scholarly men though they may have been, have been poor advertisements for the humanitarianism of the Boston Brahmin class—the class to which Aldrich attached himself during his New England residence. But it is unfair and historically inaccurate to judge all New England by this minority group in a localized region. In fact the Boston and Cambridge Brahmins themselves have produced their liberals; Samuel Adams and Oliver Wendell Holmes, Jr., alone are ample counterpoises for the narrowness of Mather and Lowell.

But on the New England countryside, particularly in later years, the spirit of tolerance has been more pervasive than in the metropolis. From Roger Williams and Thomas Hooker through Ethan Allen, Whittier, Thoreau, and Edward Bellamy the village, not only in New England but in all Yankee America, has been the nursery of liberalism. The lesser New England writers that we have been discussing here—Rowland Robinson, Celia Thaxter, Sarah Orne Jewett—represented educated village opinion and feeling. Far from being leaders, they were led by the prevailing sentiments of their communities. "Foreigners," a Negro, or a Jew, wishing to find in America an environment where they could lead a life reasonably unhampered by the prejudice of their neighbors would look far before finding a more favorable spot than some small New England township. Their children would have a better experience in school, they would themselves stand a better chance of recognition in the politics, churches, fraternal organizations of the town than perhaps anywhere else in America. Dorothy Canfield's story in *Raw Material* of the sensitive southern Negro who found in a small Vermont town the only happiness of his life is by no means an isolated case. "There is very little caste feeling in our valley", Canfield explains, "and not a bit of color prejudice."[25] As Samuel Williamson pointed out in a *New York Times* article, the chief danger to Negros, the Italians, the Portuguese, or the Swedes in such a community is not that of ostracism but of becoming Yankees themselves. Perhaps it is not so desirable to be made into a Yankee, but it is probably better than to be treated as a pariah or even than to join forces with one's own kind and wage war to the death with the original inhabitants, as sometimes happens in the cities.

XII. AFTERMATH AND RENASCENCE

> The leaves on the old, old maples were all new to life, hung young, soft, transparent to the sun. And when—long months from now—their turn came to die, to be buried, to be forgotten—the next June would clothe the ancient trees in a glory for which death is but a passing episode.
>
> DOROTHY CANFIELD FISHER, *Seasoned Timber*[1]

By 1900 the indigenous literary movement of rural New England was nearing extinction. Celia Thaxter, Lucy Larcom, Rose Terry Cooke, and Rowland Robinson were dead. Mary Wilkins Freeman had moved, gladly, to New Jersey, where she was writing little except trash. Sarah Orne Jewett, identifying herself more and more with the Back Bay, had written her best work and was useful now primarily as a companion for Annie Fields and as a mentor for Willa Cather.

More somberly significant was the fact that the most promising poet ever to emerge from the area, Edwin Arlington Robinson, had before the age of thirty fled, literally to save his sanity, from the Maine town of Gardiner. Before his departure for New York he had left two volumes of poetic observations on up-country New England life—volumes to be ranked only with the work of Emerson and Emily Dickinson. Well read in New England small-town and rural letters from Hawthorne's *House of Seven Gables* to Mary Wilkins Freeman's *Pembroke,* he had used many of the well-known themes, seasoning them well, to be sure, with the tartness of his European favorites Hardy, Crabbe, and Zola. Yet Robinson did not achieve full recognition till after the war, and when recognition did come it was not primarily for his regionalism, which indeed had been becoming less important in his work with his continuing absence from Gardiner. The New England countryside was left without any considerable author.[2]

But despite a growing disrepute that it was laboring under, New England local-color writing did not vanish completely. A number of writers, in what George Santayana stigmatized as the Genteel Tradition, were still turning out pretty stories in dialect. The excessive moralizing and sentimentality that only occasionally hampered the authors of the previous generation now became the rule. In contrast to the honesty of Rowland

Robinson or Sarah Orne Jewett and the realism of Rose Terry Cooke and the early Mary Wilkins the trend of the later writers was toward the goody-goody—a total submergence in the Genteel.

Such a writer is Annie Trumbull Slosson. As there is no crime or immorality involved in being Genteel, one should approach Slosson for what she was—a short-story writer of very slender yet definitely discernible talent. Born in the seaport town of Stonington in extreme eastern Connecticut, Slosson was educated in Hartford. After her marriage she lived in New York; yet her ties with Stonington were always of the strongest and most sentimental, and she formed other ties with New England through her summerings in New Hampshire and Vermont.[3]

Her interests were varied and conventional for her time and place. An amateur naturalist like Rowland Robinson and Celia Thaxter, she managed to gather during her lifetime specimens of thirty-five thousand different kinds of insects—a collection that just before her death in 1926 she bequeathed to the American Museum of Natural History in New York. Another hobby, and one having literary consequences, was her china collecting. Her first book, *The China Hunters Club*, which was published in 1878, is a strange yet rather tasteful concoction of information on various types of old china to be found in New England, interspersed with sentimental dialect stories of Yankee rural life. Roughly, the plan is to give a description of some pieces of crockery discovered by one of the members of the club and then have the farm-woman owner of the piece nasally render the story behind it. For example, one cream pitcher in the shape of a cow had been the hiding place of a billet-doux, the discovery of which saved the life of a lovesick maiden. The sentimentality of these stories, however, accords with the sentimental picturings on much of the china, so that the book is to a degree artistically effective.

In her most impressive work, *Dumb Foxglove and Other Stories*, published in 1898, Slosson has hit upon a theme that would have borne rich fruit had she been able to confine her gushiness ever so slightly. These are stories of conscience—of women who try to square their more humanitarian instincts with their Calvinistic religion. One woman who loves animals suffers spiritual conflict because contrary to the teachings of her church she hopes and believes the souls of animals will enter heaven.[4] Another woman who prefers cooking to anything else feels guilt because she hopes that in heaven she will be able to cook rather than pursue "higher things."[5] Yet whatever excellences these stories have were largely neutralized by Slosson's lavish use of such phrases as "dear little thing" and "sweet, good creature."

The low-water mark of Slosson's writing and of the whole tradition that she represented is found in *A Local Colorist*. Realizing that her slight vein of talent has been worked out, she here resorts to parodying her own style—the excessive interest in dialect, the preoccupation with nature study, the sentimentality of her plots. When a tradition's vitality consists solely in the possibilities it offers for parody that tradition is probably near extinction.

A literary movement of which Slosson was a major spokeswoman could not be termed precisely flourishing. Yet the genre was to make a deathbed recovery into a life fully as vigorous as its former one and perhaps more important for the nation as a whole. In 1913, a year after the appearance of her abortive *A Local Colorist*, appeared Frost's *A Boy's Will*, to be quickly followed by *North of Boston* and *Mountain Interval*. Now there are three significant facts about Frost's first book. It was printed in England; it was written by a man; its author had spent the first ten and most impressionable years of his life far from New England. In other words, in the United States Yankee local-color writing was in such justifiably ill repute that a serious practitioner of the genre couldn't find a publisher; the almost exclusively feminine monopoly on this type of writing had been broken; and a broader background of experience was being brought to bear on the interpretation of New England life.

In the national expansion after the Civil War the energies of the men throughout the nation had been drained into so-called practical channels like building railroads, chasing the Indians from their Western reservations, and vanquishing the Spanish. In the general scramble for wealth and power the women had been left at home as guardians of the old ways and ideals. This was especially true in the country sections of New England, where the exodus of men had been enormous and where the older ways and ideals had been more firmly established because of the antiquity and remoteness of the region. To a woman living in her ancestral colonial mansion in Maine the transcontinental railroad and the Carnegie steel mills were indeed nebulous even if she owned stock in them; and insofar as they were realities at all they were evil, since they were inimical to the older ways of the village.

Nor did the rural women fight an entirely losing battle, for in recent years, at least, an increasing number of men have come over to their side. To mention but a few men who have recently been writing in New England or about New England, there are (in addition to Frost) Robert P. Tristram Coffin, John Marquand, James Gould Cozzens, Frederic van de Water, and Le Grand Cannon. The women writers still outnumber the men, of course, but the literary culture of the region is no longer almost exclusively feminine.

That much writing about New England in the past generation has been done by people born elsewhere is even more significant. The "New England" writer is as often as not a person of New England heritage perhaps but of non–New England birth and upbringing. Of the authors mentioned above Coffin alone was born and reared in the region. Among the women, Dorothy Canfield Fisher and Jean Stafford are Westerners by birth and education. Only Maine, which in addition to Coffin can count Mary Ellen Chase, Gladys Hasty Carroll, Kenneth Roberts, Ruth Moore, and Edna Millay as natives, produces its own writers in any quantity. The values that New England once contributed in such abundance to the nation and which were celebrated so copiously in the writings of the post–Civil War generation are being rediscovered. That this is being done in New England more than in any other part of the country does not mean that the section is the sole depository of these values. Willa Cather and Ellen Glasgow, to mention but two, are evidence to the contrary. The centering of activity in this corner of the nation is surely in great part due to the beauty of the countryside and the picturesqueness of the villages— the attractive physical surroundings serving as symbols for the ideas exploited. Nevertheless, the members of the New England group are in basic agreement as to principles, and these principles are identical with those of the earlier writers. Self-sufficiency, individualism, harmony with environment, tolerance are as much the themes of such authors as Robert Frost and Gladys Hasty Carroll as they were of Sarah Orne Jewett and Rowland Robinson. Herein New England regionalism of the present differs from that of the South, if you except an occasional writer like Stark Young. In Erskine Caldwell, William Faulkner, and Eudora Welty the emphasis seems to be on the lack of values—on degeneracy, violence, lunacy—the picture afforded being, of course, extremely unreal though symbolically effective. In New England a Tolstoy-like veneration for country people exemplified earlier in the works of Jewett, has held its ground to the exclusion of more somber tendencies of Freeman and the naturalism of E. A. Robinson. Still the pessimistic strain in New England literature has died lingeringly—and perhaps it would have been better if it had not died at all. Frost has written "A Servant to Servants" and "Home-Burial," both grimly tragic. Edith Wharton, an outstanding example of an outsider, a summer resident, contributing to the literature of the region, outshadowed in *Ethan Frome* and *Summer* the gloom of Freeman's darkest stories. And finally Eugene O'Neill, though only slightly connected with New England, used Yankee scenes and characters in "Desire Under the Elms" and "Mourning Becomes Electra."

Still, if one were seeking the typical in recent New England writing, one would certainly not go to Eugene O'Neill or Edith Wharton. A more promising choice would be Dorothy Canfield, and perhaps most representative of this most typical author is *Seasoned Timber*, published in 1939. Here, as in so many of her novels and stories, Canfield pictures life as she sees it in the Green Mountain valley that she has made her home. The spirit of tolerance and fair play is everywhere evident in her community. Greater value is set on ideals than on monetary profit. The idealism and independence of the Vermont villager is identical with the best that the old cultures of Europe had to offer in the past. And hovering above the whole life of the village like a guardian angel is the beauty of the mountains, a beauty that is reflected in the calmness of soul and handsomeness of physique of those who live within its influence. This and generations of experience with self-government in the town meeting have bred a sense of solidarity, a group-independence, with the aid of which the community is able to retain its ideals against the centralizing and standardizing forces of the times.

NOTES

For full bibliographical details of the works cited in these notes see the Bibliography.

Chapter One

1. Sarah Orne Jewett, *A White Heron and Other Stories*, p. 25.
2. Fred Lewis Pattee, *Side-Lights on American Literature*, pp. 163ff.
3. Seth Hubbell, *A Narrative of the Sufferings of Seth Hubbell & Family, in His Beginning a Settlement in the Town of Wolcott, in the State of Vermont* (Danville, Vt.: E. & W. Eaton, Printers, 1824), reprinted in Barrows Mussey, ed., *We Were New England*, pp. 115ff. The quoted passage is in the last paragraph of Hubbell's narrative.
4. Timothy Dwight, *Travels in New England and New York*, 1:265, 4:206–07 and 212–17.
5. Dwight, 4:251; also James F. Cooper, *Notions of the Americans*, 1:94.
6. Mussey, p. 48f. See also Van Wyck Brooks, *The World of Washington Irving*, pp. 29, 64, and 80; Noah Webster, *Dissertations*, p. 288; J. Hector St. John de Crèvecoeur, *Letters from an American Farmer*, pp. 48–91. In the *Knickerbocker* 44(August 1854):200, F. W. S., a correspondent writes: "The State of Vermont, rock-ribbed and rough as it is, is as much distinguished for substantial blessings as any other in the great confederation. Education is universal, and the necessary comforts of life very equally diffused, while pinching poverty and pampered luxury are alike unknown."
7. Harriet Beecher Stowe, *The Pearl of Orr's Island*, p. 120.
8. For Lucy Larcom see *A New England Girlhood*, Chapters 6–9; for Nichols see Barrows Mussey, pp. 195ff.; for Dickens see *American Notes*, Chapter 4.
9. H. F. Wilson, *The Hill Country of Northern New England*, pp. 113–14. The passage is quoted by Wilson from Charles C. Mott, "A Good Farm for Nothing," *The Nation*, 49:406–08. See earlier chapters of Wilson's book for a fuller treatment of economic conditions in rural New England in the nineteenth century.
10. Charles W. Eliot, *John Giley, passim.*
11. Lucy Larcom, pp. 93ff. Similar descriptions of seaport life may be found in George Lunt's *Eastford; or, Household Sketches* and *Old New England Traits*, in both of which the author depicts life in Newburyport, Massachusetts, as he knew it in his boyhood during the early nineteenth century.
12. Stowe, p. 291.

13. See Sarah Orne Jewett's description of a New England seaport in *A Country Doctor;* also Mary Ellen Chase's authentic and beautifully written *Silas Crockett, Mary Peters, A Goodly Heritage,* and *A Goodly Fellowship* (Chapter 1); also T. B. Aldrich's *An Old Town by the Sea* and T. W. Higginson's *Oldport Days.*

14. Van Wyck Brooks, *New England: Indian Summer,* p. 100.

15. Timothy Dwight, *Travels in New England and New York,* 4:335.

16. Brooks, *New England: Indian Summer,* pp. 100ff.

17. Vernon Parrington, *Beginnings of Critical Realism in America,* pp. 60–69.

18. Henry James, *Hawthorne,* p. 34.

19. Henry James, *The American Essays of Henry James,* pp. 257 and 278.

20. Brooks, *New England: Indian Summer,* p. 99n.

CHAPTER TWO

1. John Greenleaf Whittier, *Prose Works,* 1:460–61.

2. Oscar Cargill, *Intellectual America: Ideas on the March,* pp. 687–88. Though during his youth O'Neill spent much time in the city of New London, Connecticut, his contact with the native rural New England mind and temperament was limited.

3. *Atlantic Monthly,* 25(April 1870):504–12.

4. Thomas Wentworth Higginson, "Americanism in Literature," *passim.*

5. Sarah Orne Jewett, *Letters,* p. 78.

6. *Ibid.,* p. 250.

7. Elizabeth Stuart Phelps, *Chapters from a Life,* p. 263.

8. *Ibid.,* pp. 264–65.

9. Elizabeth Stuart Phelps, *The Madonna of the Tubs,* p. 92.

10. William Dean Howells, *Their Wedding Journey,* pp. 254–55.

11. Henry Ward Beecher, *Norwood: or, Village Life in New England,* p. 2. See also Rudyard Kipling's contrast between the urban and the rural people of New England in "One Side Only," *The Times* (London), November 29, 1892, p. 8.

12. John Macy, "The Passing of the Yankee," p. 618; see also Van Wyck Brooks, *New England: Indian Summer,* pp. 13–14 and 45–52.

13. John Greenleaf Whittier, Introductory Note to "Mogg Megone," *Complete Poetical Works,* p. 1.

14. *Ibid.,* pp. 325–26.

15. *Ibid.,* p. 326

16. Whittier, *Prose Works,* 1:468–69.

17. Forrest Wilson, *Crusader in Crinoline,* p. 164; and Ima Honaker Herron, *The Small Town in American Literature,* pp. 76–79.

18. Annie Fields, *Authors and Friends,* pp. 199–200. See also Harriet Beecher Stowe, the Preface to *Old town Folks.*

19. Stowe, *The Pearl of Orr's Island,* pp. 387–88.

20. *Ibid.,* pp. 347–48.

21. Charles E. Stowe, *Life of Harriet Beecher Stowe,* p. 334.

22. Forrest Wilson, p. 529.

23. Barrows Mussey, ed., *We Were New England*, p. 31.
24. Forrest Wilson, pp. 243 and 247.
25. Stowe, *The Pearl of Orr's Island*, pp. 240–41.
26. S. Foster Damon, Introduction to Rowland Robinson's *Sam Lovel's Boy.*

Chapter Three

1. Rowland E. Robinson, *Vermont: A Study of Independence*, p. 365.
2. Rowland Robinson, *Out of Bondage and Other Stories*, pp. 247–55. The best sources of biographical and critical material are in the introductions of the Centennial Edition of Robinson's works, ed. Professor Llewellyn R. Perkins, 7 vols. (Rutland, Vt.: Charles E. Tuttle, 1933–1937). This edition is as fine a job as has been done with a minor author in America. More specifically, the biographical material in my chapter has been drawn from Mary Robinson (Rowland Robinson's daughter), "Rowland Robinson," which serves as an introduction to *Out of Bondage and Other Stories*. Also worth consulting are Lincoln Bailey, "The Chronicler of Davis Folks," and Julia C. R. Dorr (a Vermont novelist of some note), "Rowland Robinson," as well as the article on Robinson in the *Dictionary of American Biography*.
3. John Greenleaf Whittier, *Complete Poetical Works*, p. 98.
4. Barrows Mussey, *We Were New England*, p. 17.
5. Rowland Robinson, *Sam Lovel's Boy*, with *Forest and Stream Fables*, p. 131.
6. Rowland Robinson, *Uncle Lisha's Shop*, and *A Danvis Pioneer*, p. 215.
7. Rowland Robinson, *Danvis Folks*, and *A Hero of Ticonderoga*, p. 37. For a discussion of Robinson's literary techniques see Professor S. Foster Damon, "Introduction," *Sam Lovel's Boy.*
8. Robinson, *Uncle Lisha's Shop*, p. 122.
9. Robinson, *Sam Lovel's Boy*, p. 38.
10. Robinson, *A Danvis Pioneer* (in same volume as *Uncle Lisha's Shop*), p. 110.
11. Robinson, *Danvis Folks*, p. 20.
12. Robinson, *Uncle Lisha's Shop*, p. 122.
13. *Ibid.*
14. Robinson, *Sam Lovel's Boy*, pp. 24–25. Robinson's handling of dialect is ably discussed by Duane Leroy Robinson, "Foreword," *Sam Lovel's Camps and Other Stories;* by Walter Pritchard Eaton, "Foreword," *Danvis Folks;* and by Dorothy Canfield Fisher, "Introduction," *Uncle Lisha's Shop*. For comments on Lowell's inadequacies see George Philip Krapp, *The English Language in America*, 1:231ff.
15. Robinson, *Sam Lovel's Camps and Other Stories*, p. 16.
16. Robinson, "Author's Note," *Danvis Folks*, p. 16. Some of the dialectical words observed by Robinson—for example, *toro*—were found as late as the 1930's by fieldworkers for Hans Kurath, *Linguistic Atlas of New England*. See also Hans Kurath, *The Word Geography of the Eastern United States.*
17. Robinson, *Uncle Lisha's Shop*, pp. 194–95.
18. See Arthur, Schomberg, "Foreword," *Out of Bondage and Other Stories.*
19. Robinson, *Uncle Lisha's Shop*, p. 118.
20. Robinson, *Out of Bondage and Other Stories*, pp. 137–47.

21. Mary E. Wilkins Freeman, *A New England Nun and Other Stories*, pp. 81–98.
22. Robinson, *Out of Bondage and Other Stories*, pp. 166–78.
23. *Ibid.*, pp. 83–96.
24. Robinson, *Uncle Lisha's Outing*, pp. 221–58.
25. Robinson, *In New England Fields and Woods*, with *Sketches and Stories*, p. 122.
26. Robinson, *Sketches and Stories* (in same volume with *In New England Fields and Woods*), pp. 194–95.
27. Robinson, *Uncle Lisha's Shop*, pp. 247–48.
28. Arthur Wallace Peach, "Introduction," *Sam Lovel's Camps and Other Stories*, pp. 13ff.
29. Robinson, *Sketches and Stories*, pp. 210–12.
30. Robinson, *Out of Bondage and Other Stories*, p. 164.
31. Reprinted in Bernard DeVoto, *Forays and Rebuttals*, pp. 138–58.

Chapter Four

1. Sarah Orne Jewett, "Preface," *Deephaven*, pp. 4–5.
2. Grant Overton, *Women Who Make Our Novels*, pp. 78–82. See Henry James, *Hawthorne*, Chapter 1, for a discussion of American writers' search for a past.
3. Willa Cather, "148 Charles Street," in *Not Under Forty*, pp. 52–75.
4. For a detailed description of 148 Charles Street see M. A. DeWolfe Howe, *Memories of a Hostess*, *passim*, but especially Chapter 2.
5. Henry James, *The Bostonians*, p. 183. See F. O. Matthiessen and Kenneth Murdock, eds., *The Notebooks of Henry James*, for James's interest in Sarah Orne Jewett.
6. Jewett, *Deephaven*, p. 5.
7. *Ibid.*, pp. 5–6.
8. Cather, "148 Charles Street," *passim*. F. O. Matthiessen, *American Renaissance*, pp. 210–11, discusses Jewett's prose style.
9. For the biography and criticism of Sarah Orne Jewett see Richard Cary, ed., *Appreciation of Sarah Orne Jewett: 29 Interpretive Essays*; Richard Cary, *Sarah Orne Jewett*; Edward M. Chapman, "The New England of Sarah Orne Jewett"; Edward Garnett, "Sarah Orne Jewett's Tales," in *Friday Nights*, pp. 89–98; C. Hartley Grattan, "Sarah Orne Jewett"; F. O. Matthiessen, *Sarah Orne Jewett*; Fred Pattee, *American Literature Since 1870*, pp. 231–35; Martha Hale Shackford, "Sarah Orne Jewett"; Jean Sougnac, *Sarah Orne Jewett*; Charles M. Thompson, "The Art of Miss Jewett"; Margaret F. Thorp, *Sarah Orne Jewett*; Helen M. Winslow, *Literary Boston Today*, pp. 63–72. Collections of Jewett's letters are: *Sarah Orne Jewett Letters*, ed. Richard Cary; *Letters of Sarah Orne Jewett*, ed. Annie Fields; *Letters of Sarah Orne Jewett Now in Colby Library*, ed. Carl Weber. An extremely useful reference tool is Gwen L. Nagel and James Nagel, eds., *Sarah Orne Jewett: A Reference Guide*.
10. Jewett, *Letters*, ed. Annie Fields, p. 111. Other references to Jewett's *Letters*

in this chapter are to Fields's edition.

11. *Ibid.*, p. 132.
12. *Ibid.*, p. 33.
13. Oliver Wendell Holmes, *Elsie Venner*, Chapter 1.
14. Jewett, *Deephaven*, p. 3.
15. Jewett, *Letters*, p. 165.
16. *Ibid.*, pp. 38–39.
17. *Ibid.*, pp. 194ff.
18. Jewett, *Country By-Ways*, p. 116.
19. Jewett, *Deephaven*, p. 3.
20. *Ibid.*, pp. 3–4.
21. *Ibid.*, p. 103
22. *Ibid.*, p. 241.
23. Jewett, *Letters*, p. 113.
24. Jewett, *Deephaven*, pp. 246–47.
25. *Ibid.*, p. 266.
26. Harriet Beecher Stowe, *Oldtown Folks*, pp. 1–10.
27. Jewett, *The Story of the Normans*, pp. 365–66.
28. Jewett, *Country By-Ways*, p. 117. Cf. Lucy Larcom's statement concerning her native Beverly: "Her spirit was that of most of our Massachusetts coast towns. They were transplanted shoots of Old England" (*A New England Girlhood*, p. 117).
29. Jewett, *Country By-Ways*, p. 118.
30. Jewett, *Letters*, pp. 207–208.
31. Jewett, *The Queen's Twin and Other Stories*, pp. 1–37.
32. Jewett, *Deephaven*, p. 117.
33. Lucy Larcom, *A New England Girlhood*, p. 117.
34. *Ibid.*, p. 118.
35. Jewett, *Deephaven*, pp. 82–101.
36. *Ibid.*, p. 84.
37. *Ibid.*, p. 49.
38. *Ibid.*, p. 82. The Biblical reference is to Proverbs 30:26.
39. *Ibid.*, p. 225.
40. *Ibid.*, pp. 93–94. George Lunt in *Old New England Traits*, pp. 144–45, gives examples of what he considers old English pronunciations in Newburyport, Massachusetts, a town much like Deephaven.
41. Jewett, *The Story of the Normans*, p. 363.

Chapter Five

1. Ralph Waldo Emerson, *Essays*, First Series, p. 89.
2. Sarah Orne Jewett, *A White Heron and Other Stories*, p. 21.
3. *Ibid.*, p. 22.
4. *Ibid.*, p. 84.
5. Emerson, *Essays*, First Series, p. 120.
6. Jewett, *A White Heron and Other Stories*, pp. 122–23. See also James Fenimore Cooper's statement in *Notions of the Americans*, 1:94: "I have

nowhere else [than in New England] witnessed such universality of that self-respect which preserves men from moral degradation."

7.   Willa Cather, *Not Under Forty*, pp. 76–95.
8.   Jewett, *The Country of the Pointed Firs*, p. 78.
9.   Jewett, *Letters*, ed., Annie Fields, p. 54.
10. Jewett, *The Country of the Pointed Firs*, p. 233.
11. *Ibid.*, p. 231.
12. H. M. Winslow, *Literary Boston of Today*, p. 70.
13. Jewett, *The Country of the Pointed Firs*, p. 127.
14. Jewett, *Letters*, ed. Annie Fields, pp. 246–50.
15. Jewett, *The Country of the Pointed Firs*, p. 110
16. Ben C. Clough, "Poor Nancy Luce."
17. Helen Hunt Jackson, *Mercy Philbrick's Choice*, p. 283. For life of Helen Hunt Jackson see Ruth Odell, *Helen Hunt Jackson*.
18. Helen Hunt Jackson, *Saxe Holm's Stories*, First Series, pp. 313–50.
19. Emily Dickinson, *Selected Poems of Emily Dickinson*, p. 54.
20. *Ibid.*, p. 38.
21. Mary E. Wilkins Freeman, "Amanda Todd: The Friend of Cats," in *People of Our Neighborhood*, pp. 57–68.
22. Winslow, pp. 70–72.
23. Mary E. Wilkins Freeman, *A New England Nun and Other Stories*, pp. 173–74.
24. Jewett, *The King of Folly Island and Other People*, p. 20. The theme of the title story may have been suggested by the life of Celia Thaxter's father. See below, Chapter Eleven.
25. *Ibid.*, p. 31.
26. *Ibid.*, pp. 81–114.
27. *Ibid.*, p. 37.

Chapter Six

1.   Ralph Waldo Emerson, *Poems*, p. 142.
2.   In Alice Brown, *Meadow-Grass*, pp. 1–17. For life and criticism of Alice Brown see Grant Martin Overton, *The Women Who Make Our Novels*, pp. 49–54; Fred L. Pattee, *American Literature Since 1870*, pp. 240–42; Charles Miner Thompson, "The Short Stories of Alice Brown"; Dorothea Walker, *Alice Brown*; Blanche Colton Williams, *Our Short Story Writers*, pp. 1–21.
3.   Ralph Waldo Emerson, *Society and Solitude*, p. 125.
4.   Alice Brown, *Meadow-Grass*, p. 1.
5.   *Ibid.*, p. 15.
6.   *Ibid.*, p. 19.
7.   *Ibid.*, pp. 28–29.
8.   *Ibid.*, p. 204.
9.   Sally Pratt McLean, *Cape Cod Folks*, p. 60.
10. Charles W. Eliot, *John Gilley*, pp. 22–23.
11. Henry James, *The American Scene*, p. 20.

Chapter Seven

1. Harriet Beecher Stowe, *Poganuc People*, p. 95.
2. *Ibid.*
3. *Ibid.*, p. 98.
4. The story of this character has been known for years to the author, who lived on an adjacent farm. A more extensive account may be found in Cornelius Weygandt, *New Hampshire Neighbors*, pp. 244ff. I know of no book, however, in which the stone house described in the following paragraph is mentioned. Despite his Freudianism, Eugene O'Neill in *Desire Under the Elm* has a character, Ephraim Cabot, who illustrates well the effects of granite on the personality of a New England farmer.
5. For biographical and critical material on Rose Terry Cooke see Harriet Prescott [Spofford], "Rose Terry Cooke"; Harriet Prescott Spofford, *A Little Book of Friends*, pp. 143–56; the article on her in *Notable American Women, 1607–1950*. Bibliographies are Jean Downey, "Rose Terry Cooke: A Bibliography," and Susan Toth, "Rose Terry Cooke (1827–1892)," a bibiographical essay.
6. Rose Terry Cooke, *Somebody's Neighbors*, pp. 153–92.
7. *Ibid.*, p. 362.
8. *Ibid.*, p. 351.
9. *Ibid.*, p. 229.
10. *Ibid.*, pp. 233–34.
11. *Ibid.*, p. 242.
12. *Ibid.*, p. 243.

Chapter Eight

1. Mary E. Wilkins Freeman, *A New England Nun and Other Stories*, p. 243.
2. Rudyard Kipling, *Something of Myself*, p. 127.
3. Rollin L. Hartt, "A New England Hill Town," p. 564.
4. Hartt, *passim.*
5. For biographical and critical material on Freeman the following are useful: Marie Thérèse Blanc [Th. Bentzon], "Un Romancier de la Nouvelle-Angleterre"; Edward Foster, *Mary E. Wilkins Freeman*; John Macy, "The Passing of the Yankee"; Fred Lewis Pattee, *American Literature Since 1870*, pp. 235–40, and the chapter "On the Terminal Moraine of New England Puritanism" in *Side-Lights on American Literature*; James H. Quina, "Character Types in the Fiction of Mary Wilkins Freeman"; Charles Miner Thompson, "Miss Wilkins: An Idealist in Masquerade"; Susan A. Toth, "A Defiant Light: A Positive View of Mary Wilkins Freeman" and "Mary Wilkins Freeman's Parable of a Wasted Life"; Perry D. Westbrook, "Mary E. Wilkins Freeman (1852–1930)" [a bibliography], and *Mary Wilkins Freeman*; Blanche Colton Williams, *Our Short Story Writers*, pp. 160–81; and Larzer Ziff, *The American 1890s*, pp. 292–96.
6. Freeman, "An Honest Soul," in *A New England Nun and Other Stories*, p. 160.

7.   Freeman, "An Honest Soul," in *A Humble Romance and Other Stories*, p. 86. For another reconciliation of these two opposing views see James Gould Cozzens, *The Last Adam*.

8.   In Freeman, *A Humble Romance and Other Stories*, pp. 92–106.

9.   *Ibid.*, p. 390.

10.   *Ibid.*, pp. 396–97.

11.   See Robert Frost's poem, "A Servant to Servants."

12.   Freeman, *Pembroke*, p. 19.

13.   *Ibid.*, p. 298.

14.   *Ibid.*, p. 297.

15.   *Ibid.*, p. 315.

16.   Edwin Arlington Robinson, *Untriangulated Stars*, pp. 174–75.

17.   See Chapter Two.

18.   Freeman, *The Jamesons*, p. 177.

19.   Sarah Orne Jewett, *Letters*, ed. Annie Fields, p. 195.

20.   Marie Thérèse Blanc, "Un Romancier de la Nouvelle-Angleterre," *passim*. See Carl Weber, "New England Through French Eyes Fifty Years Ago," for details concerning Marie Thérèse Blanc's relations with Jewett.

21.   Freeman, *A New England Nun*, pp. 97–98.

22.   Sarah Orne Jewett, *A Native of Winby and Other Stories*, pp. 177–218.

23.   Rowland E. Robinson, *Out of Bondage, and Other Stories*, pp. 137–47.

24.   Freeman, *A New England Nun*, p. 17. Louisa, the "nun" in the story, voluntarily fences herself away from full participation in life, as Freeman makes amply clear by two symbols—that of Louisa's caged canary and that of her old dog Caesar, which has been chained fourteen years because as a puppy he bit some one. In a letter written to a friend on July 4, 1886, Freeman tells of seeing just such a dog chained for many years by an elderly woman.

25.   E. A. Robinson, pp. 174–75.

26.   R. W. Emerson, *Essays*, First Series, p. 117.

27.   Blanche Colton Williams, *Our Short Story Writers*, p. 169.

28.   Freeman, *A New England Nun*, p. 468.

29.   Williams, p. 170.

30.   Freeman, *A New England Nun*, p. 28.

31.   *Ibid.*, p. 33.

32.   Freeman, *Six Trees*, pp. 64–65.

Chapter Nine

1.   Nathaniel Hawthorne, *The American Notebooks*, p. 260.

2.   Oscar Laighton, *Ninety Years at the Isles of Shoals*, p. 101. Oscar Laighton was Celia Thaxter's brother and a poetaster who achieved publication in the *Atlantic*.

3.   Celia Thaxter, *The Poems of Celia Thaxter*, pp. 45–48. This edition of Thaxter's poems, collected and prefaced by Sarah Orne Jewett, contains the bulk of her adult verse. Oscar Laighton edited under the title *The Heavenly Guest* additional of his sister's poems, which had been found among papers

in Sarah Orne Jewett's possession and returned to the Thaxter family on her death. Laighton includes in this volume many reprints of interesting articles on Thaxter and her work, as well as a biographical introduction by himself. Jewett also edited the juvenile poetry and prose of Celia Thaxter.

Laighton's *Ninety Years at the Isles of Shoals* and the material he includes in *The Heavenly Guest* are useful sources of information concerning Thaxter's life and critical reception. But the best story of her life can be gleaned from her own writings: *Among the Isles of Shoals, An Island Garden*, and *Letters of Celia Thaxter*, ed. Annie Fields and Rosa Lamb. Other writings on Thaxter include: Richard Cary, "The Multicolored Spirit of Celia Thaxter"; Rosamond Thaxter, *Sandpiper: The Life and Letters of Celia Thaxter* (the best biographical source, written by Celia Thaxter's granddaughter); Dorothy M. Vaughan, "Celia Thaxter's Library"; and Perry D. Westbrook, "Celia Thaxter: Seeker of the Unattainable." Nathaniel Hawthorne, *The American Notebooks*, pp. 256–75, and Frank Preston Stearns, *Sketches of Concord and Appledore*, pp. 223–52, contain general comments on the life of the Thaxters on the Isles of Shoals.

4.   Henry David Thoreau, *Cape Cod*, pp. 11–14.

5.   Matthew Arnold, "Empedocles on Etna," *Poetical Works*, p. 233. For discussions of this outlook in English Victorian poetry see Lionel Trilling, *Matthew Arnold*, Chapter 3, and Joseph Warren Beach, *The Concept of Nature in English Nineteenth-Century Poetry*, pp. 406–503. The poems of Wordsworth and Cowper quoted *supra* may be found in any reliable edition of each poet's work.

6.   Celia Thaxter, *Among the Isles of Shoals*, pp. 7–15.

7.   Thaxter, *Poems*, p. 2.

8.   Thaxter, *Among the Isles of Shoals*, pp. 22–23.

9.   Elizabeth Stuart Phelps (Ward), *Chapters from a Life*, pp. 177–78.

10.   Thaxter, *Poems*, p. 3.

11.   Thaxter, *Among the Isles of Shoals*, p. 31.

12.   Thaxter, *Poems*, p. 17. See also "An Early Letter by Celia Thaxter."

13.   Mary T. Higginson, *Thomas Wentworth Higginson*, pp. 108–109. (See Rosamond Thaxter, *Sandpiper*, pp. 34–36, for Celia's age at the time of the wedding and a more detailed and accurate account of the proceedings.)

14.   Thaxter, *Letters, passim*, and Laighton, *Ninety Years at the Isles of Shoals*, pp. 88ff. and 99.

15.   Samuel T. Pickard, *Life and Letters of John Greenleaf Whittier*, 2:519–21.

16.   Thaxter, *Letters, passim*.

17.   Thaxter, *Among the Isles of Shoals*, pp. 141–42.

18.   *Ibid.*, p. 105.

19.   Thaxter, *Letters*, p. 56.

20.   For an account of this inscription see George W. Cooke, *A Guide-Book to the Poetic and Dramatic Works of Robert Browning*, p. 195. The epitaph may be found in any edition of the complete poems of Robert Browning.

21.   Thaxter, *Among the Isles of Shoals*, p. 16.

22.   *Ibid.*, p. 150.

23.   Thaxter, *Letters, passim*.

24.   In addition to Browning's analysis in "Mr. Sludge," the interested reader

will find in William B. Carpenter's *Mesmerism, Spiritualism, Etc.* an objective and fascinating account and explanation of the nineteenth-century outbreak of spiritualism. See also Henry James, *The Bostonians*, and William Dean Howells, *The Undiscovered Country*, for fictional treatments of the fad.

25. Hawthorne, *The American Notebooks*, p. 260.
26. Stearns, pp. 240–42.
27. Thaxter, *Letters*, p. 88.
28. *Ibid.*, p. 90.
29. Annie Fields, *Authors and Friends*, p. 254.
30. Thaxter, *Letters*, pp. 141–42.
31. M. A. DeWolfe Howe, *Memories of a Hostess*, pp. 129–31.
32. For one of several exposés of the activities of Mme. Blavatsky, the founder of Theosophy, see Carl Eric Bechofer-Roberts, *The Mysterious Madame*.
33. Thaxter, *Letters*, p. 219.
34. *Ibid.*, p. 178.
35. *Ibid.*, pp. 168–69.
36. Thaxter, *Poems*, p. 177.
37. Thaxter, *The Heavenly Guest*, p. 25.
38. Thaxter, *Letters*, p. 160.
39. Thaxter, *Poems*, pp. 65–66.
40. Thaxter, *The Heavenly Guest*, p. 8.
41. *Ibid.*, p. 52.
42. Thaxter, *Poems*, p. 139.
43. Thaxter, *Letters*, p. 138.
44. For example, in the story "Where's Nora?," in Sarah Orne Jewett, *The Queen's Twin and Other Stories*, pp. 73–117.
45. "A Memorable Murder" was first published in the *Atlantic Monthly*, May 1875.
46. Herman Melville, *Billy Budd and Other Prose Pieces*, p. 45.
47. See William W. Ellsworth, *A Golden Age of Authors*, pp. 88ff., and Henry Steele Commager, *A St. Nicholas Anthology*.
48. Van Wyck Brooks, *New England: Indian Summer*, pp. 52–55.
49. Thaxter, *Letters*, pp. 95–96; and, for a slightly different account, Stearns, pp. 249–50.
50. Pickard, 2:600–01.
51. *Ibid.*, pp. 578–79.
52. *Ibid.*, p. 565.
53. *Ibid.*, p. 564.

Chapter Ten

1. Henry David Thoreau, *The Variorum Walden*, ed. Walter Harding, p. 90.
2. See sources mentioned in Chapter One, note 8.
3. Lucy Larcom, *A New England Girlhood*, p. 17. For the life of Lucey Larcom see also Daniel D. Addison, *Lucy Larcom: Life, Letters, and Diary*.
4. Larcom, pp. 94–99. See George Lunt, *Old New England Traits* and *Eastford; or Household Sketches* for pictures of Newburyport closely resembling

Larcom's description of Beverly.

5. Larcom, p. 47.
6. *Ibid.*, p. 19.
7. Addison, p. 259.
8. Charles Dickens, *American Notes*, p. 78. A similar account—for what it is worth —is Davy Crockett, *The Autobiography*, pp. 180ff. Oscar Cargill, *Intellectual America*, pp. 537–44, briefly summarizes the place of the American woman in the factory system.
9. Larcom, p. 243.
10. Dickens, p. 80.
11. Jonathan Edwards, *Representative Selections*, p. 56.
12. Harriet Beecher Stowe, *The Minister's Wooing*, pp. 265–66. In a short tale, "The Yankee Girl," Stowe dilates at length on the New England girl, in whom she finds a "union of womanly delicacy and refinement with manly energy and decision, womanly ingenuity and versatility in contrivance, with manly promptness and efficiency in execution" (p. 63).
13. Timothy Dwight, *Travels in New England and New York*, 4:334–37.
14. Thomas Wentworth Higginson, *Malbone*, p. 35.
15. Harold F. Wilson, *The Hill Country of Northern New England*, pp. 67–68.
16. Larcom, pp. 9–10.
17. Lucy Larcom, *An Idyl of Work*, p. ix.
18. Francis A. Westbrook, *Industrial Management in This Machine Age*, pp. 377–78.
19. Larcom, *An Idyl of Work*, p. 15.
20. Larcom, *A New England Girlhood*, pp. 200–01.
21. Larcom, *An Idyl of Work*, pp. 136–37.
22. Larcom, *A New England Girlhood*, p. 199.
23. Quoted by Addison, pp. 7–8.
24. Stowe, *The Minister's Wooing*, p. 83.
25. Larcom, *An Idyl of Work*, pp. 135–36.
26. Lucy Larcom, *Poems*, p. 145.
27. Larcom, *An Idyl of Work*, pp. 141–42.
28. William Dean Howells, *Annie Kilburn*, pp. 149–50.
29. *Ibid.*, p. 170.
30. Larcom, *An Idyl of Work*, pp. 178–79.
31. T.W. Nichols, in Barrows Mussey, *We Were New England*, pp. 195ff.
32. Larcom, *An Idyl of Work*, pp. 118–19.
33. Vernon Parrington, *The Beginnings of Critical Realism in America*, pp. 50–59.
34. Mary E. Wilkins Freeman, *The Portion of Labor*, pp. 562–63.
35. Larcom, *An Idyl of Work*, pp. 138–39.

Chapter Eleven

1. Ralph Waldo Emerson, *Journals*, 8:226.
2. Quoted in Vernon Parrington, *The Beginnings of Critical Realism in America*, p. 59.

3. *Ibid.*

4. *Ibid.*

5. *Ibid.*, p. 54. See John P. Marquand, *The Late George Apley*, and Cleveland Amory, *The Proper Bostonians*, for the class-consciousness and xenophobia of New England old-line families. See William Dean Howells, *The Rise of Silas Lapham*, for the rift between city and rural life and values.

6. Parrington, p. 62.

7. Harold F. Wilson, *The Hill Country of Northern New England*, pp. 161ff.

8. Rudyard Kipling, *Something of Myself*, p. 129.

9. Rowland Robinson, *Vermont: A Study of Independence*, p. 328.

10. *Ibid.*, p. 330.

11. Celia Thaxter, *Among the Isles of Shoals*, p. 184.

12. Annie Fields, *Authors and Friends*, pp. 234–35.

13. In Sarah Orne Jewett, *Strangers and Wayfarers*, pp. 79–115.

14. In Jewett, *A Native of Winby and Other Stories*, pp. 219–52.

15. *Ibid.*, pp. 253–309.

16. In Jewett, *The Queen's Twin and Other Stories*, pp. 73–117.

17. Jewett, *Strangers and Wayfarers*, pp. 87–88.

18. Parrington, p. 62.

19. Jewett, "The Gray Mills of Farley," in *American Local Color Stories*, ed. H. R. Warfel and G. H. Orians, pp. 363–82.

20. *Ibid.*, p. 380.

21. *Ibid.*, p. 376.

22. *Ibid.*, p. 365.

23. *Ibid.*, p. 373.

24. *Ibid.*, p. 366.

25. Dorothy Canfield (Fisher), "Fairfax Hunter," in *Raw Material*, pp. 113–14.

26. Samuel T. Williamson, "New England Isn't That Way," *New York Times Magazine Section*, August 31, 1947, p. 12, col. 3.

Chapter Twelve

1. Dorothy Canfield Fisher, *Seasoned Timber*, p. 485.

2. Emery Neff, *Edwin Arlington Robinson, passim.*

3. There is very little biographical material available concerning Slossom other than the *Who's Who* entry for 1926 and very brief obituary notices.

4. In the story "Anna Malann," *Dumb Foxglove and Other Stories*, pp. 85–117.

5. "Dumb Foxglove," in *Dumb Foxglove and Other Stories*, pp. 3–43.

BIBLIOGRAPHY

The following list contains entries for all works cited in the notes and for most of those referred to in the text but not cited in the notes. No attempt has been made to compile an exhaustive bibliography of the period or subjects discussed in the book.

ADDISON, DANIEL DULANEY. *Lucy Larcom: Life Letters, and Diary.* Boston: Houghton, Mifflin, 1895.

ALDRICH, THOMAS BAILEY. *Marjorie Daw and Other Stories.* Boston: Houghton Mifflin, 1887.

――――. *An Old Town by the Sea.* Boston: Houghton, Mifflin, 1893.

――――. *The Story of a Bad Boy.* Boston: Houghton, Mifflin, 1870.

――――. *Unguarded Gates and Other Poems.* Boston: Houghton, Mifflin, 1895.

AMORY, CLEVELAND. *The Proper Bostonians.* New York: E. P. Dutton, 1947.

ARNOLD, MATTHEW. *Poetical Works.* New York: Thomas Crowell, 1897.

BAILEY, HENRY LINCOLN. "The Chronicler of Danvis Folks." *New England Magazine,* New Series, 23 (December 1900): 430–37.

BEACH, JOSEPH WARREN. *The Concept of Nature in English Nineteenth-Century Poetry.* New York: Macmillan, 1936.

BECCHOFER-ROBERTS, CARL ERIC. *The Mysterious Madame.* New York: Brewer and Cuarran, 1931.

BEECHER, HENRY WARD. *Norwood; or, Village Life in New England.* New York: Charles Scribner, 1868.

BLANC, MARIE THÉRÈSE [Th. Bentzon]. "Un Romancier de la Nouvelle-Angle-terre." *Revue des Deux Mondes* 136(August 1896):544–69.

BRAND, ALICE GLARDEN. "Mary Wilkins Freeman: Misanthropy as Propaganda." *New England Quarterly* 50(March 1977):83–100.

BROOKS, VAN WYCK. *New England: Indian Summer.* New York: E. P. Dutton, 1940.

――――. *The World of Washington Irving.* Philadelphia: Blakiston, 1945.

BROWN, ALICE. *Meadow-Grass.* Boston: Copeland & Day, 1896.

――――. *Tiverton Tales.* Boston: Houghton, Mifflin, 1896.

BURNS, ROBERT. *The Poems and Songs of Robert Burns.* London: J. M. Dent, 1905.

CANFIELD, DOROTHY. *Raw Material.* New York: Harcourt, Brace & Co., 1923.

――――. *Seasoned Timber.* New York: Harcourt, Brace, 1939.

CARGILL, OSCAR. *Intellectual America: Ideas on the March.* New York: Macmillan, 1941.

CARPENTER, WILLIAM B. *Mesmerism, Spiritualism, Etc.* New York: D. Appleton, 1889.

CARROLL, GLADYS HASTY. *As the Earth Turns.* New York: Macmillan, 1946.

CARY, RICHARD, ed. *Appreciation of Sarah Orne Jewett: 29 Interpretive Essays.* Waterville, Me.: Colby College Press, 1973.

————. "The Multicolored Spirit of Celia Thaxter." *Colby Library Quarterly,* Series 6, No. 12 (December 1964), pp. 512–36.

CATHER, WILLA. *My Antonia.* Boston: Houghton, Mifflin, 1949.

————. *Not Under Forty.* New York: Alfred A. Knopf, 1936.

CHAPMAN, EDWARD M. "The New England of Sarah Orne Jewett." *Yale Review* 3(October 1913):157–72.

CHASE, MARY ELLEN. *A Goodly Fellowship.* New York: Macmillan, 1939.

————. *A Goodly Heritage.* New York: Macmillan, 1932.

————. *Mary Peters.* New York: Macmillan, 1934.

————. *Silas Crockett.* New York: Macmillan, 1935.

CLOUGH, BEN C. "Poor Nancy Luce." *New Colophon* 2(September 1949):253–65.

COMMAGER, HENRY STEELE. *A St. Nicholas Anthology.* 2 vols. New York: Random House, 1948–1950.

COOKE, GEORGE WILLIS. *A Guide-Book to the Poetic and Dramatic Works of Robert Browning.* Boston: Houghton, Mifflin, 1891.

COOKE, ROSE TERRY. *Somebody's Neighbors.* Boston: James R. Osgood, 1881.

————. *Steadfast.* Boston: Ticknor, 1889.

COOPER, JAMES FENIMORE. *Notions of the Americans.* Philadelphia: Carey, Lea & Carey, 1832.

COZZENS, JAMES GOULD. *The Last Adam.* New York: Harcourt, Brace, 1933.

CRÈVECOEUR, J. HECTOR ST. JOHN DE. *Letters from an American Farmer.* New York: Fox, Duffield, 1904.

CROCKETT, DAVID. *The Autobiography of David Crockett.* Edited by Hamlin Garland. New York: Charles Scribner's, 1923.

DEVOTO, BERNARD. *Forays and Rebuttals.* Boston: Little, Brown, 1936.

DICKENS, CHARLES. *American Notes and Pictures of Italy.* Vol. 28 of *The Works of Charles Dickens* (Gadshill Edition). 34 vols. Edited by Andrew Lang. London: Chapman & Hall, n.d.

DICKINSON, EMILY. *Selected Poems of Emily Dickinson.* Introduction by Conrad Aiken. New York: Modern Library, n.d.

DORR, JULIA C. R. "Rowland Robinson." *Atlantic Monthly* 87(January 1901):117–22.

DOWNEY, JEAN. "Rose Terry Cooke: A Bibliography." *Bulletin of Bibliography* 21(May–August and September–December 1955):159–63 and 191–92.

DWIGHT, TIMOTHY. *Travels in New England and New York.* 4 vols. Edited by Barbara Miller Solomon. Cambridge, Mass.: Belknap Press of Harvard University Press, 1969.

EDWARDS, JONATHAN. "Sarah Pierrepont." In *Jonathan Edwards: Representative Selections.* Edited by Clarence H. Faust and Thomas H. Johnson. New York: American Book Co., 1935.

ELIOT, CHARLES W. *John Gilley.* Boston American Unitarian Association, 1899.

ELIOT, GEORGE. *Adam Bede.* New York: Charles Scribner's Sons, 1917.

ELLSWORTH, WILLIAM W. *A Golden Age of Authors.* Boston: Houghton, Mifflin, 1919.

EMERSON, RALPH WALDO. *Essays.* First Series. Vol. 1 of *The Complete Works of Ralph Waldo Emerson.* 12 vols. Edited by Edward Waldo Emerson. Boston:

Houghton, Mifflin, 1903–1904.

———. *The Journals of Ralph Waldo Emerson*. 10 vols. Edited by Edward W. Emerson and W. E. Forbes, Boston: Houghton, Mifflin, 1909–1914.

———. *Poems*. Vol. 9 of *The Complete Works of Ralph Waldo Emerson*. 12 vols. Edited by Edward Waldo Emerson. Boston: Houghton, Mifflin, 1909–1914.

———. *Society and Solitude*. Boston: Fields, Osgood, 1870.

FIELDS, ANNIE. *Authors and Friends*. Boston: Houghton, Mifflin, 1897.

FOSTER, EDWARD. *Mary E. Wilkins Freeman*. New York: Hendricks House, 1956.

FREEMAN, MARY E. WILKINS. *A Humble Romance and Other Stories*. New York: Harper & Bros., 1887.

———. *The Jamesons*. New York: Doubleday and McClure, 1899.

———. *A New England Nun and Other Stories*. New York: Harper & Bros., 1891.

———. *Pembroke*. New York: Harper & Bros., 1894.

———. *People of Our Neighborhoods*. New York: International Association of Newspapers and Authors, 1901.

———. *The Portion of Labor*. New York: Harper & Bros., 1901.

———. *Six Trees*. New York: Harper & Bros., 1903.

FROST, ROBERT. *Collected Poems*. New York: Henry Holt, 1939.

F. W. S. "Letters from the Green Mountains." *Knickerbocker* 44(August 1854):200.

GARNETT, EDWARD. *Friday Nights*. New York: Alfred A. Knopf, 1922.

GRATTAN, C. HARTLEY. "Sarah Orne Jewett." *Bookman* 49(May 1929):296–98.

HARTT, ROLLIN LYNDE. "A New England Hill Town." *Atlantic Monthly* 83(April and May 1899):561–74 and 712–20.

HAWTHORNE, NATHANIEL. *The American Notebooks*. Edited by Randall Stewart. New Haven: Yale University Press, 1932.

HERRON, IMA HONAKER. *The Small Town in American Literature*. Durham, N.C.: Duke University Press, 1939.

HIGGINSON, MARY T. *Thomas Wentworth Higginson*. Boston: Houghton, Mifflin, 1914.

HIGGINSON, THOMAS WENTWORTH. "Americanism in Literature." *Atlantic Monthly* 25(January 1870):56–63.

———. *Malbone*. Boston: Fields, Osgood, 1869.

———. *Oldport Days*. James R. Osgood, 1873.

HOLMES, OLIVER WENDELL. *Elsie Venner*. Boston: Houghton, Mifflin, 1892.

———. *The Guardian Angel*. Boston: Houghton, Mifflin, 1895.

HOWE, M. A. DEWOLFE. *Memories of a Hostess*. Boston: Atlantic Monthly Press, 1922.

HOWELLS, WILLIAM DEAN. *Annie Kilburn*. New York: Harper & Bros., 1889.

———. "Reviews and Literary Notes" (unsigned). *Atlantic Monthly* 25(April 1870):504–12.

———. *The Rise of Silas Lapham*. Boston: Houghton, Mifflin, 1912.

———. *Their Wedding Journey*. Boston: James R. Osgood, 1875.

———. *The Undiscovered Country*. Boston: Houghton, Mifflin, 1880.

HUBBELL, SETH. *A Narrative of the Sufferings of Seth Hubbell & Family in His Beginning a Settlement in the Town of Wolcott, in the State of Vermont*. Danville, Vt.: E. & W. Eaton, Printers, 1824.

JACKSON, HELEN HUNT. *Mercy Philbrick's Choice*. Boston: Roberts Bros., 1876.

———— . *Saxe Holm's Stories*. First Series. New York: Charles Scribner's Sons, 1878.

JAMES, HENRY. *The American Essays of Henry James*. Edited by Leon Edel. Vintage Books, 1956.

———— . *The American Scene*. New York: Harper & Bros., 1907.

———— . *The Bostonians*. New York: Modern Library, 1956.

———— . *Hawthorne*. Ithaca, N.Y.: Cornell University Press, 1956.

———— . *The Notebooks of Henry James*. Edited by F. O. Matthiessen and Kenneth Murdock. New York: Oxford University Press, 1947.

JEWETT, SARAH ORNE. *Country By-Ways*. Boston: Houghton, Mifflin, 1881.

———— . *A Country Doctor*. Boston: Houghton, Mifflin, 1884.

———— . *The Country of the Pointed Firs*. Boston: Houghton, Mifflin, 1910.

———— . *Deephaven*. Boston: Houghton, Mifflin, 1893.

———— . "The Gray Mills of Farley." In *American Local Color Stories*. Edited by H. R. Warfel and G. H. Orians. New York: American Book Co., 1941, pp. 363–82.

———— . *The King of Folly Island and Other People*. Boston: Houghton, Mifflin, 1888.

———— . *Letters*. Edited by Annie Fields. Boston: Houghton, Mifflin, 1911.

———— . *Letters of Sarah Orne Jewett Now in Colby Library*. Edited by Carl Weber. Waterville, Me.: Colby College Press, 1947.

———— . *The Life of Nancy and Other Stories*. Boston: Houghton, Mifflin, 1895.

———— . *A Marsh Island*. Boston: Houghton, Mifflin, 1885.

———— . *A Native of Winby and Other Stories*. Boston: Houghton, Mifflin, 1894.

———— . *The Queen's Twin and Other Stories*. Boston: Houghton, Mifflin, 1901.

———— . *Sarah Orne Jewett Letters*. Edited by Richard Cary. Waterville, Me.: Colby College Press, 1956.

———— . *The Story of the Normans*. New York: G. P. Putnam's Sons, 1887.

———— . *Strangers and Wayfarers*. Boston: Houghton, Mifflin, 1891.

———— . *The Tory Lover*. Boston: Houghton, Mifflin, 1901.

———— . *A White Heron and Other Stories*. Boston: Houghton, Mifflin, 1886.

JUDD, SYLVESTER. *Margaret: A Tale of the Real and Ideal. . . .* Boston: Phillips Sampson, 1857.

KIPLING, RUDYARD. "One Side Only." *The Times* (London), November 29, 1892, p. 8.

———— . *Something of Myself*. Garden City, N.Y.: Doubleday, Doran, 1937.

KRAPP, GEORGE PHILIP. *The English Language in America*. 2 vols. New York: Century, 1925.

KURATH, HANS. *The Word Geography of the Eastern United States*. Ann Arbor: University of Michigan Press, 1949.

———— . *Linguistic Atlas of New England*. 3 vols. and a *Handbook*. Providence: Brown University Press, 1939.

LAIGHTON, OSCAR. *Ninety Years on the Isles of Shoals*. Boston: Beacon Press, 1930.

LARCOM, LUCY. *An Idyl of Work*. Boston: James R. Osgood, 1875.

———— . *A New England Girlhood*. Boston: Houghton, Mifflin, 1889.

———— . *Poems*. Boston: Fields Osgood, 1869.

LOWELL, JAMES RUSSELL. *The Complete Poetical Works of James Russell Lowell*. Edited by Horace E. Scudder. Boston: Houghton, Mifflin, 1897.

LUNT, GEORGE. *Eastford; or, Household Sketches.* Boston: Crocker and Brewster, 1855.

———. *Old New England Traits.* New York: Hurd and Houghton, 1873.

MCLEAN, SALLY PRATT. *Cape Cod Folks* Boston: DeWolfe, Fiske, 1904.

MACY, JOHN. "The Passing of the Yankee," *Bookman* 73(August 1931):616–21.

MARQUAND, JOHN P. *The Late George Apley.* New York: Random House, 1940.

MATTHIESSEN, FRANCIS OTTO. *American Renaissance.* New York: Oxford University Press, 1941.

———. *Sarah Orne Jewett.* Boston: Houghton, Mifflin, 1929.

MELVILLE, HERMAN. *Billy Budd and Other Prose Pieces.* Edited by Raymond Weaver. New York: Liveright, 1928.

MUSSEY, BARROWS, ed. *We Were New England.* New York: Stackpole Sons, 1937.

NAGEL, GWEN L., AND NAGEL, JAMES, eds. *Sarah Orne Jewett: A Reference Guide.* Boston. G. K. Hall, 1977.

NEFF, EMERY. *Edwin Arlington Robinson.* New York: William Sloane Associates, 1948.

ODELL, RUTH. *Helen Hunt Jackson.* New York: Appleton-Century, 1939.

O'NEILL, EUGENE. "Desire Under the Elms." In *Nine Plays.* New York: Liveright, 1932.

———. "Mourning Becomes Electra," *In Nine Plays.* New York: Liveright, 1932.

OVERTON, GRANT MARTIN. *The Women Who Make Our Novels.* New York: Dodd, Mead, 1928.

PARRINGTON, VERNON LOUIS. *The Beginnings of Critical Realism in America.* Vol. 3 of *Main Currents in American Thought.* 3 vols. New York: Harcourt, Brace, 1930.

PATTEE, FRED LEWIS. *A History of American Literature since 1870.* New York: Century, 1915.

———. *Side-Lights on American Literature.* New York: Century, 1922.

PHELPS, ELIZABETH STUART. *Chapters from a Life.* Boston: Houghton, Mifflin, 1896.

———. *The Gates Ajar.* Boston: James R. Osgood, 1873.

———. *Hedged In.* Boston: Fields, Osgood, 1870.

———. *The Madonna of the Tubs.* Boston: Houghton, Mifflin, 1887.

———. *The Silent Partner.* Boston: James R. Osgood, 1871.

PICKARD, SAMUEL T. *Life and Letters of John Greenleaf Whittier.* 2 vols. Boston: Houghton, Mifflin, 1894.

QUINA, JAMES H., JR. "Character Types in the Fiction of Mary Wilkins Freeman." *Colby Library Quarterly,* Series 9, No. 4(December 1970), pp. 432–39.

ROBINSON, EDWIN ARLINGTON. *Collected Poems.* New York: Macmillan, 1937.

———. *Untriangulated Stars: Letters of Edwin Arlington Robinson to Harry DeForest Smith.* Edited by Denham Sutcliffe. Cambridge, Mass.: Harvard University Press, 1947.

ROBINSON, ROWLAND EVANS. *Danvis Folks,* and *A Hero of Ticonderoga.* Rutland, Vt.: Charles E. Tuttle, 1934.

———. *In New England Fields and Woods,* with *Sketches and Stories.* Rutland, Vt.: Charles E. Tuttle, 1937.

———. *Out of Bondage and Other Stories.* Rutland, Vt.: Charles E. Tuttle, 1936.

———. *Sam Lovel's Boy,* with *Forest and Stream Fables.* Rutland, Vt.: Charles E. Tuttle, 1936.

————. *Sam Lovel's Camps and Other Stories*. Rutland, Vt.: Charles E. Tuttle, 1934.

————. *Uncle Lisha's Outing, The Buttles Gals,* and *Along Three Rivers*. Rutland, Vt.: Charles E. Tuttle, 1934.

————. *Uncle Lisha's Shop* and *A Danvis Pioneer*. Rutland, Vt.: Charles E. Tuttle, 1933.

————. *Vermont: A Study of Independence*. Boston: Houghton, Mifflin, 1892.

SCOTT, WALTER. *The Heart of Midlothian*. London: H. Frost, 1910.

SEDGWICK, CATHARINE MARIA. *Hope Leslie, or Early Times in the Massachusetts*. New York: White, Galaher, and White, 1827.

————. *A New-England Tale: or, Sketches of New-England Characters and Manners*. New York: E. Bliss & E. White, 1822.

————. *Redwood: A Tale*. New York: E. Bliss & E. White, 1824.

SHACKFORD, MARTHA H. "Sarah Orne Jewett." *Sewanee Review* 30(January 1922):20–26.

SLOSSON, ANNIE TRUMBULL. *The China Hunters' Club*. New York: Harper, 1878.

————. *Dumb Foxglove and Other Stories*. New York: Harper & Bros., 1898.

————. *A Local Colorist*. New York: Charles Scribner's Sons, 1912.

SOUGNAC, JEAN. *Sarah Orne Jewett*. Paris: Jouve et Cie., 1937.

SPOFFORD, HARRIET PRESCOTT. *A Little Book of Friends*. Boston: Little, Brown, 1917.

————. "Rose Terry Cooke." In *Our Famous Women* (Hartford, Conn.: A. D. Worthington, 1884), pp. 174–206.

STEARNS, FRANK PRESTON. *Sketches from Concord and Appledore*. New York: G. P. Putnam's Sons, 1895.

STOWE, CHARLES E. *Life of Harriet Beecher Stowe: Compiled from Her Journals and Letters*. Boston: Houghton, Mifflin, 1889.

STOWE, HARRIET BEECHER. *The Minister's Wooing*. New York: Derby and Jackson, 1859.

————. *Oldtown Folks*. Boston: Fields, Osgood, 1869.

————. *The Pearl of Orr's Island*. Boston: Houghton, Mifflin, 1896.

————. *Poganuc People*. Boston: Houghton, Mifflin, 1890.

————. *Sam Lawson's Oldtown Fireside Stories*. Boston: Houghton, Mifflin, 1897.

————. "The Yankee Girl." In *Regional Sketches: New England and Florida*. Edited by John R. Adams (New Haven, Conn.: College & University Press, 1972), pp. 62–74.

THAXTER, CELIA. *Among the Isles of Shoals*. Boston: James R. Osgood, 1879.

————. "An Early Letter by Celia Thaxter." *Old-Time New England* 37(April 1947):101–103.

————. *The Heavenly Guest*. Edited by Oscar Laighton. Andover, Mass.: Smith and Coutts, 1935.

————. *An Island Garden*. Boston: Houghton, Mifflin, 1895.

————. *Letters*. Edited by A[nnie] F[ields] and R[osa] L[amb]. Boston: Houghton, Mifflin, 1895.

————. "A Memorable Murder." *Atlantic Monthly* 35(May 1875):602–15.

————. *Poems*. Boston: Houghton, Mifflin, 1896.

THAXTER, ROSAMOND. *Sandpiper: The Life and Letters of Celia Thaxter*. Francestown, N.H.: Marshall Jones, 1963.

THOMPSON, CHARLES MINER. "The Art of Miss Jewett." *Atlantic Monthly*

94(October 1904):485–97.

———— . "Miss Wilkins: An Idealist in Masquerade." *Atlantic Monthly* 83(May 1899):665–75.

———— . "The Short Stories of Alice Brown." *Atlantic Monthly* 98(July 1906):55–65.

THOREAU, HENRY DAVID. *Cape Cod.* Boston: Houghton, Mifflin, 1893.

———— . *The Variorum Walden.* Edited by Walter Harding. New York: Twayne Publishers, 1962.

THORP, MARGARET F. *Sarah Orne Jewett.* Pamphlets on American Writers Series. Minneapolis: University of Minnesota Press, 1966.

TOTH, SUSAN A. "A Defiant Light: A Positive View of Mary Wilkins Freeman." *New England Quarterly* 46(March 1973):82–93.

———— . "Mary Wilkins Freeman's Parable of Wasted Life." *American Literature* 42(January 1971):564–67.

———— . "Rose Terry Cooke" [critical bibliography]. *American Literary Realism, 1870–1910* 4(Spring 1971):170–76.

TRILLING, LIONEL. *Matthew Arnold.* New York: W. W. Norton, 1939.

———— . *The Middle of the Journey.* New York: Viking Press, 1947.

VAUGHAN, DOROTHY M. "Celia Thaxter's Library." *Colby Library Quarterly,* Series 6, No. 2 (December 1964), pp. 536–49.

WALKER, DOROTHEA. *Alice Brown.* New York: Twayne Publishers, 1974.

WEBER, CARL J. "New England Through French Eyes Fifty Years Ago." *New England Quarterly* 20(September 1947):385–96.

WEBSTER, NOAH. *Dissertations.* Boston: I. Thomas, 1789.

WESTBROOK, FRANCIS A. *Industrial Management in This Machine Age.* New York: Thomas Y. Crowell, 1932.

WESTBROOK, PERRY D. "Celia Thaxter: Seeker of the Unattainable." *Colby Library Quarterly.* Series 6, No. 12 (December 1964), pp. 499–512.

———— . "Mary E. Wilkins Freeman" [critical bibliography]. *American Literary Realism, 1870–1910* 2(Summer 1969):139–42.

———— . *Mary Wilkins Freeman.* New York: Twayne Publishers, 1967.

WEYGANDT, CORNELIUS. *New Hampshire Neighbors.* New York: Henry Holt, 1937.

WHITTIER, JOHN GREENLEAF. *The Complete Poetical Works.* Boston: Houghton, Mifflin, 1880.

———— . *Prose Works.* 2 vols. Boston: Houghton, Mifflin, 1882.

WILLIAMS, BLANCHE COLTON. *Our Short Story Writers.* New York: Dodd, Mead, 1920.

WILLIAMSON, SAMUEL T. "New England Isn't That Way." *New York Times Magazine,* August 31, 1947, pp. 12 and 19.

WILSON, FORREST. *Crusader in Crinoline: The Life of Harriet Beecher Stowe.* Philadelphia: J. P. Lippincott, 1941.

WILSON, HAROLD FISHER. *The Hill Country of Northern New England: Its Social and Economic History (1790–1930).* New York: Columbia University Press, 1936.

WINSLOW, HELEN M. *Literary Boston Today.* Boston. L. C. Page, 1903.

ZIFF, LARZER. *The American 1890s.* New York: Viking Press, 1966.

INDEX

184

Q7